The Complete Guide to

DIVINATION

The Complete Guide to

DIVINATION

How to Foretell
the Future Using the
Most Popular Methods
of Prediction

Cassandra Eason

THE CROSSING PRESS
BERKELEY, CALIFORNIA

The Crossing Press
www.crossingpress.com

A Division of Ten Speed Press
P.O. Box 7123
Berkeley, CA 94707
www.tenspeed.com

Library of Congress Cataloging-in-Publication Data

Eason, Cassandra.
  The complete guide to divination : how to foretell the future using
the most popular methods of prediction / Cassandra Eason.
     p. cm.
Originally published: London : Judy Piatkus (Publishers) Ltd., 1998.
Includes bibliographical references and index.
  ISBN 1-58091-138-2
  1. Divination. I. Title.
  BF1751.E27 2003
  133.3—dc21
                              2003011013

First published in the United Kingdom in 1998 by
Judy Piatkus (Publishers) Ltd.
5 Windmill Street
London W1P 1HF

Cover design by Lisa Buckley Design
Cover illustration by Joel Nakaruma/Images.com, Inc.
Text design by Toni Tajima
Text production by Chloe Nelson

First printing this edition, 2003
Printed in the United States

1 2 3 4 5 6 7 8 9 10 — 07 06 05 04 03

contents

INTRODUCTION

The intellect has little to do on the road to discovery. There comes a leap in consciousness, call it Intuition or what you will; the solution comes to you and you don't know how or why.

—ALBERT EINSTEIN

THE WISDOM that can be attained through casting runes, choosing tarot cards, or using any of the other "self-discovery" methods described in this book is timeless and beyond reason and logic. It is that of the divus, or god, within us all, sometimes described as the Higher or Evolved Self, whose knowledge is drawn from a pool of the experience of all humankind in all times and places, past, present, and future. The psychologist Carl Gustav Jung discussed the "two-million-year-old-man" contained in everyone—we can reach this repository of wise counsel through divination.

What Does Science Say?

Dr. Dean Radin at the University of Nevada, Las Vegas, has found startling evidence of the existence of psychic and divinatory powers. His telepathy experiments involved subjects who attempted to transmit one of four randomly selected images into the mind of someone in a sealed, soundproof room. By chance alone, it was estimated that the people guessing the projected images would on average pick out the correct image in one in four cases. Yet, in more than twenty-five

1

hundred tightly controlled trials, Dr. Radin found an overall rate of accuracy better than one in three.

Telepathy is a thing of the present. What of the future? Dr. Radin also tested that most common kind of premonition: the sudden sense of impending doom that we have just before an accident or when we pick up an envelope and know—against all reason—that it contains bad news.

There is always a temptation to be wise after the event, and many people might say they had a feeling of unease before a tragedy even if they did not. So Dr. Radin decided to measure something that could not lie: the bodily reactions of his subjects. When we say that we "felt cold" just before an event or "felt a sinking in the stomach," we are not just using figures of speech. Unease can cause physiological changes. Our heart rate drops, we experience increased perspiration, and the pupils in our eyes dilate. Less noticeable but more easily measured are decreases in the electrical resistance of our skin and the volume of blood passing through our fingers.

Dr. Radin hypothesized that if people could really sense when they were about to have an emotional shock, it might be possible to detect these physiological changes a few instants before impact. His subjects were wired up, then placed in front of computer screens that were programmed to present a series of emotionally shocking scenes, mixed randomly with a much larger number of innocuous scenes of cheerful people and pleasant landscapes. He found that his subjects' physiological responses changed significantly for a shocking image, but remained flat for the innocuous ones.

What was unexpected was that the physiological changes appeared up to three seconds *before* the emotional images were shown, while the screen was still blank. This confirmed that the test subjects could sense the content of the next picture several seconds before it was shown.

Dr. Radin's research is described in his book *The Conscious Universe* (see Further Reading).

The Hand of Fate

FIRST WITCH *All hail, Macbeth! hail to thee, thane of Glamis!*
SECOND WITCH *All hail, Macbeth! hail to thee, thane of Cawdor!*
THIRD WITCH *All hail, Macbeth, that shalt be king thereafter.*

—WILLIAM SHAKESPEARE, *MACBETH*

The three witches on the stormy heath who greet Macbeth with a prophecy of his future greatness represent an image that appears in several cultures: in classical mythology, for instance, the Three Fates controlled men's destiny. Yet the witches were not foretelling a fixed future, but one that depended on the deliberate decisions made by Macbeth and the Thane of Cawdor. Macbeth was already Thane of Glamis. His elevation to Cawdor resulted because the former thane committed an act of treachery, thereby forfeiting his life and title. As a favorite of King Duncan, Macbeth was a likely candidate to replace him.

As for becoming king, the seeds of ambition were already in Macbeth, as was the ability to kill Duncan. The hags merely revealed one potential path, which Macbeth could have rejected.

Fate can change anyone's life in an instant, through a lottery win, an unexpected promotion, a layoff, illness, or bereavement, or falling in love. Yet most examples of so-called fate are at least partly the results of our own or others' actions.

For instance, you cannot win the lottery unless you buy a ticket, nor can you gain promotion unless another person leaves a post vacant by choice or a senior manager decides to create a new position. Even illness may be caused by a genetic or personal weakness or by the asocial habits of others.

What is more, our reaction to fate is crucial in deciding our future path, and sometimes there can be several options, which in turn affect future opportunities or obstacles in different ways.

Divination can reveal unconsidered paths and guide us to the best action or reaction, using the deeper knowledge that is out of conscious reach. These inspirational insights can be masked by a carefully formulated argument, expert advice, or the doubts and anxieties, guilt and obligations that can cloud decisions.

The Web of Fate

According to the Vikings, whose method of divination is explored in Section Two, our fate is not preordained but is determined by our own actions past and present—and those of our forebears who made us what we are. Each decision or action alters the pattern of the web of our personal fate that is constantly being woven. In the Norse tradition, the cosmic web of fate was created by the three Fates or Norns, who were believed to oversee even the fortunes of the gods.

The first Norn is called Urdhr and speaks of the past, which influences not only our own present and future, but also that of our descendants. The second Norn, Verdhandi, tells of present deeds and influences, also strongly implicated in our future direction.

Skuld, the third Norn, talks of what will come to pass, given the intricate web of past and present interaction. Our future fate, or *orlog,* is constantly being changed as each new day adds to the web of inter-action. The web is continually being torn apart and rewoven in ever more intricate patterns as the future becomes the present and ultimately the past.

How Divination Works

Divination is not a statistically accurate, mathematical method; it taps into the same instinctive processes that alert a mother to a child's danger even if her child is far away.

However, divination can take incredibly complicated forms. One reason for this is to give the intuition time to work, and for some people, following a long ritual can provide the time they need. Equally, the best inspirations sometimes occur in seconds, and if a method is too complex, the anxiety created can actually be counter-productive. If we accept, as Jung said, that nothing occurs by chance, then every method, however simple, is really governed by synchronicity or meaningful connections. This is how we end up with the "right cards," the right runes, or the right *I Ching* reading. It is a process of psychokinesis in which our unconscious knowledge influences the "fall of the dice." By the laws of the cosmos such information is provided in response to the individual's need to know an answer. This is why psychic gamblers are few and far between.

ASKING THE RIGHT QUESTIONS

The hardest part of divination is asking the right questions. To demand certainties or precise timescales is to ignore the complexity of the future. It is also to disregard our own influence on our future or that of external circumstance and other people. Had Macbeth asked the witches if kingship would bring him long-term happiness, his destiny might have been very different.

Sometimes you may start with one question, but get an answer to an entirely different one (usually the question you needed to ask but had not realized or acknowledged). You can ask questions on any level and about any subject as long as the question is important to you or the person for whom you are asking, for need and emotion are the channels along which psychic energies flow most easily.

Sometimes there is no definite question or it is one that you cannot easily formulate. In this case, let the divinatory tools act as a focus for your unvoiced wishes and anxieties.

INTERPRETING THE ANSWERS

Divination can be equally successful for yourself or others and not at all unlucky to practice as an art of self-exploration. When you read for someone else, or another person interprets a reading for you, there should be a two-way flow of psychic energy, so the reading becomes a joint endeavor. Do not feel that you are on trial or that you need to provide an entire life history unprompted, for that is guaranteed to stop your natural flow of inspiration. The other person has a question, decision, or dilemma and your function is to help the questioner find a resolution.

Make sure the questioner shuffles, deals, or casts whatever you are using as a focus for divination and then, after explaining the basic method and interpretation, you can ask the person for whom you are giving the reading how he or she would apply the meanings to the current situation. What you lose in mystique you gain in trust. Even if you are working as a professional psychic counselor, as in any other area of expertise, a good practitioner takes the client's own interpretation as a basis for the whole consultation.

Sometimes people can press you to make definite predictions or to tell them what to do. It can be tempting to promise good news if someone is ill or desperately unhappy or to offer warnings if you can see that the present course seems to be leading to disaster. However, taking over the fate of another person is a very grave responsibility, and there are other ways of being positive and supportive.

How to Use This Book

In this book, I have described ten basic methods of divination. Each can be used separately or they can be combined in different ways for a fuller life review. There may be one form that instantly attracts you or with which you are already familiar. Each section of the book is entirely self-contained and they can be read in any order. Some may not seem right for you or you may decide to put them aside until a later date. Most people discover one system at which they almost instinctively become expert and two or three others that, with a little practice, become almost second nature. On the other hand, you may find that you can use all ten with equal skill.

At the back of the book, there is a Further Reading section in case you want to find out more about any of the subjects mentioned. The books listed range from beginners' guides to quite complex interpretations. They offer alternative perspectives, for divination is not a precise science or even a technology to be mastered; it is more akin to bringing to the surface your dreams, hopes, fears, and hidden wisdom. On the deepest level, the meanings seem startlingly familiar to almost everyone, being recalled from a distant source rather than learned for the first time.

MAKING A PSYCHIC TREASURE BOX

With the exception of a tarot pack and ten small crystals, all the other equipment you need can be improvised or bought incredibly cheaply. Making runes, tree staves, or *I Ching* stones can be as simple as drawing symbols on pebbles or as complex as carving out and varnishing symbols on the appropriate kind of wood. From earliest times, men and women have created divination tools from the natural world around them—from clay, stone, crystal, wood, and bone. In creating their own divination sets, seekers of wisdom have etched and imposed their essence on the most humble and the most precious substances. Some of the most accurate and moving readings I have experienced have been in circles drawn with a stick in sand or scribbled on the back of an envelope on a long train journey.

If you wish, you can create a beautiful treasure box of your divinatory materials, containing perhaps a crystal pendulum, crystals that have personal significance, and a tarot pack wrapped in dark silk. Whenever possible, whatever you buy, find, or make, make the occasion a positive, spiritual one so your divination is endowed from the beginning with good vibrations. Watch the sun filtering through the leaves in the forest; hear the waves crashing on the shore. As you run your hands through a box of crystals in a New Age store, feel the energies rising and see your own special crystal gleaming like a star.

The treasure box itself may "appear" at an unexpected time and place—at a garage sale or as a gift—and can be made of wood, metal, or any other material. Best of all are those you make yourself, whether from a particularly beautiful gold or silver box from a Christmas or birthday present or a strong cardboard box covered with fabric or painted. It should be large enough to contain the different systems, plus any cloths or charts you have made, and candles in white or purple that you can light while carrying out your readings.

Plain silk scarves make an excellent base for permanent circle cloths. You need separate bags, pouches, or small boxes for your different kinds of stones and crystals. Some people wrap the contents of the entire box in dark silk.

The magic is in you, not in your tools, but having a treasure box indicates that this is a separate, special part of your life.

ENERGIZING RITUALS

With any new form of divination, and when first using your box, especially if you have acquired it from someone else, there are some very simple rituals that can both offer psychic protection and energize your artifacts. These are based on the ancient elements Earth, Air, Fire, and Water, once regarded as the basis of all life and still recognized as symbolizing the qualities of sensation, thought, intuition, and feeling in Jungian psychology. Together they make up an integrated world-view and a fifth element, different and greater, that is a synthesis of the other four.

To perform an energizing ritual

1. Place your stones, cards, and any permanent charts or cloths on a silver foil circle, for the magical intuitions of the moon.

2. Around the circumference of the circle, at regular intervals, arrange nine small brass or gold-colored objects, coins, or circles of gold paper (nine being a sacred number of perfection and completion).

3. Pass a dish of salt over the nine objects in a clockwise direction for the grounding power and protection of the Earth. As you do so, visualize magical standing stones and ancient circles, tall jagged rocks, mountains, vast sandy plains.

4. Next move a lighted incense stick of pine for energy and clarity of thought or sandalwood for psychic and healing powers around the circumference. These offer the keen perceptions and searching insights of Air. As you do so, visualize mighty winds, fresh breezes, birds soaring high, forests of dancing leaves.

5. For the inspiration and creativity of Fire, light a golden, yellow, or red candle and raise this above the center of the moon disc. See the crackling fires of the great festivals, the dazzling sun at noon, the lightning flash.

6. Finally, sprinkle a few drops of water steeped with rose petals, or rose or lavender essential oil for harmony and sensitivity to the deeper emotions of those for whom you may read. As you summon the power of Water, feel the spray from a gushing waterfall, hear the tide breaking on a stony beach, see soft sunlight dappling a still, dark pool.

7. Leave the circle and divinatory objects on a windowsill for a sun and moon cycle of twenty-four hours, then return them to the box.

PROTECTIVE AND CLEANSING RITUALS

If you avoid carrying out divination, or indeed any psychic work, when you feel exhausted or negative, your explorations should be entirely harmonizing and positive. However, because you become more sensitive to atmospheres the more psychically evolved you are, it is important to establish a psychic space in which to work and to close down this area after you finish so you are not awake all night.

Even in a public place, in your mind's eye you can draw around yourself with a glowing amber crystal a clockwise circle, beginning in the north, that completely encloses you in golden light. When you finish giving a reading, close down the circle in a counterclockwise direction. Begin again in the north by visualizing a dark crystal, such as a smoky quartz or obsidian, overwriting the golden light and leaving you at peace. If you are reading for someone else, you can enclose them in a separate circle of protection, so that if they do have negative vibes through sadness or anxiety, these are enclosed and dispelled at the end of the reading.

If you have read for someone else, pass your crystal pendulum or an amethyst over your runes, tree staves, or cards to draw off any negative feelings and then wash the pendulum or crystal under running water. Afterward, rest the pendulum or crystal in black silk for a while. In the companion to this book, *The Complete Guide to Psychic Development* (see Further Reading), there are more detailed examples of psychic protection.

Some people invoke four archangels to stand in each corner of the room before beginning any psychic work. Create your own image of Michael, the Archangel of the Sun and the warrior; Gabriel, the messenger; Raphael, the traveler with his pilgrim's staff; and Zadkiel, the Angel of Wisdom. Alternatively, ask your personal guides, God, the Goddess, or a named chosen deity for protection, or invoke the blessing of Light and Benevolence before beginning psychic work.

Remember afterward to thank your psychic guardians and to visualize them moving farther away to watch you through the night.

Certain crystals have natural protective powers that have been used from the time of the ancient Egyptians. You will use some of these in your crystal divination work, but you can also buy large unpolished chunks of crystal that double for meditation work.

Place them in the corners of the room or on the four corners of the table on which you are working, or on the table or floor directly in front of you, whenever you give a reading to act as a psychic shield from any unintentional negativity. Protective crystals include black agate, amethyst, bloodstone, carnelian, garnet, black and red jasper, lapis lazuli, tigereye, topaz, and turquoise.

PSYCHIC TIMES AND PLACES

You can carry out divination at any time in any place. However, transition times—sunrise, noon, sunset, and midnight—are especially powerful, as is the day the crescent moon first appears in the sky and the first day of the full moon cycle. These are all listed in the weather section of many newspapers.

Section One

DIVINATION BY SELECTION

Chapter 1

Tarot Cards

WITH IMAGES such as the Devil and Death, it is hardly surprising that tarot cards are sometimes dubbed "terror cards." Indeed, during radio and television broadcasts, I have been telephoned by terrified listeners who have been told by clairvoyants—mercifully a tiny minority—that someone in the family would die because the Death card appeared or that the Tower of Destruction (inherently a card of liberation) was heralding financial ruin.

Taking the Terror out of Tarot

Antonia, a successful woman in her thirties, was initially disturbed when the three cards shown above appeared in this sequence during a reading I gave her. However, I was able to reassure her that the cards did not predict any future catastrophe, but referred to a hidden, existing conflict in her life and that the symbols were actually quite positive. Antonia said she knew what the cards were referring to—a very destructive relationship with a lover who was far less successful than

13

her in material terms but somehow managed to make Antonia feel inferior, inadequate, and unattractive.

We deduced that the Devil card represented her hidden anger and frustration, which she had turned on herself by bingeing on food and crash dieting. Death indicated what she already knew, but had not acknowledged—that it was time to bring the relationship to an end. (She had held onto it out of fear that no one could possibly love her.)

The Ace of Wands, a card that symbolizes new beginnings, offered reassurance that she could exist as an independent and fulfilled individual in her own right. The cards did not tell Antonia what would happen, because the choice was hers. After a great deal of thought, she decided to break up with her boyfriend. It was painful, but a few months later she telephoned me to say that she had made a major career move and, for the first time in more than a year, felt happy.

What Are Tarot Cards?

The tarot pack comprises seventy-eight highly illustrated cards, twenty-two Major cards, or Trumps as they were traditionally called, forty numbered cards in four suits, and sixteen Court cards. The first twenty-two cards form the Major Arcana (*arcana* means "hidden wisdom") and many people use these alone, because they represent the main archetypes known to humankind in all times and places: the father, the mother, the wise man, the fool or child, the trickster, the divine sacrifice, the judge, the hero, and the virgin.

The cards can be used for divinations, meditation, visualization, and sometimes as a focus for rituals to attract or repel the qualities inherent in each, reflecting the medieval belief that all cards were invented by the devil.

More than any other form of divination, the tarot has been unfairly regarded as a dark form of magic. But as Antonia discovered, tarot cards are really only a set of symbols for interpreting unconscious needs and wishes and anticipating future paths.

The problem lies not with the cards, but with the way they are used. On one occasion, I was contacted by a woman in great distress. She was in her midthirties and trying for a baby. During a reading at a psychic fair, she had been told that the Queen of Swords was a warning of trouble with her reproductive system. This increased her anxiety, and stress is a factor that has been shown to affect fertility adversely. Therefore, her clairvoyant's prediction of trouble was self-fulfilling. As I said in the Introduction, any form of magic, divination, and ritual can have negative connotations if used by someone with less-than-honest intent. For this reason, it is best to consult only clairvoyants who are personally recommended. Even better is to read the tarot cards for yourself and your friends and if you do turn professional, to interpret any obstacles as challenges to be overcome rather than irrevocable bad news.

The History of the Tarot

Tarot cards are now mainly associated with magic and divination, but for a long time they were used for card games. The origin of the tarot is uncertain. It seems to be a medieval creation, although the images and themes are much older. The Bibliothèque Nationale in Paris has seventeen ornate cards, sixteen of them tarot Trumps, originally believed to have been made for Charles VI of France around 1392, but now thought to be Italian, dating from about 1470.

One suggestion is that tarot cards sprang from the north of Italy in the valley of the Taro River which is a tributary of the River Po. This could have influenced the Italian name for the cards, *tarrochi*, and the French name *tarot*. The modern tarot pack comes directly from an Italian version, the Venetian or Piedmontese Tarot, which has twenty-two Trumps. The same form is found in the French pack, called the Tarot of Marseilles, which is still popular. Both designs were in popular use by about 1500 in northern Italy and France.

The four suits represented the different strata of society: the swords were the aristocracy; cups or chalices for the clergy and monastic orders; coins for the merchants; and batons for the peasants.

Other explanations link the origin of the name with the Celtic Tara—the sacred Hill of the High Kings of Ireland from ancient times until the sixth century A.D. This view was given credence by Robert Graves, the historian and novelist, who believed that the twenty-two tarot Trumps were derived from the ancient twenty-two-symbol Tree Alphabet of the Celts (see Tree Divination in Section Two).

Another theory claimed that the Gypsies brought the tarot with them in their long trek to Europe from India via the Middle East. Certainly the Arabic word *tariqua,* meaning "the way of wisdom," bears some resemblance to *tarot.* And the ancient Egyptian word *tarosh* means "the royal way." The Egyptian connection was established in 1781, a period when Egypt was seen as the source of all knowledge. Antoine Court de Gebelin, a French Protestant clergyman who became fascinated by the occult, visited friends and found them playing tarot cards. He identified the cards as containing the secrets of the priests of ancient Egypt, hidden in the symbols to protect this wisdom from invading barbarians.

A third root was seen in the Kabbalah, the source of Hebrew esoteric wisdom. *Torah* is the Hebrew name for the first books of the Old Testament. In 1856, Eliphas Levi, a former Catholic priest whose real name was Louis Constant, linked each Major Arcana card with one of the twenty-two letters of the Hebrew alphabet. He also connected each of the ten numbers in the suits with one of the ten aspects of God reflected in the Kabbalistic Tree of Life.

The greatest influence on modern tarot reading is Arthur Edward Waite, who joined the Order of the Golden Dawn in 1891. The tarot was important to the Golden Dawn, who traced their traditions back to the mysterious Rosicrucians of the seventeenth century, who in turn drew on alchemical and Kabbalistic traditions dating back to Moses, who learned his ancient wisdom in Egypt. The Rider Waite Tarot pack, with its illustrated Minor Arcana, was intended to promote visions as well as to be used for divination. Waite associated the four suits with the four sacred objects of the Holy Grail quest: the cup, the dish, the lance, and the sword. Many of his cards reflect the romantic Arthurian background of the Grail legends.

The darker associations of the tarot came from the occultist Aleister Crowley who broke away from the Order of the Golden Dawn. Crowley believed he was the reincarnation of Eliphas Levi and added sexual and negative connotations to magic and the tarot. This has done the cards and their spiritual symbolism great disservice and, sadly, this is the aspect out of all the countless positive associations that is too frequently remembered.

Which Pack Should You Choose?

Contrary to popular belief, it is not at all unlucky to choose your own tarot pack. It is worth going to a large bookshop or New Age store and spending time studying the different packs. Unless you have a strong preference, it is often easier to choose a set of cards with an illustrated Minor Arcana, as many people find that the symbols for each number and the detailed Court cards help stimulate their intuition, especially if they are unfamiliar with the tarot. Conversely, I find that when reading playing cards, the lack of images and stylized Court cards is not a problem, because, as with the runes and the Tree Alphabet, different psychic faculties come into play. Many tarot packs are based on the Rider Waite pack, which is probably the most straightforward and stimulating.

The Morgan Greer and Mythic Tarot both have illustrated Minor Arcanas. The Classic and Marseilles packs have plain number cards, and their Major card imagery is quite static. Those who find the Waite-type packs too flowery may prefer them. I have also seen reproductions of the early Italian packs that can be large and usually beautiful and brilliantly colored. If you initially choose the Astrological Tarot (one of the American Indian or Egyptian versions or the round Motherpeace card), you may find problems with correspondences with the standard packs, which can make learning a general tarot method more difficult.

I taught the tarot in classes at my local college and those with unusual packs, perhaps incorporating a different system and card numbering, struggled with the correspondences. Eventually you may buy several packs because at different times, each addresses a special need. Packs for beginners, with the meanings on the top, are limiting and tend to stifle your natural creativity in reading.

The Major Arcana

The order of the first twenty-two cards comprising the Major Arcana may vary slightly according to the pack you buy. These cards contain the essence of the system, and you can make very accurate readings using these cards alone. The spreads most suitable for Major Arcana readings are indicated.

If you have never read the tarot before, spread the twenty-two Major Arcana pictures in a circle, faces upward, beginning (or ending) with the Fool. In some versions, the Fool is numbered zero, symbolizing that he is the beginning and the end in a never-ending cycle. Concentrate on a question about an issue that really matters to you, then pick up the three cards to which you are most drawn. Place them in a row in the order you chose them, starting at the left.

Look at each card in turn, without worrying what it ought to mean, and let ideas flow into you. You may find that images form in your head, as divinatory forms often stimulate our underutilized pictorial store of wisdom that can get lost in the world of words. You might like to record your impressions either in writing, sketches, or on a tape recorder. Alternatively, read for a sympathetic friend or family member who also does not know the meanings of the cards. You will find that this is probably the most accurate reading you do, because you are relying on the vast well of unconscious wisdom and imagery, uncluttered by expectations.

Interpreting the Cards

Some tarot readers interpret cards as either positive or challenging according to whether the card is dealt upright or reversed (upside-down). In my own experience, this does not seem a true psychic choice, because the card may have been previously returned to the pack incorrectly or shuffled by someone who, like myself, is not dextrous.

Each card contains in itself the potential for creative or stultifying results, according to future actions. Usually one aspect of meaning predominates and this can be interpreted according to the other cards and, most importantly, to the intuitive feel for the whole reading. This cannot be taught, but comes with practice and with trusting initial impressions even if these seem counter to conventional meanings. The feminine cards apply equally to men and women, as they refer to an aspect in their anima, their gentler "feminine" side. The same is true of male cards. Sometimes tarot readers identify Major cards as actual personalities; for example, the Empress can be seen as a mother figure, the Fool as someone immature, and the Hierophant or Pope as an authority figure such as a bank manager or judge.

If this connection occurs spontaneously, especially if you are only using the Major Arcana in a reading, it is probably a valid one. However, in a full-pack reading, Major cards tend to refer to qualities and courses of action, with Court cards referring to specific personalities, and Minor numbered cards to specific situations.

The Meanings of the Major Arcana

Here is a list of the accepted meanings of the Major Arcana. Take these only as a guide, not as something set in stone, as this will limit your own powers of intuition.

THE FOOL

The Fool is the first and sometimes last card. He is represented in the act of preparing to leap off a cliff or set off on a journey, the first step taken by man into the world at birth, as Wordsworth said, "trailing clouds of glory." The fool is accompanied by his dog, Instinct. In literature, he's the Fool of Shakespeare's *King Lear,* who is not afraid to speak the unvarnished truth though he may suffer for it.

He's Jung's inner child, the essential self stripped of worldly trappings, the real person that integrates our competitive and caring sides. In alchemy, he is the divine hermaphrodite, the philosopher's stone, the offspring of the marriage of King Sol and Queen Luna.

Positive Interpretation Untapped potential, a step into the unknown that will bear fruit, enthusiasm for a new venture, seizing an unexpected opportunity that may involve change (either actual or adopting a new perspective)

Challenging Aspects Indecisiveness, irresponsibility, inability to stick to one's course, gullibility

THE MAGICIAN

The Magician or Juggler is the card of creative energies and is the archetypal innovator/trickster who holds the key to enlightenment. Some associate him with Mercury, the god of travel, communication, and health, who carried the power of healing in his caduceus (his staff entwined with serpents). Mercury was also the god of commerce and thieves. In many tarot packs, the Magician is pictured as one of the ancient alchemists who manipulates the four elements from which the fifth, Ether or Spirit, is created. He links the everyday sphere with the magical and spiritual world beyond and seeks the all-powerful philosopher's stone that can turn base metals into gold and might hold the key to immortality.

Positive Interpretation Creativity, originality, using inspiration rather than logic to find a solution, versatility

Challenging Aspects Deviousness, unreliability, using manipulative tactics to persuade others against their will, unpredictability

THE HIGH PRIESTESS OR POPESS

The High Priestess represents the spiritual, mysterious aspects of the feminine principle and gets her name from the legendary Pope Joan in the ninth century. She is often associated with virgin goddesses such as the Moon Goddess, Artemis, or the Celtic Brigid (patroness of healers and poets). In some packs, she is called Juno, wife of the supreme Roman god Jupiter, in her sense as the abstract, wise feminine principle of divinity rather than the sensual Mother Goddess. The High Priestess is frequently portrayed between two pillars, whether darkness and light, with her crescent moon at her feet, or mercy and severity; behind her a veil leads to the unknown.

Positive Interpretation Spirituality, detachment from trivial concerns, independence from the approval of others, trusting intuition

Challenging Aspects Self-centeredness, indifference to the emotional needs of others, obsession with detail

THE Empress

The Empress is the card of motherhood and mothering. She represents the Mother Goddess and Earth Mothers typified by Ceres; Demeter, the Classical Corn Goddess; Cerridwen of the Celts, Goddess of the full moon; or Frigg in the Norse legends, Goddess of women and mothers; and the northern housewife. In many tarot packs, the Empress is portrayed surrounded by corn, fruit, and flowers and may be seen in the aspect of the early mother status in the full flower of pregnancy.

Positive Interpretation Motherhood, nurturing those who are vulnerable, fertility (in ventures as well as human reproduction), creative giving and empathy with others' problems and weaknesses

Challenging Aspects Martyrdom on the altar of others' wishes, possessiveness, loss of individual identity, preoccupation with the lives of others

THE Emperor

The Emperor is the card of fathering, determination, and early power. He is the ultimate authority figure before whom all bow, Father God, and consort to the Empress Mother. The Emperor is the All-Father of many traditions: Zeus in classical mythology, the Norse Odin the Wise One or Woden in the Anglo-Saxon tradition. He is pictured enthroned, often in battle dress, for he is an experienced warrior as well as the leader of his people. But although he is the giver of law and decisions, his laws may not always be just, and his decisions are not always wise.

Positive Interpretation Focused energy in carrying through objectives, logic, assertiveness, confidence

Challenging Aspects Overcritical attitude toward the weakness of others, dominance and disregard of others' wishes, aggressiveness and impatience

The Hierophant or Pope

The Hierophant or Pope represents traditions of all kinds and accumulated spiritual wisdom. In the classics, he is Saturn or the Saxon's Seater, the God of Limitation and Fate. In some tarot packs, he is called Jupiter, the Roman name for Zeus. He mirrors the Emperor, his alter ego, but in wisdom and knowledge rather than authority. His wisdom is that of conventional and learned insight gained through application.

Positive Interpretation Seeking wisdom from a wise source, whether a person or book; adhering to traditional values on an uncertain path; learning by application and altruism

Challenging Aspects Inability to go against conventional behavior; unwillingness to accept innovations; being dominated by redundant fears, rejections, and prohibitions

The Lovers

This is the card of love and emotions, relationships and the family. The Lovers are usually portrayed with a third party present, whether Venus, Cupid, an angel, or even the devil. The Lovers may represent Adam and Eve or the alchemical sacred marriage of King Sol and Queen Luna. The third person, usually a woman, suggests choice between partners, family members, or earthly and spiritual love. In such cases, the youth is seen as the Fool on his journey through life. Originally, the Lovers were a family group with a child between them who became Cupid. The family aspect is not one to be ignored.

Positive Interpretation Happiness in love or through relationships, emotional or love choices that bring satisfaction, new love or friendship involving the need for trust or commitment

Challenging Aspects Problems in love or relationships that should not be ignored, isolation, unwelcome choices in love or family

THE CHARIOT

The Chariot is the card of change, challenge, and also of triumph. Apollo the Sun God rode his golden chariot across the sky so the day might progress. Mars, the young God of War, rode his fiery chariot into battle, and conquering Roman generals used them to return to Rome for their "triumph," a victory procession through the streets in which they rode in a chariot. Whether black and white horses or sphinxes pull the chariot, the card indicates that the rider has harnessed opposing powers to gain the impetus to succeed.

Positive Interpretation Making positive and often sudden change, overcoming obstacles to success by integrating opposing factors, taking the action required to achieve an objective

Challenging Aspects Impulsive decisions, restlessness leading to change for its own sake, wavering between extremes

JUSTICE

Justice appears later in the Rider Waite pack, but because the majority of packs have it in this position, I have placed the card after the Chariot. Justice is the card of principles and speaking true, sometimes connected with official matters of all kinds, not only legal, but also a personal desire for what is right in matters large and small. In Egyptian tradition, after death a person's heart was weighed against a feather from the head of Ma'at, Goddess of Truth and Justice. If the scales balanced, the heart was free from sin and the deceased might pass to the afterlife. Justice is often pictured with scales and a blindfold, an indication that justice should be impartial.

Positive Interpretation Tackling officialdom using facts and accurate details, need for action to right an injustice, upholding vital principles

Challenging Aspects Accepting injustice in exchange for a quiet life, unfairness to others, putting principles before people

THE HERMIT

The Hermit, the archetypal wise old man, is the card of the inner voice and withdrawal from the outer to the inner world. Although he is wise, it is the wisdom of quiet contemplation and inner illumination, as shown by the lantern he carries in many tarot packs. His wisdom is that favored by Buddhist teachings: seeking answers to your own questions. He is the gate to the collective well of unconscious wisdom, Jung's two-million-year-old man in us all.

The Hermit is identified as Hermes Trismegistus, the semi-mythological patron saint of alchemy. According to the old texts, Hermes Trismegistus (Hermes thrice-greatest), who was probably a real though semidivine being, held "three parts of the wisdom of the whole world." The answers to immortality were there to be found through spiritual as well as physical searchings not set in any book.

Positive Interpretation Listening to the inner voice, withdrawing from the world's demands for creative renewal, seeking solitude and letting the answer come

Challenging Aspects Ignoring the wisdom and advice of others, opting out from situations, failure to communicate

THE WHEEL OF FORTUNE

The Wheel of Fortune represents the input of the unexpected, both good and bad, into someone's life and his or her response to fortune or misfortune. The Wheel of Fortune varies in tarot packs, the key aspect being who is turning the Wheel. For example, it may be the blindfolded Goddess Fortuna, suggesting that humans are subject to the whims of fate. Others show the Egyptian jackal-headed god Anubis, Conductor of Dead Souls, or the Egyptian god Amon, Controller of Destiny and Life, who is linked with the Sun God. The Wheel may be regarded as the Sun Wheel. In the Buddhist philosophy, the Wheel of Birth, Death, and Rebirth is turned by a person's own actions in different incarnations, so this symbol contains the elements of choice and responsibility. This card never predicts that either good or bad fortune will strike, but usually refers to a fear of disaster, hope of fortune, or some twist of fate that occurred at the time of the reading.

Positive Interpretation An unexpected opportunity or challenge that, if followed, promises good results; a person who may offer a new outlet for your talents, making a supreme effort to advance your cause

Challenging Aspects Allowing others to influence your destiny unduly, a feeling of helplessness and inability to control events, waiting for the magical solution to turn up

STRenGTH, Force, or ForTITUDe

Strength, which is interchangeable in its position with Justice, is symbolic of the strength and courage to overcome adversity (maybe that of the Wheel of Fortune) or the endurance and patience to see a relationship through to fruition or a natural ending. Sometimes Strength is depicted as a woman closing a lion's jaws, not with brute strength but with persuasion and quiet determination. She is Cyrene, a maiden of Artemis, the waxing moon goddess, whom Apollo the Sun God saw fighting and winning a battle against a lion. As a reward, he took her to the realm of the gods. Other tarot packs depict Heracles wrestling with a lion. He was unable to overcome the lion with arrows, but eventually strangled it. Thereafter, he wore the lion skin, which endowed him with the strength and courage of the lion.

Positive Interpretation Courage to overcome opposition, patience and perseverance under difficulty, hidden strengths

Challenging Aspects Fear of facing opposition to plans, being too patient in a hopeless situation, not listening to the arguments of others

THE HANGED MAN

THE HANGED MAN.

The Hanged Man is the card of sacrifice or voluntary loss to gain greater advantage. In traditional tarot packs, the Hanged Man is often represented by the Norse god Odin, the All-Father who hung by his feet from the world tree, Yggdrasil, for nine days and nights without food or water in search of wisdom. At last, Odin saw the runes beneath him and, in reaching down for them and letting go of all his worldly expectations, found he was free. The tree may be seen as a living entity, giving life as well as taking it. The Hanged Man is a symbol of rebirth and renewal, just as the old Corn Gods in many traditions were cut down in the autumn to be reborn in the spring in the new seed so the crops would grow. Many religions have the divine sacrifice as a central tenet. Contrary to some gloomy tarot readers, this card in no way presages loss, but a letting go, whether an inner change in perspective or a decision to carve out a better life by giving up immediate advantage or making a great effort that will not bring instant rewards.

Positive Interpretation Making a long-term advantageous plan or commitment that will require great input or short-term loss, giving up unrealistic plans or redundant ways of living, unselfish actions

Challenging Aspects Inability to let go in an unfulfilling situation, sacrificing personal happiness for an unworthy cause, concentration on short-term gain and ignoring the long-term view

DEATH

DEATH.

The Death card is the card of natural change and progression, and as such, its positive meaning far outweighs any negative connotations. Death is sometimes portrayed as the medieval Grim Reaper with scythe, as a black skeleton, or as a knight in black armor with a skull revealed through the helmet. All are seen to fall before him: bishop, king, lovely maiden, the lovers, and a child who, unlike the others, is not afraid. Many of these figures also appear either in the Sun card or the

Judgment card. The *Memento Mori,* the Death's head symbol, was carried by people in medieval and Tudor times as a talisman and reminder that death was ever present. Because health care is now so advanced in the Western world and most people live into old age, the concept of death has become taboo, and so the Death card is an unwelcome reminder that our lives are finite.

Positive Interpretation Natural change points; endings that, if accepted, will lead to new beginnings; indications that decisions or changes that have been deferred can now be made

Challenging Aspects Change in a particular area may be long overdue, reluctance to move forward, undue pessimism about the future

Temperance

TEMPERANCE.

This is the card of harmony, healing, and moderation. Temperance is one of the four Christian virtues and also one of the classical virtues. It is associated with time, in the sense of letting time heal and allowing things to pass in their own time. Usually, the figure is seen pouring water from one container to another or from fountain to jug and back again, to symbolize the interplay between unconscious and conscious, mind and body, self and others, and the constantly flowing path of time. Temperance is also associated with Iris, Goddess of the Rainbow and messenger between the underworld, earth, and heaven. She is also depicted as an angel, sometimes holding the key to the heavenly city, the key being moderation, acceptance, and peace.

Positive Interpretation The need to let events take their course; finding a compromise; healing, whether by others or to others

Challenging Aspects Concentrating on other people's harmony to the detriment of one's own, opting out of making unpopular decisions, being too naive about others' motives and intentions

THE DEVIL

This card has nothing to do with black magic or evil, but reflects the shadow side of the human personality and the importance of acknowledging negative thoughts and emotions. The Devil is a Judeo-Christian concept. Milton's Satan was a fallen angel of light, a power to be eradicated. This contrasts with some Oriental and Western philosophies that evil is the opposite pole of good and that gods of evil (such as Loki in the Norse tradition) are a necessary facet of creation. Incorporated in many of the demonic images is the goat-footed pagan Pan, the Horned God of Nature. He represents natural instincts, Freud's id that, if unbridled, would destroy humankind's civilized world. Nevertheless, as Freud recognized, these basic instincts are necessary for survival and procreation, providing a source of root energy and drive necessary for action. The enslaved figures that are depicted often hold their own chains. Were they to use their negative aspects to bring about positive change, they would be free from the thrall of their inner darkness. If we destroy or project onto others our shadow side, we lose an integral part of ourselves.

Positive Interpretation Using negative feelings to bring about change and put right injustices, accepting that negative feelings about a person or situation are justifiable, acknowledging a negative influence or situation

Challenging Aspects Repressing justifiable anger and resentment so they turn into depression or self-hate, allowing the negativity of others to affect us, continuing in destructive patterns or relationships while blaming others

THE TOWER

The Tower is a symbol of liberation from restrictions and stagnation; the new beginning promised in the Death card, with which it frequently appears in readings. In some packs, it is called the Tower of Destruction or *La Maison Dieu,* which is not (as literally translated) the house of God but a corruption of Diefel, the biblical

Tower of Babel. The Tower of Babel was built by Noah's descendants in an attempt to climb up to the heavens to avenge themselves on God for sending the flood. As a punishment, God sent down a confusion of tongues, and henceforward it was said that different languages caused discord among humankind. In fact, this was in itself a liberation so that diversity, not only of expression but of ideas, could germinate to prevent stagnation. A lightning bolt cleaves the tower. However, those who fall from it are not destroyed but freed from a prison, like Rapunzel in the fairy story. What is destroyed is the narrow perspective of life viewed from narrow windows and the false security that comes from limited horizons. This card does not predict coming disaster, but points out weaknesses of which the questioner is aware, the cracks that are already appearing, which, if recognized, can offer relief from stagnation.

Positive Interpretation Liberation from restrictions, a widening of possibilities, the apparent destruction of plans that did not have firm foundations, the chance to build a more secure future

Challenging Aspects Loss of a temporary refuge from reality, fear of losing familiar if restricting routines, temporary setbacks and disruption that cannot be avoided

THE STAR

THE STAR.

The Star is the card of hope, of inspiration, of the illumination that heralds a happier future. Stars have been a symbol of promise in many cultures. For the ancient Egyptians, the appearance of Sirius heralded the annual flooding of the Nile, which brought fertility to the parched land. The magi followed their star to Bethlehem. The Norse god Tyr, God of Courage and War, who sacrificed his sword arm to save the other gods by binding Fenris Wolf, is known as the Star or Spirit Warrior. Some tarot packs show the Star as a naked maiden, pouring water on the earth to nourish it. In the same way, practical action nourishes dreams and hopes. Although we are wishing on a star, those dreams most likely to come true are those that we make come true ourselves.

Positive Interpretation Signs of hope after a difficult period, pursuing dreams that can come true with effort and belief in oneself, finding sudden inspiration that heralds future happiness

Challenging Aspects Pinning hopes on unrealistic expectations of perfection in people or situations, being attracted by surface glamour or excitement, spending so much time wishing that real opportunities are missed

THE MOON

The Moon card is a symbol of mystery, magic, and the cycle of life, with its ebbs and flows, its constant promises of renewal and new beginnings. The Moon Goddess was worshiped from early times in her three aspects that reflected the life cycle of maiden, mother, and wise woman (birth, growth, fruition; wisdom, death, and rebirth) that are mirrored in the seasons. To Artemis, the Virgin Goddess, and Selene, the Mother, the High Priestess, and Empress of the earlier cards, the symbol of the moon adds the third dimension—that of the Crone, Hecate, hag of the night; the wisdom of experience and acceptance of endings in the dark of the moon, to return as new life in the crescent. The wolves seen baying on some of the cards are a primitive call of nature. The crayfish, one of the oldest surviving creatures, who cohabited with the dinosaurs, crawling out of the water is the envoy of timelessness. This, then, is a very special card, containing elements of many of the others.

Positive Interpretation Trusting dreams, visions, and psychic insights; using imagination rather than logic; using the natural ebbs and flows of energies to know the right time to act and the right time to wait

Challenging Aspects Living purely in a world of dreams, following the easy path, being unnecessarily secretive

THE SUN

The Sun is the card of pure energy, optimism, joy, and success in the world's terms; the alter ego of the Moon. Sun Gods have a central role in many mythologies: the Egyptian Ra who ferried the solar boat across the sky each day; Helios of the Greeks, who was regarded as the sun himself and ascended the heavens in the morning in a chariot, drawn by winged snow-white horses, and in the evening plunged into the ocean; Quetzalcoatl, the Aztec plumed serpent deity of the sun. The Summer Solstice, the longest day of the year, is heralded as the day of maximum power, and pagan ceremonies—from Druidic observances at stone circles, aligned to the dawn sunrise, to the American Indian Sun Dance—acknowledge the powerful energies associated with solar light and warmth.

Positive Interpretation The perfect moment to seize an opportunity; unfulfilled potential; the energy and ability to succeed in any action or plan

Challenging Aspects Competitiveness in a destructive sense, obsession with perfection, exhaustion due to burnout

JUDGMENT

Judgment or the Angel is the symbol of reconciliation and of spiritual renewal. It symbolizes the day of reckoning, not in the medieval sense of the allotting of rewards and punishments, but self-judgment—recognition of one's own and others' worth and accepting the weakness and folly both of ourselves and others. Once the books are balanced, any redundant feelings of bitterness, anger, guilt, or a sense of failure in the world's terms can be left behind, as the essential person refined through experience is ready to move forward. Essentially, Judgment is the card of freedom. This card centers around the Day of Judgment where figures—often a trinity of man, woman, and child portrayed on the Death card—are seen rising from the grave. St. Michael, Archangel of the Sun, is depicted blowing a golden trumpet, restoring life. He is the "light-bringer."

Positive Interpretation The ability to evaluate the success of a particular venture or life generally, in terms of personal satisfaction rather than the world's terms; the ability to forgive and forget, both our own mistakes and those of others; using experience, good and bad, to avoid future mistakes

Challenging Aspects Not learning from the past; living life on other people's terms; dwelling on past mistakes and wrongs; making hasty judgments about a situation or person

THE WORLD

The World is the card of expanding horizons and limitless possibilities and also of movement, whether involving actual travel or being open to new fields and ideas. In the center of what is sometimes portrayed as an ellipse, the cosmic egg is the dancer, "at the still point of the turning world," as T. S. Eliot said in his *Four Quartets*. The dancer is sometimes flanked by the symbols of the four Evangelists, Matthew, Mark, Luke, and John, also representing the zodiac signs Aquarius, Leo, Taurus, and Scorpio. These are the signs of the four elements of Air, Fire, Earth, and Water that are integral to the tarot. In a sense, the dancer is the synthesis of the four elements, the elusive philosopher's stone, key to immortality, or perhaps the Fool refined and transformed.

Positive Interpretation New horizons and the beginning of an exciting phase, whether mental or physical; the need to move further afield or to try new ventures; a sense of completeness and self-worth

Challenging Aspects Ignoring what is of value close to home; frenetic activity to fill every moment, which leaves no time for contemplation; refusing to expand the boundaries of possibility

Reading the Cards

Once you master the cards of the Major Arcana, you can read the tarot, although some people find that learning the rest of the cards does add to the quality and detail of readings.

Choose a pack of tarot cards, either the full seventy-eight or the first twenty-two Major cards. Think of a specific question or ask the person for whom you are reading to concentrate on a general issue. If the person tells you the question, it is not cheating, but use the tarot as a tool to provide as much relevant information as possible about an important matter.

* Shuffle the cards and place them facedown. Either divide the pack into three and deal from the one that feels right, or take cards at random from the whole pack so that you cannot see the faces until you have picked the required number.

* Turn them over one at a time and read each card before turning over the next, or look at the whole spread together before beginning the reading. The latter is easier for me, because I can then get an overview before reading the individual cards. There are no rights and wrongs, and if you are trying to follow someone else's rules, you may block your own intuition.

* If you are reading for someone else, get them to shuffle, place, and turn over the cards.

USING THREE, SIX, OR NINE CARDS

When I first began reading, I found it intrusive to assign meanings to certain positions in a layout and simply took three, six, or nine cards from a shuffled pack, facedown. This is still my favorite format and a good one if you are still learning the cards, as it enables you to build up a picture. It is ideal either with the Major cards or the whole pack.

The first row of three cards is placed from the left-hand corner nearest the dealer. If you are using a six- or nine-card spread, continue dealing, with the second row placed directly above the first, also from left to right. The third row also runs from left to right.

As with any reading, however simple or complex, it can be helpful to look at the initial layout and let the impressions take shape in your mind. Look for patterns of cards that seem linked, such as the Empress and the Emperor, the Hanged Man and Death. You may find two related groups. This patterning becomes more evident when you add the Minor Arcana, and, in time, grouping in your mind's eye becomes automatic. This initial impression may disagree with the individual card meanings. But trusting this first and most powerful insight is the key to successful tarot reading and, indeed, any divination. The cards are building blocks. Considered as a whole, as Gestalt psychologists say, they may be very different from the sum of their parts.

A Horseshoe Spread

This five-card layout does assign significance to the position of the cards, and this can be of special help in answering more specific questions or issues. The spread varies according to different practitioners, so if the assigned positions do not feel right, experiment until the format works for you. Use the Horseshoe layout with either the Major Arcana or a complete pack.

Deal five cards in a horseshoe formation:

Card 3

Card 2   **Card 4**

Card 1   **Card 5**

Read the cards from the bottom left upward and down the other side of the horseshoe, progressing from the situation at the beginning of the reading to possible advantage as a result of decision to initiate change or to wait. You may begin with a specific issue in mind or you may find that if you let your mind go blank, the first card dealt will provide the real question.

Card 1 This represents the present position in which you find yourself and a choice, dilemma, or predominant question about some aspect of your life.

Card 2 Represents present influences. These are all the people and circumstances that have contributed to your present position and who would be affected by any decision or change you make.

Card 3 Unexpected influences. These are the hidden factors that influence you, your past successes, and all the messages you carry from parents, past lovers, and so on. They also include those factors you can see out of the corner of your eye, just beyond the horizon, that come into play according to whether you decide to change or preserve the status quo.

Card 4 Suggested action or decision to wait, both of which will alter the path that you would have followed if you had let events or others dictate the future.

Card 5 Possible outcome of intervention.

Sample Tarot Card Reading

Anna was eighteen and her parents were eager for her to take up a place at university to read history. However, Anna had been working on Saturdays and during school holidays at a local retail store and out of the blue had decided to train as an assistant manager. Anna's parents were angry and upset, but Anna pointed out the number of graduates who were unemployed and said that by the time she would have left the university, she could be fully trained and earning a good salary. Jan, Anna's mother, asked me to read her cards. I used the Major Arcana only for Jan's reading, as I felt that the issue was more complex than it seemed on the surface.

Card 1 Present Position

The Hanged Man. Who was making the sacrifice? Anna, giving up her chance of an academic future, or Jan, losing the dream she had had since Anna was a little girl and had written her first story?

Card 2 Present Influences

The Lovers. Anna's change of career would affect the whole family, not least Jan's relationship with her husband Keith. Why? The next card revealed more.

Card 3 Unexpected Influences

The Tower of Destruction or Liberation. What was being destroyed? Jan and Keith's expectations of an academic daughter. Jan admitted that Keith's amorous interests were wandering and he had indulged in several affairs. However, Anna's need for a stable home and financial support for three more years ensured that Keith, who adored his daughter, would stay around at least until Anna graduated. Jan had not worked outside the home for years and said she did not know how she would cope with a working daughter. But could or should the marriage be saved?

Card 4 Suggested Action

The High Priestess, the alter ego of motherhood, detachment, was the essential Jan, who was in fact a gifted caterer and made wedding cakes for friends that had been featured in the local press.

Card 5 Possible Outcome

The Sun, for Anna certainly, if she followed her own route to happiness and, if necessary, made her own mistakes. But this was Jan's reading and showed futures in which she would blossom, in which Anna might regret her decision, Keith might leave Jan, or she might decide the faithless Keith was not worth sacrificing her own life for. It even showed the answer to the question she was really asking. You cannot live your life through others or hold back the inevitable, but you can wisely choose your own path.

The Minor Arcana

The Minor Arcana comprises fifty-six cards, four more than a conventional playing card pack. There are forty numbered cards, from ace (or one) to ten in each of four suits, as well as sixteen Court cards.

THE FOUR SUITS

The four tarot suits—Pentacles (coins or discs), Cups (dishes or chalices), Wands (batons or staves), and Swords—correspond to the four traditional playing card suits: diamonds, hearts, clubs, and spades. But the tarot suits also represent what the ancients regarded as the four elements of which all life was composed: Earth, Water, Fire, and Air and the spiritual and psychological qualities associated with these elements.

Pentacles or Discs correspond to the element *Earth* and the attribute called sensation by the psychologist Jung. They refer to the everyday practicalities of life, financial matters, and the domestic sphere. A predominance of this suit indicates that progress will be step by step, but results will be real and long lasting.

Cups or Chalices are linked with the element *Water,* the attribute Jung called feeling. They talk of emotions, relationships, and empathy with others. A predominance of Cups suggests that the most effective response to a current joy or sorrow in your life should come from the heart, not the head.

Wands or Staves are associated with the element *Fire,* the attribute Jung called intuition. They speak of creativity, originality, and individuality. A predominance of Wands indicates that you should seek an immediate solution, using your enthusiasm and imagination.

Swords are linked with the element *Air,* the attribute Jung called thinking. They speak of limitations and obstacles, but also the power to initiate change, especially under difficult circumstances. A predominance of Swords suggests that logic and determination are the way to overcome problems.

THE NUMBER CARDS

Rather than containing a positive or challenging aspect within each card, the numbers themselves highlight either obstacles or progress that vary from suit to suit.

The Aces herald a beginning or an unexpected event or change, always advantageous. They are the cards of optimism.

* The Ace of Pentacles speaks of a new beginning on a material or practical level that may involve learning a new skill or an opportunity for financial gain.

* The Ace of Cups represents either a new relationship, whether a friendship, romance, or pregnancy, or a new stage in a relationship.

* The Ace of Wands promises positive change, whether travel or a new interest or job opportunity.

* The Ace of Swords promises a new start, perhaps after a setback or delay, and the power to succeed through logic and determination.

The Twos deal with partnership issues, both with balancing different priorities and reconciling conflicting demands. They are the cards of duality.

* The Two of Pentacles talks about the need to juggle the practical demands of everyday life, the logistics of balancing work and home or family commitments, and also balancing the books and deciding on financial priorities.

* The Two of Cups indicates that the relationship aspect is dominant: the deepening of a relationship, whether love or friendship, the mending of a quarrel, or a period of harmony in a relationship.

* The Two of Wands is the card of choosing between alternatives that demand a period of reflection before action, whether a career move or a new interest or project.

* The Two of Swords appears if neither of two alternatives appeals. It is better to use logic to decide rather than do nothing and wait for someone else to choose for you.

The Threes involve cooperation and increase, whether a gain or the need for extra input. They are the cards of unity.

* The Three of Pentacles is an assurance that practical efforts you have made have not been wasted and that working with others, rather than alone, is the key to success at this time.

* The Three of Cups promises celebration: a birth or addition to the family, a family gathering, a get-together with absent friends, or a period of emotional happiness in the family.

* The Three of Wands marks the widening of horizons and the formulating of definite plans, and promises that a period of waiting or stagnation will soon be over.

* The Three of Swords represents the problematic aspect of relationships involving more than two people, whether emotional or in the workplace. Apparent rejection or being passed over can open new fields if you don't give way to emotional blackmail.

The Fours are the cards of organization and stability; they offer reassurance that a venture or relationship is secure. They are the cards of security.

* The Four of Pentacles poses the question "Is it better to hold on to what has been partially achieved or attained in a practical or material sense?" The alternative is to risk what has been achieved in the real hope of greater gain.

* The Four of Cups expresses vague discontent with an existing situation on the emotional front or a general desire for something more exciting, the pursuit of which may put at risk an existing relationship or friendship.

* The Four of Wands represents success and recognition of achievement, but prompts the question "What is the next stage?" for there is an inner restlessness that will not be content for long.

* The Four of Swords speaks of the ghosts in our head; the fears and doubts that may seem very real and that can paralyze us into inaction and cause retreat from action. The battles are best fought in the real world.

The Fives involve communication and versatility, but can lead to restlessness and uncertainty. They are the cards of instability.

★ The Five of Pentacles talks of the need for practical help or advice with money matters and suggests that help will come from an unexpected source, as usual sources may prove uncooperative.

★ The Five of Cups reflects a disappointment or emotional setback, but says that it is important to keep this in perspective and see what can be salvaged, as the loss is only partial and may even be restored.

★ The Five of Wands warns there may be a fair amount of opposition to your immediate plans or personal ambitions. It's always worth arguing for what you want or believe in.

★ The Five of Swords implies that the odds may seem insurmountable, but the answer lies in finding another subtle tactic.

The Sixes reflect peace and harmony and events that turn out better than expected, although there is an element of escapism and idealism. These are the cards of integration.

★ The Six of Pentacles promises that financial or practical help will be offered—although it may be that if you are the one helping others, you are asked to give too much or too frequently.

★ The Six of Cups is the card of nostalgia, of looking back on peaceful, sunlit days, perhaps through rose-tinted spectacles, perhaps a relationship or friendship you have left behind. It may not be too late to rekindle the past. However, it may also be that children or old people bring happiness to your life.

★ The Six of Wands is a card that heralds promotion or recognition of your worth and says that you are on the right path and should not doubt yourself.

★ The Six of Swords says that calmer times lie ahead after a period of unrest or uncertainty, so long as you leave behind any bitterness or regrets. This card is sometimes said to indicate travel.

The Sevens deal with wisdom acquired through experience, principles, and decision making. They are the cards of noble action.

*   The Seven of Pentacles expresses doubts at the sheer immensity of the task undertaken, either financially or in the practical sphere. There are no shortcuts, but it may be important to find temporary respite from money and work worries.

*   The Seven of Cups involves the need to choose between several options or paths, between success in the world's terms or emotional satisfaction. It may be necessary to consider the less certain path in which emotional and spiritual fulfillment may offer less-tangible rewards. The only danger lies in indecision.

*   The Seven of Wands says you may find it hard to stand by your principles and decisions, especially if you are facing a lot of backbiting or rivalry. However, your own satisfaction is probably worth more to you than the wholehearted approval of others.

*   The Seven of Swords warns that there may be less-than-honest behavior among those around you, including gossip and petty spite. Use stealth and avoidance tactics to defeat any opposition.

The Eights are the cards of overcoming obstacles and abandoning what may be redundant. They are the cards of positive change.

*   The Eight of Pentacles is sometimes called the apprentice card, of learning new skills or adopting old ideas to create firm foundations for success.

*   The Eight of Cups says that sometimes it is important to start again emotionally if you are in a destructive situation; this may involve walking away or breaking the old patterns. A phase of a relationship may be ending physically, or there may be a change in emphasis not caused by you. Sometimes it may be helpful to step back emotionally for a while.

*   The Eight of Wands, the "up and flying" card, heralds complete change: travel, a house move, or even a turnabout of ideas or beliefs that may involve physical uprooting or a sudden enlightenment or burst of enthusiasm, usually in response to some obstacle or setback.

*   The Eight of Swords suggests that you may feel trapped by the demands of others or by old guilts and responsibilities that you

thought you'd left behind. Use your head, not your heart, to face the inner fears that are the real obstacle to your happiness.

The Nines speak of courage and determination to succeed whatever the odds, also of self-reliance or total isolation. They are the cards of supreme effort.

* The Nine of Pentacles is the card of security and independence in a material sense or in the sense of a determination to not rely on others to solve a crisis. It promises material success through one's own resources and efforts.

* The Nine of Cups is the card of self-confidence and emotional self-reliance; not loneliness or isolation, but an ability to be happy in one's own company and sure of one's own worth. It assures you happiness and happy relationships come from self-love, which is very different from selfishness.

* The Nine of Wands, the "bloody but unbowed card," promises that success is very near, whether in your career or personal life, and that you are in a strong position to achieve your ambitions if you make a supreme effort.

* The Nine of Swords is a card that reflects rather than predicts doubts and despair. As with similar Sword cards, the worst fears are within, and one can magnify them to the point at which no solution seems possible. There may be many problems in the outside world that demand resolution. Only by facing them with courage, breaking out of the isolation, and seeking support will the darkness dissipate.

The Tens herald completion, which can either represent perfection or endings before new beginnings and new hope. These are the cards of fulfillment.

* The Ten of Pentacles shows the culmination of hard work and practical effort and says happiness lies in the domestic world and the home itself, whether finding the ideal home or making the present one comfortable.

* The Ten of Cups gives the same message on the emotional plane. Happiness lies in stable relationships, togetherness, and family bliss rather than dreams of perfect love and passion.

The next two cards are much more about the end-before-the-beginning aspect of the Tens.

* The Ten of Wands talks of a heavy burden or worry that is soon to be lifted. It is a question now of off-loading any unnecessary responsibilities imposed by others and accepting that you have gone as far as you can or should. You should move forward, free of any restricting obligations.

* The Ten of Swords, "the darkest hour is before the dawn" card, continues from the Nine of Swords and has the morning breaking, promising a new and better tomorrow, the light at the end of the tunnel. It is time to accept that some aspect of your life is ending, and it is a time to regret and allow yourself to be sad and rest before moving on. The sun will shine again for you.

Reading the Number Cards

You can read the number cards as part of the whole pack or with the Court cards alone in the same way as a playing card set. Some people remove the Court cards altogether, finding that these "personality cards" detract from the twenty-two Trumps.

* If you use the Major Arcana, see whether there is a predominance of Major or Minor cards (about four to one if you use the Court cards). If there are proportionately more Major cards, then the reading is concerned with wider-ranging issues or matters of significance to the questioner.

* If you use the Minor Arcana, notice whether any suit predominates. A predominant suit can give you a focus for the readings. For example, a number of Cups suggests that matters of the heart are the prime concern, or the questioner may have endowed the issue with emotional significance, even if money or career are under consideration. If any suit is absent, for example, Pentacles,

this may indicate that financial incentives or problems would not affect any decision that was reached. If a number is repeated, it may indicate a particular theme running through the reading. For example, two or more fours would suggest that security/stagnation was a central concern.

THe PYramID spreaD

This in-depth spread is best done with both the Major and the Minor cards. I have used an example from a real reading with a full pack in which no Court cards turned up. It is spread from a shuffled or mixed pack, from the right, in four rows ending at the center top. As it is a layout involving steps, it may be better to turn the cards over one at a time as you read them.

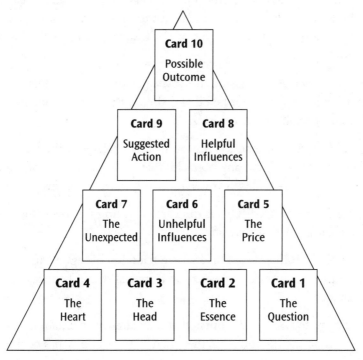

The pyramid is a sacred shape, found in places as geographically distant as Egypt and South America. The greatest attention has been focused on the Great Pyramid of Cheops at Giza in Egypt, built around

2700 B.C., which seems to be the repository of strange physical phenomena and also psychic and healing powers. It has been suggested that pyramids acted as transformers of cosmic energy. The Pyramid spread is therefore especially good for spiritual matters or major life changes.

Card 1 The Question that is being posed, either openly or consciously.

Card 2 The Essence, sometimes called the Root of the Matter, is the deeper, often unformed question or unconscious wish or fear.

Card 3 The Head or Logical Considerations. Careful analysis, which stems from deduction and detecting a pattern, is a vital skill for the tarot reader. Likewise, in any reading, what the conscious mind can deduce from given facts is part of the equation.

Card 4 The Heart of the Matter. This is what the questioner feels, and while the emotional response alone is not the best indicator of possible action, what someone knows in his or her heart is right is too powerful an indicator to ignore.

Card 5 The Price. Any decision, however positive, involves loss as well as regret for the options not taken and the cost (not only monetary, but also emotional) of any decision.

Card 6 Unhelpful Influences. This can be any advice or criticism, however well-intentioned, and any obstacles that stand in the way of fulfilling a goal, even self-doubts. Swords frequently turn up in this position.

Card 7 The Unexpected. This is the card of seeing just over the next horizon to a factor that may affect your decision.

Card 8 Helpful Influences. This may be friends, colleagues, an unexpected source of help, or even your own special strengths that enable you to succeed.

Card 9 Suggested Action. A course that may alter or maintain the status quo, but which the questioner, rather than outside events, has decided.

Card 10 Possible Outcome, the Crown of the Reading. This card suggests the possible consequence of the proposed action. It is not a card of fixed fate, because circumstances and our response to them are constantly changing (see the chapter on the *I Ching*).

Sample Tarot Card Reading

Tony was in his fifties and unmarried with no immediate family. He had discovered that he was seriously ill and unlikely to live to old age. Consequently, Tony had taken early retirement and wanted to use his savings and pension to travel around Central and South America and visit the remains of the ancient civilizations, especially the Mayan and Aztec sun temples. However, his friends advised Tony to hold on to his money, as he might need it to ease his life as he became progressively worse. Doctors said that treatment might offer him a few extra months of reasonable health, but there was no chance of a cure. Tony selected from the full Major and Minor Arcana.

Card 1 The Question

The World: should he expand his horizons in travel?

Card 2 The Essence

The Two of Pentacles: should Tony hold on to his money or take what will be his last opportunity to fulfill his dreams?

Card 3 The Head

The Hermit: listen to the inner voice that in this case would suggest that logically Tony will only have one opportunity.

Card 4 The Heart of the Matter

The Four of Cups: Tony's discontentment with friends who were trying to protect him, but did not understand his urgent sense that time was running out. Tony wanted to be alone to sort out his feelings.

Card 5 The Price

The Nine of Swords: the price of moving away from his friends was facing alone the fears that came in the night; fears that were very real, of pain and ultimately his premature death.

Card 6 Unhelpful Influences

The Ten of Swords: the well-meaning insistence of those around him that the future was not as black, that there was always hope. For Tony, this false hope was actually holding him back from making major changes in his life. Until others could accept that he would not get better, Tony felt unsupported.

Card 7 The Unexpected

The Empress: for Tony, there was the hope that he would meet someone, male or female, who would understand his position and support him in both the happy and darker days to come. He hoped that by traveling he might meet this person. Tony had always held back from emotional involvement. Now it was suddenly important.

Card 8 Helpful Influences

The Eight of Pentacles: learning new skills. Tony had almost decided to begin crash courses in Spanish and Portuguese and also to improve his skills with a video recorder so he could record his travels. Tony commented that there were many things he could still do while he felt fit.

Card 9 Suggested Action

The Eight of Wands: the up and flying card. Tony knew what he wanted to do. The reading confirmed the rightness of his decision.

Card 10 Possible Outcome

Ace of Swords: a new beginning under difficulty? Was remission round the corner? Always a possibility, said Tony, though he felt it better for him not to hope. But another new beginning was a project he had not even acknowledged to himself: writing an account of his travels and the insights he acquired, to leave as a legacy whether published or not.

I lost touch with Tony and do not know if he went on his journey. However, he had such determination that I shall look for his account on the bookshelves.

THE COURT CARDS

There are sixteen Court cards—four more than in a playing card deck because the Jack takes on two aspects, the Page and the Knight. The Court cards can have different names, such as Princess and Prince, Daughter and Son, and even Priestess and Shaman, instead of the traditional Queen and King, but most keep the traditional titles. These Court cards usually refer to personalities who are dominant or difficult in our lives or represent aspects of our own personalities that are significant or needed at a particular time.

As you read about each Court card, you may find it helpful to note characters you have met over the years whom they resemble.

The Pages These are the cards of the Earth and may refer to a child or gentle teenager of either sex. But if the person is not identified during a reading, the card can represent an undeveloped aspect of the questioner's personality as tentative ideas or dreams. On the challenging side, they can represent a person of any age who is childish.

* The Page of Pentacles is a reliable, hardworking, and studious young person who is loyal and stoical. However, this Page can be unimaginative and unwilling to try new things.

* The Page of Cups is a dreamer: kind, sympathetic, and upset by the troubles of others; easily hurt and sensitive to the needs of others. However, he or she can be unworldly and unable to accept criticism.

* The Page of Wands is quick-witted, curious, imaginative, and eager to try anything new. Ideals are untainted by the desire for worldly success, and enthusiasm for life is unbounded. However, the Page of Wands is easily distracted and becomes discouraged at the first sign of difficulty.

* The Page of Swords is clever, observant, humorous, and aware even at a young age of life's limitations and injustices. However, he or she can be devious and careless of others' feelings.

The Knights Knights are older teenagers, especially boys, and men and women in their twenties who may not have formed a stable emotional unit. If the Knight in a reading is not identified, he or she may be part of a new facet of the questioner that is emerging to act out of character or to take up a cause. The challenging aspect is the immature person of any age who pursues his or her own desires at the expense of others. The Knights are the cards of Air and in any suit are regarded as messenger cards that herald news in the area of the next card in a reading.

* The Knight of Pentacles is the most stable of the Knights, tempering restlessness and crusading with a vein of reality and a respect for the world. The challenging aspect is that this Knight may lack the vision to explore wider horizons.

*   The Knight of Cups is the original knight in shining armor. He or she offers excitement, sentiment, and romance, and his or her quest is for perfection in others—as well as in his- or herself. The challenging aspect of the Knight of Cups is shallowness of feelings and inconstancy in affections.

*   The Knight of Wands is the great communicator and innovator who devises brilliant schemes and loves travel and risk of any kind. The challenging aspect of this Knight is that he or she can flit from one project or job to the next, never completing anything. He or she can also be liberal with the truth.

*   The Knight of Swords has perhaps the most impetus and determination of all, challenging injustice and showing courage against the most powerful odds. The challenging aspect is obsessiveness and a willingness to sacrifice others for his or her cause.

The Queens The Queens represent a more mature woman, whether a mother or a female authority figure, symbolizing female fertility and wisdom. If there is no Queen whom you recognize, the card may stand for your own nurturing side, not only in relationships, but in any situation in which your anima is the predominant function. The Queens are the cards of Water. The challenging aspect is in possessiveness or living other people's lives for them.

*   The Queen of Pentacles, sometimes called the Queen of Health and Home, is a woman (or man) who deals with practical and financial affairs in such a way as to make whatever or whoever she is queen of comfortable and secure. She cares for the sick, the old, and the troubled, not by dispensing advice, but by coming up with real solutions. She is incredibly hard-working. The challenging aspect is that she can become obsessed with order or take over the responsibilities of others and become a martyr.

*   The Queen of Cups is naturally intuitive and peace-loving, totally in tune with the feelings of others and the natural world.

She represents fertility and creativity in their widest sense. Her challenging aspect is in emotional possessiveness and in seeking ideal rather than real relationships.

* The Queen of Wands is the wise woman, independent, authoritative, but also intuitive and imaginative. She is at the hub of activities, with her enthusiasm and ability to weld together disparate people and interests. However, she does not live through her family, though she may be happily married and a mother. Her challenging aspect is in her impatience with those who seem weak or lack vision and her inability to let others take the lead.

* The Queen of Swords is the disappointed woman, whether in relationships or the workplace, whose own past or present sorrows can make her bitter and overcritical. The love and kindness still exist beneath the surface, and she may prove an unexpected and powerful ally in adversity. Her challenging aspect is her inability to express love and gratitude and in being unforgiving.

The Kings The Kings represent mature or older men or male authority figures. They embody power, achievement, paternalism, and responsibility. If you do not recognize the King in your reading, it may represent your own ultimate animus—your own desire and drive to succeed. These are the Fire cards. The Kings' challenging aspects are domineering ways and inflexibility.

* The King of Pentacles has succeeded either financially, in business, or in a practical, methodical way and is firmly rooted in his domestic world of which he sees himself as benign lord and master. He works hard for his family or to make a comfortable base and is honest and generous. His challenging aspects are that he can be overcautious, obsessed by detail, and materialistic.

* The King of Cups is the most approachable of the Kings. Popular and benign, he puts people above property or achievement. He may be spiritual, religious, or involved in the caring

professions, but is invariably the dreamer who believes in the goodness of humanity to the end of his days and is constantly striving for perfection. His challenging aspects are sudden bursts of anger and flirtatiousness in view of his lifelong struggle for ideal love.

★ The King of Wands is a man of vision: persuasive, an expert communicator, and the driving force behind many ventures; energetic and eager to share his considerable knowledge and wisdom. He lives life to the fullest and expects others to do the same. His challenging aspects are selfishness and lack of loyalty in favor of innovation.

★ The King of Swords may appear to outsiders totally rigid and lacking sympathy with humanity, but his strength is in his strong sense of responsibility and in using logic and clear thought to succeed. This King is associated with authority figures such as bank managers, government officials, judges, lawyers, and doctors, both male and female. His challenging aspects are pedantry and calculated cruelty to opponents.

A COURT CARD READING WITH FOUR CARDS

Shuffle the sixteen Court cards and place them facedown in a circle. Select four cards and place them in a pile. Dealing from the top, place a card facedown nearest to you. Read this and then place the second card directly above the first, reading this before placing the third, until you have the four cards in a vertical line.

Card 4 Who will you become?

Card 3 Who will oppose you?

Card 2 Who will help you?

Card 1 Who are you now?

Sample Court Cart Reading

Anita felt she was being cast in the role of wicked stepmother by her husband Ken's mother, who constantly referred to his ex-wife Gaynor in glowing terms. The older woman ignored the fact that Gaynor had moved in with another man, leaving Ken with two young boys. The boys stayed with their mother and her new partner on weekends, but Granny seemed hell-bent on proving how inadequate Anita was, even though she coped with a full-time job and the children. Ken did not want to get involved as he was afraid of his mother's sharp tongue. Using the Court cards, Anita drew the following:

Card 4
The Queen of Wands

Card 3
The Knight of Cups

Card 2
The Queen of Swords

Card 1
The Queen of Pentacles

Card 1 Who is Anita now?

The Queen of Pentacles is the role Anita occupies at the moment: caring for Ken and the boys, working, and trying to please her difficult mother-in-law.

Card 2 Who will help?

The Queen of Swords. Not the obvious candidate for this card, Ken's mother, but the other opponent, Anita concluded, the much-vaunted

Gaynor. Anita had sporadic, but not unfriendly contact with Ken's ex-wife, although her mother-in-law's attitude made her feel very hostile toward her predecessor.

Card 3 Who will oppose the resolution of the problem?

The Knight of Cups, whom Anita identified as her lovely but very immature husband who wanted to keep everybody happy and secretly enjoyed having women—including his mother—fighting over him.

Card 4 Who could Anita become if she overcame her present feelings of inadequacy?

The Queen of Wands, independent of the need of approval from her mother-in-law once she saw through her power game.

Anita took the boys to their mother's new home and had a chat with Gaynor, only to discover that the mother-in-law had been driving her wild with tales of Anita's virtues. Gaynor explained that one of the problems with her marriage to Ken had been his inability to stand up to his mother's interference. Realizing that Ken could not change, Anita kept in direct contact with Gaynor to minimize the effects of the mother-in-law's troublemaking.

The Tarot and the Zodiac

There are many correspondences between tarot and astrology and these have given rise to different systems. Each sign has a planetary ruler. According to the Golden Dawn system, each sign and its ruling planet have a corresponding tarot card and color. In addition, each of these signs is associated with one of the twelve Houses or areas of relevance that appear on many zodiacal wheels of the year. This House maintains its significance whether or not its own sign is currently in it.

This system avoids most of the complications of many astrological spreads that can detract from the tarot meanings. Yet it keeps the element of unconscious selection that is the key to inner astrology, whereby symbolic rather than predetermined connections are made with the powers inherent in the Sun Signs and Planets.

Each House has its own associated Sun Sign and Planetary tarot card from the Major Arcana. When you read the tarot using a zodiac wheel, it pinpoints the area to which the card is referring and, according to the order in which it is dealt, can offer insight into your inner astrology. Below is a list of popular associations, including colors. You might like to make a tarot wheel and use it to pinpoint the Major Arcana cards you select unseen from the pack. You can, if you wish, color the segments in the suggested rainbow shades that merge throughout the spectrum. More detailed explanations of the Houses are given after the chart. Each House has two tarot cards associated with it: first, the Sun Sign card, reflecting personal issues; and second,

House	Area	Color	Sign and Card	Ruling Planet and Card
First House	The unique self	Red	Aries—Emperor	Mars—Tower
Second House	Financial matters	Red/Orange	Taurus—Hierophant	Venus—Empress
Third House	Communication	Orange	Gemini—Lovers	Mercury—Magician
Fourth House	Domestic matters	Orange/ Yellow	Cancer—Chariot	Moon— High Priestess
Fifth House	Love and children	Yellow	Leo—Strength	Sun—Sun
Sixth House	Health; detailed matters of all kinds	Yellow/Green	Virgo—Hermit	Mercury—Magician
Seventh House	Partnerships	Green	Libra—Justice	Venus—Empress
Eighth House	Endings; psychic development	Green/Blue	Scorpio—Death	Pluto—Judgment
Ninth House	Travel; new ideas	Blue	Sagitarrius—Temperance	Jupiter– Wheel of Fortune
Tenth House	Career; officialdom	Blue/Purple	Capricorn—Devil	Saturn—World
Eleventh House	Friendship; principles	Purple	Aquarius—Star	Uranus—Fool
Twelfth House	Conflicting interests; intuition	Purple/Red	Pisces—Moon	Neptune— Hanged Man

the Planetary Ruler, reflecting issues involving others. The Magician and the Empress appear twice.

If any of these tarot cards feels wrong in a certain place, simply follow your own insights. Equally, if a House seems to suggest additional or other attributes, again adapt it according to what works for you.

The First House, Aries, March 21–April 20 The First House deals with the self, the individual, and core personality. It talks of new beginnings, change, and renewal.

The Second House, Taurus, April 21–May 21 The Second House deals with possessions and financial matters and speaks of material concerns and security of all kinds.

The Third House, Gemini, May 22–June 21 The Third House talks of relationships with equals, whether brothers and sisters or neighbors, and interaction with others. It also concerns travel and communication, learning, study, and memory.

The Fourth House, Cancer, June 22–July 22 The Fourth House revolves around the home and private world of the individual. It also talks of older people, especially relations, and all the issues involved in aging.

The Fifth House, Leo, July 23–August 23 The Fifth House concerns love, emotions, and passions. It talks of any emotional issues and strong feelings and is the house of children and younger relations.

The Sixth House, Virgo, August 24–September 23 The Sixth House talks of health, physical matters, and anything concerning detail. It also talks of work relationships, especially with those for whom you care professionally or as subordinates.

The Seventh House, Libra, September 24–October 23 The Seventh House concerns close relationships and partnerships, whether of marriage or business. It deals with the negative as well as positive aspects and the actions of rivals and with any matter connected with justice.

The Eighth House, Scorpio, October 24–November 22 The Eighth House concerns endings that form the seed of new beginnings, matters of inheritance, taxes, and debts, and psychic and mystical matters.

The Ninth House, Sagittarius, November 23–December 21 The Ninth House is an extension of the Third House and influences philosophy and far-reaching ideas, distant travel, communication, new educational fields, religion, and new ideas.

The Tenth House, Capricorn, December 22–January 20 The Tenth House concerns the outward public and social image (as opposed to the Fourth House, which deals with the inner private world of home). It talks of career matters and anything to do with officialdom.

The Eleventh House, Aquarius, January 21–February 18 The Eleventh House concerns the influence of friends and organizations and social activities. It also deals with hopes, principles, and ideals.

The Twelfth House, Pisces, February 19–March 20 The Twelfth House concerns limitations, conflicting sorrows, and difficulties. However, it is also the house of intuitive insights that can overcome any obstacles and lead to deeper happiness.

THE ASTROLOGICAL SPREAD

This method is different from the more involved spreads that are sometimes called astrological, because it uses a round clear quartz crystal (about the size of a small coin) or a pure white stone that is thrown onto the zodiacal chart to indicate into which House the card should be placed.

★ Copy or photocopy the zodiac wheel opposite so that a tarot card can comfortably fit inside each segment. Alternatively, you can throw the crystal onto the wheel in the book and place the tarot card in a similar position below it.

★ If more than one card falls in a single House, that suggests that this area is dominant.

★ If your Sun Sign appears in a reading in any position, then the issue concerns your identity and personal world.

★ If the card of your Planetary Ruler appears in any position in the reading, the matter concerns those close to you, whether in your personal or work life.

* If your Sun Sign or its Planetary Ruling card appears in the House associated with your Sun Sign, it is an indication that the issue involves a major change or decision, even if the original question seemed relatively minor.

* If a card appears in the House to which it belongs, this is an indication of harmony and appropriate action or decision making, whether actual or potential.

* Using the Major Arcana only, shuffle or mix the cards, and take a card from the pack facedown.

* Throw the crystal onto the wheel to identify the correct House. If it is on the cusp, take both Houses as an indicator.

* Place the card in the appropriate house and repeat until you have drawn four cards.

Card 1 Your current strengths

Card 2 Your current weaknesses

Card 3 The area of life you need to develop

Card 4 The card of fate

Sample Astrological Reading

David was an Aries in his late forties, a fiery administrator with a large company. Recently, he had been in conflict with Susan, a new young manager whose ambition matched his own. There had been talk of a new post being created in the company's London branch, and Susan, another Fire sign, a Leo, had made it known that she would like the job. David had been with the company for ten years and felt that he should be first in line for any promotion. The interoffice rivalry was causing tension and David had been warned (he felt unfairly) that the dissension was seen as coming from him and that this would make him unsuitable for promotion.

Card 1 Current Strengths

The Emperor in the Tenth House. This signifies career and public image. It is David's Sun Sign tarot card and so relates to him personally and to his identity. David's strengths were in his leadership and drive—a typical Emperor—but the problem was with the image he was projecting in the office. This did not reveal his positive leadership attributes and strength, but was being interpreted as an aggressive attitude, the challenging aspect of the Emperor.

Card 2 Current Weaknesses

Justice in the Third House. This signifies the area of communication. David felt he had been unjustly treated—which might have been true—but resentment and hostility on his part were only furthering Susan's cause. Susan was better at keeping her hostility away from the public gaze.

Card 3 The Area of Life You Need to Develop

The Tower in the First House. This indicates the unique qualities we all have and David's Ruling Planet card, Mars, the God of War. The matter was an important one and it also involved those around him. From what Tower did David need to be freed? His present job, at which younger and more ambitious people were finding favor. For years, a friend had been asking David to take over his overseas sales force in an expanding computer company, an area David had developed in his spare time. Here David's strengths as the Emperor could be utilized, and he would be much more independent in his decision making, another strength of the First House.

Card 4 The Card of Fate

The World in the Ninth House. This points to new ideas, far-reaching communication, and even travel. David realized that he was ready for a major career change.

Ironically, Susan did not get the new position. It was offered to David when he handed in his resignation, but he declined and the post went to an ambitious young man already in the London office.

In the next section, on playing cards, there are several spreads, such as the Celtic Cross and the Calendar spread, that can equally be used with tarot cards. It is probably easier to learn the tarot first, and its images will help you with the plainer playing cards.

Chapter 2

PLAYING CARDS

P LAYING CARDS are rife with superstition. "To be lucky at cards is to be unlucky in love"; "Beginner's luck in gambling plus borrowed money can never lose"; "If luck is against a player, he can change it by getting up and turning around three times with his chair"—these are just some of the beliefs associated with playing cards.

Playing cards are often considered unlucky, partly because of their association with the tarot or "terror" cards and partly because, historically, the evils of gambling were emphasized by various churches and at times by the State. The captains of some fishing vessels do not allow the "devil's picture books" on board. If they are used and anything goes wrong, they throw the cards overboard as a precaution.

Miners also consider them a bad omen in a pit. It is said that thieves never steal cards for fear of detection and throw away any packs found among stolen goods.

In fact, playing cards are, like tea leaves, a homely form of divination, read by firelight or candlelight, by a grandmother or grandfather, mixing words of wisdom and caution with their prophetic messages. Their simplicity makes them a perfect vehicle for the inner eye to cast images on the basic template of the meanings.

The Origin of Playing Cards

The first cards were probably invented in China. It is said that on the eve of the Chinese New Year A.D. 969, the Emperor Mu-tsung played domino cards with his wife, a game that much resembled playing cards. Chinese "money cards" are even closer to Western playing cards. The Chinese engraved copper and silver with designs and numbers based on the four suits. They copied these onto paper and used them for games. Indian cards dating from a similar time showed the Hindu gods holding scepters, swords, cups, and rings.

A key theory places the origin of European playing cards in a region in Egypt. From here, a Mameluke deck dating from around 1400 comprised fifty-two cards with four suits: swords, polo sticks, cups, and coins. Each suit was numbered from one to ten, and there were three court cards in each suit, called *malik* (king), *na'ib malik* (viceroy or deputy-king), and *thani na'ib* (second under-deputy). It seems likely that the *na'ib* court card gave the early names of European cards: *naibbe* (Italian) and *naipes* (Spanish).

Other theories suggest that Marco Polo brought cards back from his thirteenth-century expeditions to China. The Crusaders are another possible source. Another popular route is via the Gypsies, through India and Egypt, because card divination was a popular Romany art. As with the tarot, playing cards may have had several different sources. For many years, playing cards were as ornate as their tarot sisters.

The European use of playing cards was first described in detail in Switzerland in 1377 by a monk in Basle, called John of Rheinfelden. He wrote about a card deck with fifty-two cards, ten number cards, and three court cards (a king and two marshals).

It is known that playing cards were used at the French court in 1390. Odette, the mistress of King Charles VI, introduced a pack brought by Gypsies and decorated with Eastern potentates. Based on these, Odette designed her own pack, depicting members of the French court. This is how we get court cards for the picture cards. A visiting Gypsy demonstrated the oracular power of the cards to Odette and the king by correctly telling future events, as well as secrets from the past and present known only to the king and his mistress.

Four hundred years later, Napoleon planned, and believed he won, several battles and successfully wooed the Empress Josephine using the prophetic power of playing cards.

Reading Playing Cards

Traditionally, a special pack is kept for divination and, when not in use, kept wrapped in black silk and placed on a high shelf. This is believed to elevate its messages above worldly concerns.

However, for many people, the beauty of playing-card divination is that wherever you are, you can very cheaply buy a pack for an instant reading (and also a game to while away the time).

You can read the cards for yourself or for other people, and you can use a card reading for an in-depth reading or to answer a simple question.

* If you are reading for someone else, first shuffle or mix the pack yourself, and then give it to the questioner to shuffle or mix so your psychic imprints are symbolically united in the pack.

* According to conventional practice, the pack is then cut three times by the questioner (with the left hand for symbolic access to the right side of the brain, which controls intuition) and spread either in an overlapping row or in a circle. Cards can then be taken facedown at random for a reading. Or, you can simply deal the cards after shuffling or mixing if this seems more natural.

The Meanings of Playing Cards

Playing-card meanings are templates and can be adapted to an individual's own situation without changing their underlying significance. The meanings are not direct parallels with the tarot, but have echoes of the Minor Arcana. The jacks or knaves combine the Page and Knight cards of the tarot.

* If you include the joker or jokers, this card can suggest that an unexpected factor in the near future may cause a change of plans. However, the jokers are usually discarded before shuffling.

* Four of the same number means an extreme result, whether joy or sorrow.

* Three of the same kind is an indicator of the harmony of different forces.

* Two of the same kind can demonstrate, according to the suit, either a conflict of interest, a reconciliation, or new connection.

* A predominance of court or picture cards says that personalities rather than situations fill your thoughts. You may identify court cards with specific characters in your everyday world, even if the descriptions are not mirror images. Court-card types are cameos rather than actual descriptions.

Rather than each card having positive and negative aspects as the tarot does, certain playing cards are naturally positive and others challenging. For example, the nine of hearts is the wish card, promising the fulfillment of hopes and dreams. The ten of spades, sometimes called the disappointment card, traditionally heralds delays, but the overall result can still be positive.

Diamonds correspond to Pentacles or discs in the tarot. This is the suit of the ancient element Earth and the information we receive from our five senses and common sense. Diamonds in a reading refer to practical matters, money, property, and the home, the qualities of patience and placidity, children, and animals.

* The Ace of Diamonds: A new financial or practical venture; a change of home or a new home-related project; an upsurge in prosperity.

* The Two of Diamonds: Balancing two aspects of life or two areas of responsibility; coming together with another person for a mutually beneficial venture, sorting out domestic issues so that efforts and benefits are fairly divided; an extra source of income.

* The Three of Diamonds: A venture has firm foundations; a birth or addition to the family (sometimes also represented by the ace of diamonds); extra commitments or responsibilities that prove to be of long-term advantage.

- ★ The Four of Diamonds: Limitations in the financial or practical sphere and a question as to whether to take a chance or conserve what you have; decisions and choices at home or concerning children that may not be easy; a need to be patient over matters of property and finance that seem to have no imminent resolution.

- ★ The Five of Diamonds: Temporary practical or monetary obstacles may create a feeling of isolation; look for a new source of help or advice; plans should not be abandoned but modified, building on what you have achieved.

- ★ The Six of Diamonds: Documents and small print are important; keep a cautious rein on finances and avoid taking on too many commitments; a time for reflection and conserving energy rather than taking action; family matters may take up time.

- ★ The Seven of Diamonds: Harmony domestically and in financial matters; longer-term plans are favored; trust dreams and intuitive signs as well as common sense; children or animals may bring joy.

- ★ The Eight of Diamonds: You may discover a new practical or moneymaking skill; domestic or financial arrangements may change unexpectedly, and you may move or refurbish the home; channel any restlessness into tangible improvements.

- ★ The Nine of Diamonds: Put personal interests first; success lies through speculation and expanding horizons; independent thought and action are favored.

- ★ The Ten of Diamonds: Success financially or happiness in the home and family; completion of plans and practical matters or a new permanent domestic commitment.

- ★ The Jack of Diamonds: A practical, reliable younger person of either sex, whose common sense, helpful attitude, and responsibility with money make him or her seem wise beyond their years; unvarying comfort and support in good times and bad.

- ★ The Queen of Diamonds: A practical, organized older woman or one in a long-term relationship; her skills lie in making others feel at home in any setting and in sorting out problems; she is a good ally and a caring mother figure; Mother Earth incarnate.

*   The King of Diamonds: Although sometimes considered dull, this king is a reliable ally, whether a friendly bank manager, a considerate partner, or a father figure who can ensure that life runs smoothly; a family man, he can be incredibly patient, but usually shows affection through deeds rather than words.

Hearts correspond to the Cups or chalices in the tarot. They are linked to the ancient element of Water and in a reading signify love, emotion, intuition, relationships, people in their twenties and thirties, and all who are in love, whatever their age.

*   The Ace of Hearts: An important new relationship or friendship; a new beginning emotionally; a sudden burst of intuition that should be trusted; unexpected happiness; a new start after an emotional setback or broken relationship; unrequited love.
*   The Two of Hearts: A love match; a deep commitment of love, marriage, growing friendship, or mending of old quarrels; also, the coming together of two different aspects of life or two people who may not have seen eye to eye in the past.
*   The Three of Hearts: Rivalry in love or friendship; emotional conflicts in which two people seek sympathy or favor; stress caused by other people's emotional pressure and blackmail.
*   The Four of Hearts: Choices involving the emotions; general feelings of restlessness and emotional dissatisfaction; another person's commitment may be under question.
*   The Five of Hearts: Misunderstandings; a need to communicate from the heart; accepting the reality of existing relationships rather than yearning for an impossible idea; passions that may not always be wise.
*   The Six of Hearts: Harmony and quiet contentment, whether in friendship or love; the positive influence of loyal friends; accepting that differences of attitude in others are not incompatible with loving or friendly feelings; reconciliation, especially with older people.
*   The Seven of Hearts: The card of intuition, dreams, and telepathic communication; trust your instincts and inner voice;

communication will be spiritual and deep with those close; you may also find that colleagues and acquaintances are on the same wavelength and are keen to cooperate.

* The Eight of Hearts: Moving to a new phase in a relationship; beware of jealousy; the need to end any potentially destructive emotional attachments or emotional blackmail; a holiday with loved ones or friends.

* The Nine of Hearts: Emotional independence; self-confidence; known as the wish or heart's desire card, this is incredibly lucky and augurs happiness in a chosen area of life, whether in a love affair or personal venture.

* The Ten of Hearts: Emotional happiness and fulfillment through others; a card of giving emotionally to others and deriving great satisfaction from caring; a card of happy marriages and permanent relationships.

* The Jack of Hearts: A young person, an emotionally vulnerable older person, or an incurable romantic of any age who seeks perfection in love; the original knight in shining armor who may love sentiment and romance more than a real-life person.

* The Queen of Hearts: A mature woman, any woman in a permanent relationship, or a woman who nurtures others and listens to their troubles; a sentimentalist who can become so overwhelmed by others' sorrows and the emotional needs of those she loves that she may lose her own identity; without realizing it, she may hold people back from emotional independence.

* The King of Hearts: An older man who is charismatic and makes everyone feel special and of value; if faithful, he is a great romantic and very tender, but he can be easily tempted and flattered; alternatively, a social-worker-type who cares for the troubles of the world, but may find it difficult to handle his own emotions.

Clubs correspond to the tarot suit of Wands or staves. They are linked to the ancient element of Fire. In a reading, they speak of ambition, success, career, health, travel, expansion, business partnerships, communication, mature people, and business partners or work colleagues.

* The Ace of Clubs: A new beginning in a career, a new ambition, original ideas, a new perspective, or opportunity to travel; a new channel of communication; a desire for independence from a restricting situation.

* The Two of Clubs: An unusually slow card in the otherwise fast-moving suit of clubs; a time to deliberate on possible options or paths; plans involving others may seem restrictive; the need to balance the demands of career and health in which exhaustion or stress may be a factor; you may need to approach a business partnership or work relationship with care.

* The Three of Clubs: Decisions about travel and an opportunity to expand horizons; business or work commitments and opportunities may increase and will demand extra energy and input; communication may involve several people.

* The Four of Clubs: A card about moving forward in the constraints caused by others, which can be frustrating; the ability to win the trust of others is vital, so there must be clear communication and correspondence, even if this seems to slow action down; written communications, as opposed to verbal responses, may be necessary to clarify a position or intention.

* The Five of Clubs: A time to argue one's case and stand one's ground in all matters outside the home; care should be taken healthwise to avoid accidents through tiredness and carelessness, as well as stress from overinvolvement in problems caused by others; rivals may be less than open in communications; make sure you get the credit at work for your input and ideas.

* The Six of Clubs: A tranquil period at work; the opportunity should be taken for a short break from responsibility and to spend time recharging your batteries; health should be stable or improve; a time for personal creativity and networking to make contacts for future endeavors.

* The Seven of Clubs: Personal success and satisfaction; high levels of energy and creativity; ideals are important and there may be principles for which you need to fight; ultimate happiness comes from seeing beyond immediate returns to a long-term goal.

* The Eight of Clubs: A time of a sudden upsurge of energy, enterprise, changes in career, travel, and lifestyle; a time to act and to seize sudden opportunities, perhaps striking out alone in some way.

* The Nine of Clubs: Responsibilities may seem overwhelming, with too much to do and not enough time; many of the burdens can and should be delegated; self-doubt and a temporary loss of confidence may make matters seem worse than they are; it is a time to press ahead with courage and conviction.

* The Ten of Clubs: Successful completion of a goal; a chance to change direction and learn new skills, perhaps regarding communication; a dream, ideal, or overriding ambition will be realized in the near future; personal happiness, self-confidence, and independence.

* The Jack of Clubs: An energetic young person or someone who is constantly dashing from one activity to another; the jack can be inclined to lose interest if things do not go well and become absorbed in work or interests to the exclusion of other people; he or she is a great communicator, but can be liberal with the truth.

* The Queen of Clubs: A mature woman who is independent whether she is in a permanent relationship or not; she is a good organizer, energetic, and able to combine many different strands of life; however, this versatility may lead to exhaustion; she is tactful and persuasive and gets what she wants out of life, while keeping everyone happy.

* The King of Clubs: A successful, ambitious man, an innovator and powerful communicator who can be insensitive to the needs and feelings of others, usually because he is impatient to finish a task; he can generally find a way round any difficulty; this king is idealistic and will not compromise on matters of principle.

Spades correspond to the tarot suit of Swords and the ancient element of Air. They represent limitations, challenges, tradition, formal learning, justice, assessment and tradition, older people, and aging.

* The Ace of Spades: A new beginning after difficulty or sorrow; a new form of learning; a sudden recourse to justice; a new challenge that can open doors.

* The Two of Spades: Two alternatives that may not seem attractive, but between which a choice must be made; the need to use logic when there may be conflict between two people or two aspects of life; deciding which of two differing pieces of information is true.

* The Three of Spades: Malice or rivalry that can only be solved by reason; accepting challenges or overcoming obstacles that may involve time and effort, but that will lead to success; assimilating facts that seem to have no immediate use, but that may come in useful later.

* The Four of Spades: Limitations and obstacles come mainly from inner fears based on past disappointment or betrayal; injustices may be keenly felt but, unless they can be resolved, should be set aside; moving forward may involve accepting losses, however unfair.

* The Five of Spades: Be sure of your facts to avoid hidden spite and less-than-honest dealings by others; disillusionment that others may not have such high standards should not cause you to abandon your plans, although you may need to be less open about your intentions.

* The Six of Spades: Formal justice or officialdom may prove surprisingly helpful; a calm period after turbulence or self-doubts; relationships that have been difficult may dramatically improve.

* The Seven of Spades: Intuition helps when logic and expert opinion fail; maximize any advantages and do not draw back from possible conflict; justice is on your side.

* The Eight of Spades: Change is possible if you can leave yesterday behind and look to tomorrow with optimism; talk through your worries and fears, and you may find that the future holds many possibilities you had not considered; new contacts and avenues prove fruitful.

* The Nine of Spades: Courage and determination to succeed can overcome any obstacles; fears of failure or rejection are

unfounded, and battles are better fought in actuality rather than in the head; you know more than you realize.

* The Ten of Spades: Sometimes known as the disappointment card, this indicates that better times are ahead; it can sometimes indicate a natural ending after which there will be a new beginning; optimism is the key.

* The Jack of Spades: This can be a young person or immature older person who can hurt others thoughtlessly or even maliciously; he or she is usually very clever and humorous, which can manifest as sarcasm and witty criticism. However, there may be reasons for his or her distrust of life and people.

* The Queen of Spades: Known as the Queen of Sorrows, this card represents the critical, disappointed mature woman, the gossiping neighbor, disapproving mother-in-law, or the harridan in the office. However, the queen of spades can be surprisingly loyal and forceful in defending her own. She is often possessive out of a fear of being left alone.

* The King of Spades: The alter ego of the king of diamonds, this is the disapproving authority figure, the harsh judge, the over-critical father, the pedant whose own vast store of knowledge makes him impatient of other's mistakes; a perfectionist, he may fear his own vulnerability and so prefer isolation.

Sample Spreads

You can use any of the spreads in the tarot section very successfully with playing cards and vice versa. Indeed, if you wish, you can follow a tarot reading with a playing card reading. You may be surprised at the number of cards that have similar meanings.

THE MYSTICAL SEVEN SPREAD

Seven is considered a mystical and sacred number, symbolizing spirituality and magic. The circle is the most magical of shapes, used in magical rituals as a protective area in which to work and also as a place of concentrated power. The spread also incorporates the six-pointed star known as Solomon's Seal, which was considered by the alchemists to have great power.

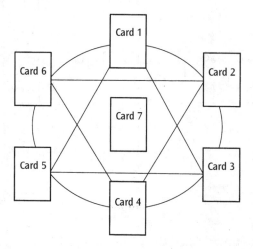

1. Shuffle or mix the cards, and either select seven cards at random from an overlapping circle of cards or choose seven cards facedown from the complete pack.

2. Place six of the cards, still facedown, in a circle, beginning at the twelve o'clock position and moving clockwise, putting the cards on the points of Solomon's Seal. Place the seventh card in the center.

3. Turn over the circle of six cards, beginning with the one you dealt first, before beginning the reading, but leave the seventh facedown.

4. Before you interpret the individual cards, note whether any suit or number is predominant and whether any suits are absent, which can be equally significant. If, for example, there is a predominance of hearts, emotional issues are to the fore. If four twos also appear, emotional and perhaps conflicting demands of different people are core issues.

5. Read the six cards in the order dealt as you would a story, seeing how the cards fit together.

6. Finally, turn over the card in the center to reveal what is just over the horizon.

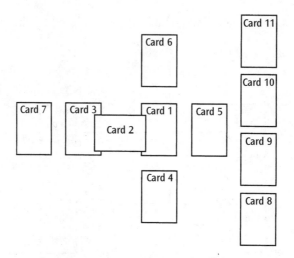

THE CELTIC CROSS SPREAD

This is also sometimes called the Gypsy spread because it is very popular among Romany clairvoyants. It can be used either for a specific question or for in-depth life readings. The Celtic Cross may look very complicated, but if you divide it into three sections, it is easy to learn. I illustrate the three sections separately and then as a whole. When you read the Celtic Cross, look at the layout section by section, and then combine the information for an overall impression

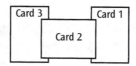

The Center of the Reading

Card 1 Present position, the circumstances surrounding the issue or question, including past matters that have led to the current situation.

Card 2 Issue dominating your life or the question you wish to ask.

Card 3 Obstacles to happiness or success.

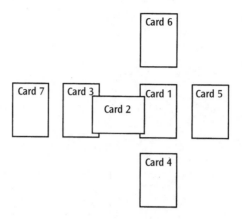

The Surrounding Square

The surrounding square represents the underlying factors, based on the ancient elements.

Card 4 Earth, the root of the matter, dealing with the practical considerations that may offer the key to a current problem or planned change.

Card 5 Air, the logical factor that can separate what is possible from what is unrealistic and help identify your strengths and potential.

Card 6 The inspirational or Fire factor, the "off the top of your head" insight that can make the missing connections in the equation; it can also reveal hidden dreams and needs.

Card 7 Water, the "heart of the matter" card, revealing what is going on under the surface, both in your own life and in the worlds of those involved; it can also reveal your true feelings, which may be very different from what you consciously thought you felt.

Pathway Cards

Card 8 Suggested action. This involves a possible change or choice you may make.

Card 9 Helpful influences. People or circumstances that can make the action or decision more likely to succeed. These influences may be unexpected.

Card 10 Short-term outcome. This refers to the outcome of any change or action in card 8.

Card 11 Long-term outcome. This may be very different from the short-term effects and needs to be considered before deciding if perhaps short-term sacrifice or possible disruption is worthwhile.

Sample Celtic Cross Reading

Andrew's long-standing girlfriend, Annie, was pregnant, but insisted that she wanted to bring up the baby alone, employing a nanny so she could return to work soon after the birth. Andrew was desperate to be involved and to be a proper father. However, Annie said he would lose interest when he discovered the hard work involved in bringing up a baby. How could Andrew persuade Annie he intended to stay around, however hard the going?

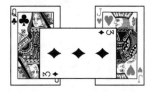

The Center of the Reading

Card 1 Present position, the circumstances surrounding the issue or question.

Annie regarded Andrew as the *jack of hearts,* immature, romantic, and a dreamer. Andrew admitted this was true to an extent. In spite of this, Andrew insisted that he was willing to assume responsibility for the unborn child for whom, to his own surprise, he felt a fierce protective love.

Card 2 The issue dominating your life or the question you wish to ask.

The *three of diamonds* referred to the impending birth, but even more to the practical question of how they could share the organizational and financial responsibilities of a new baby. The card promised potential happiness if Andrew could suggest a way to share in the day-to-day care of the new infant, which so far he had not done.

Card 3 Obstacles to happiness or success.

The obstacle was Annie's insistence on independence. However, because the *queen of clubs* can be as happy in the right relationship as alone, it was essential for Andrew to work out why Annie felt the need to exclude him. Was it something within Annie, within Andrew, or both? These were questions that had to be answered if the couple were to have a future together.

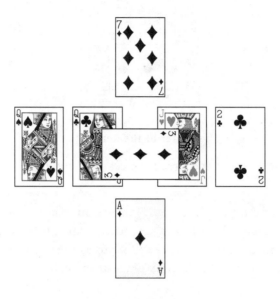

The Surrounding Square

Card 4 Earth, the root of the matter, dealing with the practical considerations.

The *ace of diamonds* is an apt card for the nitty-gritty of family life and reiterated that a new beginning for the family (the ace of diamonds is also a birth card) was only possible if Andrew could come up with practical proposals as to how the new situation could work. Only if Annie could see that she and the baby would be cared for by Andrew, and not just loved, would she be convinced that their relationship could succeed with the added strains of parenthood.

Card 5 Air, the logical factor that can separate what is possible from what is unrealistic.

The *two of clubs* suggested a business partnership between Annie and Andrew. This made sense and might hold the key: Andrew said that before the pregnancy was known, he and Annie, who were both computer experts, had talked seriously about going freelance as a partnership. They had not developed the idea as the time had not been right. Could this offer an answer as to how the new relationship might work, a working and domestic relationship combined?

Card 6 Fire, the inspirational insight that can make the missing connections in the equation.

The *seven of diamonds* promises long-term happiness in domestic matters and joy through children, but also said that Andrew should trust his intuition and dreams. Andrew found this significant because several times before the pregnancy he had dreamed about an old converted warehouse filled with computers and two school-age children running up the stairs calling him. A prediction? But what about the warehouse? A couple of weeks earlier Andrew had been sent information about converted warehouse workshops with living accommodation attached, in a country town. He had put it to one side.

Card 7 Water, the heart of the matter. The *queen of spades* held a key, not to Andrew's, but to Annie's true feelings.

The queen of spades was Annie's mother, who had been deserted by her husband when Annie was small and, thirty years later, was still a very bitter woman. Understandably, Annie found the prospect of being abandoned with a small child frightening and was desperate to maintain her independence. Andrew needed to recognize this and offer reassurances that all men were not like her father and that Annie was not her mother (who allowed initially justifiable bitterness to sour her whole life). Indeed, Annie's mother was trying to persuade Annie to return home with the baby, a move Annie knew would be disastrous.

Pathway Cards

Card 8 Suggested action; a possible change or choice you may make.

The *eight of clubs* is a card of great movement, perhaps indicating Andrew setting in motion the plan to go free-lance with Annie, involving a physical change in location to the converted warehouse or something similar.

Card 9 Helpful influences; unexpectedly helpful people or opportunities.

The *ace of clubs,* the new beginning in a career, in the position of helpful influences, referred, Andrew said, to a sizeable insurance policy that had recently matured. This would tide him and Annie over while they set up a new career venture and home together and sold their present cramped flats in the center of the city.

Card 10 Short-term outcome, referring to the outcome of any change or action in card 8.

The *eight of hearts* indicates that moving to a new stage in a relationship, becoming a family, would seem likely, but there is the warning to beware of jealousy. This might have referred to Annie's mother, who was bitterly opposed to Annie and Andrew remaining together.

Card 11 Long-term outcome. This may be very different from the short-term effects and needs to be considered in deciding if perhaps short-term sacrifice or possible disruption is worthwhile.

The *ten of hearts,* the long-term outcome, continued the prospect of family happiness and emotional fulfillment far into the future. I met Andrew in the West Country and have not seen him since. I do not know what happened, but the reading was hopeful. It did not reveal anything Andrew did not already know, albeit unconsciously, but as so often happens with readings, it put all the disparate elements in a pattern so that possible solutions and thereby potentially fortunate future paths could be initiated.

Chapter 3

THE *I CHING*

THE *I CHING* or *Book of Changes*
is more than a divination system. It is also a classic of ancient Chinese
literature that describes a way of life and represents one of the first
efforts of civilized man to understand his place in the world and the
course and meaning of his life. You can read the *I Ching* and follow
its teachings, without understanding the divination system. It is also
possible to use the divination system without a thorough knowledge
of Chinese language and history, because it is rooted in universal
human wisdom and experience.

The divinatory method involves casting coins, yarrow stalks, or
stones to create one of sixty-four basic shapes called hexagrams (each
made up of six lines, either broken or unbroken). These link to a variety of responses to match the unique qualities and situations of the
seeker. The wisdom of the *Book of Changes* suggests correct and balanced responses to a multitude of situations. Comparatively few people
in the modern Western world use the *I Ching* for personal divination,
although in China and Japan it is often consulted before business deals
as well as before making important personal decisions.

I Ching is often pronounced "Eye Ching" or even "Ee Ching."
"Eye Jing" or "Ee Jeng" are probably closer to the original sounds.
Chinese scholars differ quite widely in the way they translate the

ancient images and judgments into modern language. One problem is that written Chinese is a pictorial form of communication, and so translation into our language can actually stifle the natural flow of meaning and also miss many of the variations contained in the nuances of the hexagram.

Although I offer conventional Chinese names and interpretations of the basic sixty-four hexagrams or six-line images, the methods put forward for both casting and interpreting the hexagrams are so simple that those who equate complexity with truth may reject them.

Change—The Essence of the I Ching

The *I Ching* has been described as a map and guidebook to life's change points. The basis of its philosophy is that nothing is static; we must adapt to the ebbs and flows of change in a way that enables us to anticipate the ocean wave as it reaches the shore, so we may ride it rather than be overwhelmed by it. The Chinese believe that any quality or state reaches an extreme and tips over into its opposite: from joy to sorrow, love to hate, darkness to light, peace to war and back again. While we cannot change some events—such as the weather or earthquakes—we can influence our destiny by our reaction to such events: whether we decide to wait or act, stay or go, use emotion or logic. There must be endings so there can be beginnings; loss so there can be an appreciation of gain.

The *I Ching* is often associated with the sage Confucius, who lived during the sixth century B.C. and instituted moral and also political forms of organization that identified the superior or ideal man in terms of a wise leader or honest administrator—just but compassionate, benignly paternalistic. In the Confucian system, each person was set in his or her rightful place, deferring to those greater in age or experience and not seeking personal advantage or advancement but the general good. Advancement came as a result of right thought and conduct, which brought responsibilities as well as reward.

Fierce debates exist as to whether Confucius himself wrote many of the judgments and commentaries of the hexagram meanings or whether his followers added them. For great emperors and philosophers are said to have lived hundreds of years, a metaphor that means wise thoughts and sayings are universal and timeless.

Chinese philosophy and culture have changed remarkably little over thousands of years, and Taoism and ancestor worship are at least as powerful and older in essence than Confucianism. The spirit of the *I Ching* embraces not only Confucianism, with its emphasis on correct moral conduct, but also the more fluid concepts of *Tao,* the Way, and *Ch'i* (the life force that flows through all things).

The essence of the *I Ching* reflects the Taoist belief that we are not separate from nature and the universe, but a part of it. Life, natural forces, people, even food are made up of *yang,* the original sun concept of light, power, masculinity, assertiveness, logic, and action. It is depicted as a straight line: ——.

Yang is balanced by *yin,* the original moon concept: darkness, receptivity, femininity, intuition, acceptance, and inaction. It is depicted as a broken line: — —.

The Taoist philosophy of *wui wei* (inaction) is sometimes seen as the right course. It may be that, left to itself, society will find its natural balance. If we can observe the trends and go with the flow of the moment, we can obtain true freedom.

An Alternative Vision of Existence

Neither the *I Ching* nor Chinese philosophy generally rests on the fundamental belief that evil can or should be eradicated. Instead, it maintains that evil is as much a part of existence as good. This dualism that runs through Oriental thought can prove problematic for the Western mind, which is used to seeing the devil as a force to be overcome with the good guy living happily ever after. Though Confucianism gives social guidance as to right conduct, it recognizes that more global forces may be at work. According to the Chinese view, life is not a once-and-for-all triumph over darkness, but a swing between the polarities. When a total state of yang is reached, it changes to a yin, which accounts for the constant flux in nature and human affairs.

THE TRIGRAMS

The trigrams are the building blocks of the *I Ching*'s divinatory system. According to Chinese philosophy, everything in the universe is made up of either yang or yin or a mixture of these two forces. In the same way, the trigrams are constructed of yin and yang. They comprise eight three-line images that are the key to creating and interpreting hexagrams.

Two of the trigrams are pure yin and yang: the Sky or Heaven trigram is composed of three yangs, while Earth is made of pure yin. The other basic forces that make up the *I Ching* divinatory system—Fire, Water or the Abyss, Thunder, Wind or Wood, Mountain, and Lake or Marsh—are a combination of yang and yin.

The Origins of the I Ching

The original inspiration for the *I Ching* came from the shell of the tortoise. The long life of the tortoise—as I write, one just celebrated its 126th birthday in Australia—has made it a magical creature, not only in China but in other cultures, including the Native North American Indian. Legends abound throughout the Eastern world of giant tortoises holding up the world and the Islands of the Blest, the earthly equivalent of paradise where immortality was assured to those who resided there. The tortoise became sacred as a symbol of permanence, and high-ranking officials wore tortoiseshell girdles.

For divination purposes, the shell of the tortoise was heated until it cracked and the cracks were interpreted. Fortunately for tortoises, this mode of divination has fallen by the wayside, but it is still commemorated in the Chinese character for divination:

This is composed of two words: "interpret" and "crack"

I Ching divination in its purest form goes back some five thousand years to the time of the ruler Fu Hsi. This monarch was said to have first found the eight trigrams, which are the building blocks of the sixty-four hexagrams (each made up of two trigrams) on the shell of a tortoise. Fu Hsi, believed to be descended from P'au Ku, the

Divine Artisan, who created the mountains and earth, is credited with teaching laws, introducing fishing nets, and building the first permanent dwellings.

It is thought that the *I Ching* was first recorded in about 1700 B.C., when it took a very simple form and was probably still centered around the basic trigrams and their natural images. From this early stage comes the main method used in this section of actually making, as opposed to drawing, trigrams and hexagrams using stones or jade crystals marked with yangs and yins to retain the original connection with the earth.

The meanings continued to evolve, but the actual book was used mostly for predicting natural events until Lord Wen paired the trigrams to create hexagrams about 1122 B.C. Lord Wen was said to have been an exceedingly wise and benevolent ruler in the Chou principality in what is now the Shensi province of China. His ways were in sharp contrast to those of the last king of the Shang dynasty, Choe, who terrorized the people and squandered the wealth of the land. There was a rebellion against him, and although Lord Wen played no part in it, he was flung into prison. During his time there, he was inspired by a vision to write the hexagrams on the wall of his cell. His son, the duke of Chou, wrote commentaries and added the concept of moving or changing lines. So Confucius was a comparative newcomer when he or his followers added yet more interpretations more than five centuries later.

Some would argue that over the hundreds of years of different translations and interpretations, the essential *I Ching* has lost its core, the pearl of natural insight, in legend carried by the great seasonal dragons and often given to a child or peasant whose heart was pure and who could go straight to the heart of the matter.

Certainly it would seem a good idea when beginning the *I Ching* to approach the core meanings of the hexagrams and only to use more elaborate commentaries after digesting the basic system. Some of the most profound readings I have come across have been from absolute beginners with a handful of coins or pebbles who look not only to the written word but upward to the sky, the wind and rain, and downward to the earth and to the other forces of nature that link the urban park with the deserted mountainside or marshes of China millennia ago.

I Ching Stones or Crystals

After the tortoise method, Chinese sages developed an elaborate method of casting yarrow stalks to create hexagrams. You will find this method described fully in the books listed in Further Reading. Later methods involved tossing coins, "the Heavenly Pennies." However, I prefer to use *I Ching* stones that are marked with either a yang or yin.

You can make these from stones such as jade or equally well from stones collected from a beach, river bank, or anyplace that has positive associations for you.

MAKING THE BASIC CHING STONES

Ching stones have a yang —— on one side and a yin – – on the other. By choosing three of these stones at random, you can create trigrams, and by choosing six, you can create hexagrams. Both trigrams and hexagrams are created and read vertically from bottom to top. The top line is the last stone you put down.

To make your first set of Ching stones

★   Take either six oval pieces of jade or stones about the size of a medium coin, with a flat surface on either side, and use paint or a water-resistant permanent marker to mark the yangs and yins. Alternatively etch out the yang and yin signs with a sharp metal object and then paint the indented shape.

★   Mark each of the six stones with a broken line for yin on one side and an unbroken line for yang on the other.

★   Use a drawstring bag or purse to hold the six stones.

USING YOUR *I CHING* STONES

To make a trigram or hexagram, composed of three or six yangs and yins

1. Pick a stone from your bag and cast it onto the table or a flat surface.

2. Note whether the yang or yin faces up, as this gives you the first line of your trigram or hexagram. Place this nearest to you to form the base of the column.

3. Continue to throw until you have a vertical row of yangs and yins, each time placing the face of the pebble that fell up in the ascending column. The top line, either the third in a trigram or the sixth in a hexagram, is the last pebble you threw. For example, if your first throw is a yin, mark a yin at the bottom. If the next is a yang, mark that on top as shown in step 2 below. Another yin would give you the trigram for water as shown in step 3.

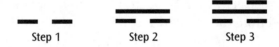

Step 1   Step 2   Step 3

THE COIN METHOD

Use three or six coins, either the old Chinese bronze kind or any coin with distinctive faces, to create a trigram or hexagram. You may want to keep these coins purely for *I Ching* readings. They need not be the same denomination. If you can get newly minted coins, then the imprints on them will be purely your own.

1. Cast each coin in turn, and use the head or blank face to represent a yang and the tail or engraved face for a yin.

2. As with the pebbles, build the trigram or hexagram from the bottom to top, but you may find it easier to draw the yangs and yins. You can use a single coin thrown three or six times if you are drawing the trigram or hexagram.

The Trigram Meanings

There are eight basic trigrams representing natural forces. From these eight, you can make up the sixty-four hexagrams. Alternatively, you can use trigram meanings in the pre-Wen tradition to give you a guiding force on a particular day, which you can symbolically tap into to guide your best action. The trigram meanings have built up over time and have various associations. These can be useful as triggers for your own visions and insights; no rigid meanings exist, for they vary according to your own worldview and also from reading to reading.

For example, ☴ can be interpreted either in a trigram or hexagram as wind, wood, or tree. If you close your eyes, you will see the picture forming in your mind, and if you let it flow and trust it, the image necessary to answer your question will emerge.

Equally, you might view ☲ as fire, lightning, or the sun, according to the question and, if in a hexagram, its corresponding trigram.

A useful way to view the trigrams is in pairs. For example, *Ch'ien* (Heaven or Sky) pairs with *K'un* (Earth), as the nuclear or source trigrams, formed from the limitless Tao. *Ch'ien,* the Great Father, and *K'un,* the Great Mother, were regarded in Chinese mythology as the creators of P'au Ku, the Divine Artisan.

FIRST PAIRING

Ch'ien, Heaven or Sky, and *K'un,* Earth, are the trigrams of the source of life.

 Ch'ien, Heaven/Sky This is the trigram of pure power and energy, of personal identity, assertiveness, directed power, and success. As an indicator of action, it advises aiming high, developing potential, and being confident and single-minded. Its key word is *achievement.*

* Attributes: strength, focused energy, creativity, logic, courage
* Animals: horse, tiger, lion
* Parts of body: head, mind, skull

* ★ Family member: father
* ★ Function: sages, military commanders, philosophers, elderly men
* ★ Associated images: outer garments, cold and ice
* ★ Direction: northwest
* ★ Season: the approach of winter
* ★ Color: white or gold
* ★ Plants: chrysanthemum, herbs
* ★ Trees: fruit trees

☷ K'un, Earth This is the trigram of pure receptivity, of considering the needs and feelings of others, of relying on intuition, unconscious wisdom, and waiting rather than acting. Its key word is *acceptance*.

* ★ Attributes: docility, receptivity, intuition, nurturing, patience
* ★ Animals: ox, cow, mare, ant
* ★ Parts of body: stomach, abdomen, womb, the unconscious mind
* ★ Family member: mother
* ★ Function: wise women, old women, ordinary people, especially in crowds
* ★ Associated images: a seamless cloak that envelops all things without question, an old cart that carries everything
* ★ Direction: southwest
* ★ Season: the approach of autumn
* ★ Color: black or dark brown
* ★ Plants: potatoes, all bulbs
* ★ Trees: tree trunks of all kinds

SECOND PAIRING

Li, Fire, and *K'an,* Water or the Abyss, are the trigrams of diffused energy.

Li, Fire This is the trigram of illumination and of clinging to whatever fuels it, whether the fire of the great
solstices, in which the emperor made offerings or the
ritual fire that cleansed what was imperfect or no longer
needed. Its key word is *inspiration*.

* Attributes: clarity, illumination, cleansing, communications,
  inspiration, clinging
* Animals: pheasant, sacred turtle, goldfish
* Parts of body: eye, the blood, speech, heart
* Family member: middle daughter
* Function: artists, young women, generous people, craftsmen
* Associated images: the sun, lightning, objects with holes, such as
  shells and armor
* Direction: south
* Season: summer
* Color: orange
* Plants: tomatoes, red and yellow peppers
* Trees: dry trees, tree hollows

 K'an, Water/the Abyss This is the trigram of fluidity, of
going with the flow, risking uncertainty and danger, and
turning into emotions. Its key word is *feeling*.

* Attributes: desire, emotion, instinct, fearlessness, danger, hardship
* Animals: pig, rat, wild boar
* Parts of body: ear, kidneys
* Family member: second son
* Function: young men, the sick and troublemakers, fishermen
* Associated images: wells, the moon, the deep, rain and rivers,
  floods
* Direction: north

* Season: winter
* Color: blue
* Plants: reeds, water lilies, lotuses
* Trees: willow, alder

THIrD PAIrING

Chen, Thunder, and *Sun,* Wind or Wood, are the trigrams of movement.

Chen, Thunder This is the trigram of natural renewal with the thunder coming out of the earth at the beginning of summer, scattering the seeds of new life. The sudden dramatic thunderstorm, which Chinese mythology claimed was dragons fighting, can be both creative in bringing refreshing rain and destructive. Its key word is *regeneration.*

* Attributes: arousal, renewal, surprise, spontaneity, initiative, male sexuality, fertility
* Animals: dragon, eagle, swallow
* Parts of body: voice, foot
* Family member: eldest son
* Function: men up to middle age, princes, inventors, musicians
* Associated images: thunderstorms, hurricanes, volcanoes
* Direction: east
* Season: spring
* Color: yellow
* Plants: all blossoming flowers
* Trees: evergreens, blossom trees, bamboo

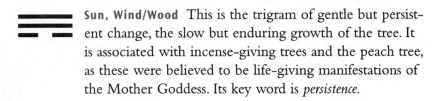

Sun, Wind/Wood This is the trigram of gentle but persistent change, the slow but enduring growth of the tree. It is associated with incense-giving trees and the peach tree, as these were believed to be life-giving manifestations of the Mother Goddess. Its key word is *persistence.*

* Attributes: gentle but determined penetration, adaptability, flexibility, endurance, justice
* Animals: cockerel, snake, tiger
* Parts of body: thigh, legs, lungs, the nervous system
* Family member: eldest daughter
* Function: women up to middle age, teachers, travelers, people engaged in business
* Associated images: trees, fragrances, clouds, ropes, webs
* Direction: southeast
* Season: the approach of summer
* Color: green
* Plants: grass, poppies, lilies
* Trees: all tall and high trees

FOURTH PAIRING

Ken, Mountain, and *Tui,* Lake or Marsh are the trigrams of stillness.

 Ken, Mountain This is the trigram of waiting, solitude, and a desire to rise above material and daily concerns. Ascending to the Jade Mountain was one way, according to Chinese mythology, whereby immortality might be reached. *Vision* is the key word of the mountain.

* Attributes: stillness, withdrawal, silence, meditation, spiritual aspiration
* Animals: dog, bull, leopard, mouse
* Parts of body: hand, back
* Family member: youngest son
* Function: boys under sixteen, prisoners, the faithful and sincere, priests, monks
* Associated images: door, opening, narrow path, walls, watchmen, watchtowers
* Direction: northeast

* Season: the approach of spring
* Color: purple
* Plants: all mountain plants
* Trees: nut trees, gnarled trees

Tui, Lake/Marsh This is the trigram of the inner world, of psychic insight, dreams, and reconciliation. Its key word is *secrecy*.

* Attributes: pleasure, joy, inner tranquility, healing, magic
* Animals: sheep, birds, deer
* Parts of body: mouth, lips that smile
* Family member: youngest daughter
* Function: women under sixteen and daughters, concubines, sorceresses
* Associated images: valleys, mist, the harvest, low-lying land
* Direction: west
* Season: autumn
* Color: red
* Plants: magnolias, gardenias, all lake plants, spices
* Trees: trees bleached with salt

Trigram Readings

It is quite possible to read the *I Ching* using trigrams only, either by casting a trigram each morning or by creating a trigram using your stones or coins in answer to a specific question. Sometimes what you think you are asking and what you need to know turn out to be very different. The *I Ching* can guide you to the core issue.

Let the images associated with the trigram, plus any associations you may develop as you work with the *I Ching,* filter through your mind. You may find that closing your eyes and visualizing the trigram shape helps trigger words and pictures that offer a way forward or an indication of the best action.

Sample Trigram Reading

Nicola, who was in her thirties, always found it difficult to cope with her younger sister Christina who, Nicola felt, was irresponsible and flitted from one job and romance to another, leaving destruction in her wake. Following the breakup of her latest romance, Christina suggested that the sisters move in together. Nicola feared she would end up doing all the chores and worrying about the bills, while Christina pursued her social life.

However, she was reluctant to refuse, as Christina said she had nowhere else to go. To try to sort out her feelings, Nicola, who had never used the *I Ching* before, cast a trigram:

Water

Considering the trigram and its implications, Nicola said she saw fast-flowing water, rafts, and true to its name, the abyss—the sudden plunging into excitement and danger: life with Christina. The question was whether that was a good thing or not, and the key word was *feeling.*

What did Nicola feel? That her own career in research and her steady relationship that someday might end in marriage were getting nowhere, and that she desired change. She decided to flat-share with Christina, but instead of acting the older, reliable, and sometimes disapproving sister to adopt some of Christina's optimism and lack of restraint. To this end, she used some of her carefully acquired savings to book a skiing holiday for herself and Christina in Canada and to risk, albeit in limited ways, plunging into the unknown.

The Hexagrams

Although trigram readings can be illuminating, many people find that hexagrams, combinations of two trigrams, offer a more profound reading. However, it is not necessary to move away from the lovely natural images. Indeed, purely intuitive hexagram readings can be very powerful and tap into your unconscious wisdom in a way that puzzling overcomplex tomes do not.

INTERPRETING THE HEXAGRAMS

By looking at the actual shape of the hexagram, you can sometimes gain an insight into its meaning.

Hexagram 20: Kuan, Earth/Wind For example, Hexagram 20, *Kuan,* Earth/Wind (the bottom trigram dictates the root name of the hexagram, although you picture the hexagram exactly as it is formed), resembles a watchtower and is traditionally called "Contemplation" or "Being Seen."

Wind

Earth

Hexagram 43: Kuai, Heaven/Lake Hexagram 43 has a single yin at the top above five yangs, and so is often called "Breakthrough" or "Resolution."

Lake

Heaven

Hexagram 23: Po, Earth/Mountain In Hexagram 23, "Splitting Apart," there is a single yang above five yins, suggesting an image of the earth crumbling away beneath the mountain.

Mountain

Earth

To interpret a hexagram

* Look at the picture made by the hexagram itself as well as the meanings of its component images.

* The ruling line was traditionally the fifth place (that is, one from the top), so if a yin is there, you know the ruling force is either gentleness or weakness.

* Lines 1, 3, and 5 are naturally yang; and 2, 4, and 6, yin. So if yang and yin occur in their appropriate places, there is harmony.

* The first two lines of the hexagram refer to earthly matters; 3 and 4 to humankind; and 5 and 6 to the spirit. Or alternatively, to body, mind, and spirit respectively.

THE ANCHOR OR SIGNIFICANT HEXAGRAMS

Four significant hexagrams may appear at times when major decisions need to be made. They represent, respectively, pure focused energy, pure acceptance, reconciliation of opposites, and irreconcilability of opposites.

Ch'ien, Heaven/Heaven

The Creative
Principle

K'un, Earth/Earth

The Receptive
Principle

T'ai, Heaven/Earth

Peace

P'i, Earth/Heaven

Stagnation

INTUITIVELY READING THE HEXAGRAMS

Once you create your hexagram, memorize its form. Close your eyes and look through your mind's eye at the images it creates, allowing your mind to roam free.

* If you have a specific question, try to interpret the images as either a strategy or an outcome of action or inaction.
* If you were making a general life inquiry, apply the images together to create a landscape of your life.
* At first you may find it easier to read the two trigrams separately, before combining them, but in time this step becomes automatic.

Sample Intuitive Hexagram Reading

Kate was a health worker who ran courses for single parents. She cared for her elderly parents and, as a single parent, brought up her three school-age children alone. Recently, she had been suffering from bad migraines. A colleague had gone sick and Kate was asked if she could take over the extra workload for a few weeks in return for extra money, which would come in useful. Should she accept, as she was being pressured to do, with the hint that refusal might damage her promotion prospects?

Kate used coins to create the Hexagram *Ta Kuo,* Excess.

Lake/Marsh

Wind/Wood

Traditional imagery sees this as the ridgepole, the main support of a house, collapsing beneath the weight of water. However, Kate saw the image as trees under a lake, quite a common picture evoked by this image. She deduced from this that, like trees left underwater after a lake floods, there was no point in trying to act; she could only wait for the water to go down. Kate did have excessive burdens, and whether you see a collapsing ridgepole or submerged tree, it was clear she could undertake no more. Julie, a member of one of my classes, saw the same hexagram as wind trapped under water and so felt that the sheer weight of still lake water (in this case, her debts) was preventing her from moving forward. She saw a built-in solution in concentrating on one area, thus making her wind into a whirlpool in the lake. It is the combination of the images that makes this hexagram different from the sum of its parts: that is, lake, stillness; and wind/wood, gentle persistence.

All these interpretations and a myriad of others are right. What is surprising is that people who have never even seen the traditional names for the hexagrams quite spontaneously come up with images and conclusions that are very close to the Chinese ones. The hexagrams form a hook on which to hang intuition's images.

Using Traditional Books of Wisdom

You have now learned all you need to know to make very accurate, personalized *I Ching* readings. However, at the end of this chapter I give a list of hexagrams in their traditional order with a quick and popularly used chart for finding your hexagram easily. There are so many translations that run into several pages that I summarized several interpretations and highlighted any special phrases, adapted from a variety of sources, to convey the essence of each hexagram.

You may find this sufficient for your hexagram interpretations, combined with your own intuitive readings. However, at the back of this book, I list some better translations and sources of the *I Ching* so you can continue your study in greater depth.

To interpret hexagrams using traditional books of wisdom

* Let your own internal imagery guide you in your unique questioning and answering before you even pick up an interpretation guide. Once you have a general concept, move on to more learned sources if this seems helpful.

* Ultimately, rely on yourself and if you read any of the Judgments or Images in a major version of the *I Ching,* use the same method of closing your eyes and letting the images on the page mingle with those from deep within your psyche.

* If something in the written text seems puzzling or irrelevant, read it out loud and let the meanings behind the words enter your consciousness.

* Do not feel tied to literal meanings, for the written *I Ching* is very cryptic, full of metaphors for truths that go beyond seemingly irrelevant statements about maidens, concubines, and wives who remain within to prepare the food for their lord husband. Is it a time to wait, to be patient, or to tread on the tail of your own tiger in the office or maybe in your home?

The Change or Moving Lines

Because change is the essence of the *I Ching,* sometimes when we make a trigram or hexagram, a new situation is already looming on the horizon. Whether we act or choose not to act, we influence the future, and the moment is in the past; today is yesterday and tomorrow today.

We all have an automatic radar that can see—out of the corner of our eye or just over the horizon—the possible results of our decisions or indecision. Change lines (also called "moving" lines) bring this knowledge of action-in-the-making into sharp focus, so we can assess and determine our present actions in the light of future possibilities.

MAKING THE TWELVE CHANGE STONES

Use twelve round, flat pieces of jade of similar size to your original *I Ching* stones, or use twelve stones with flat surfaces.

Stones 1 to 6 With paint or indelible marker, draw a yang (unbroken line) on one side of the pebble and on the other side a *changing* yin (a broken line with a cross in the middle). Do this on six stones in total.

yang

changing yin

Stones 7 to 12 Draw an ordinary yin (or broken line) on one side of the pebble and on its other side make a *moving* yang (an unbroken line with a circle in the middle). Do this on six stones in total.

yin

moving yang

It is best to use a separate bag or purse for the change stones.

READING THE CHANGE LINES

Using your change stones, make your trigrams and hexagrams in the usual way. Count the number of change lines before you read the trigram or hexagram. This reveals how stable the current situation is. If more than half the lines are changing, the situation is either likely to change rapidly or change is overdue in a particular situation or relationship.

* Read your trigram or hexagram exactly as before, interpreting moving yangs as yang and moving yins as yin.
* Record the first trigram or hexagram showing the change lines.

* Turn over each of the changing or moving lines in the trigram or hexagram, starting at the bottom. Leave the plain yins and yangs in place.

* This creates a second trigram or hexagram that indicates what is coming into your life or what needs to occur.

* If you did not have any change lines in the original trigram or hexagram, the particular situation remains stable.

I am often asked how long change will be in coming. It would be nice if the answer was a simple matter of counting the number of change lines and saying that it would happen in so many weeks, months, or days. But because we are making our own future, rather than relying on a fixed fate, it is not as simple as that. All we can say is that the greater the number of change lines, then the sooner something will happen. The additional factor is the eagerness of the questioner for change and the will to take advantage of the glimpse of the future provided by the *I Ching*.

Creating a Changing Trigram or Hexagram Using Coins

This time you need to draw the hexagram and you need three coins, as the calculations are slightly more complex. Toss the three coins together to give you the value of each line. Heads are yang and tails are yin. Assign the value of two for a yin and three for a yang.

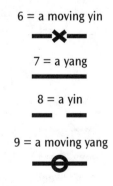

6 = a moving yin

7 = a yang

8 = a yin

9 = a moving yang

1. As with the stone casting, either think of a specific question or allow your unconscious mind to direct the focus of the reading.

2. Throw the three coins for each line until you have three or six lines. Add up the total of the coin values for each throw to show you the kind of Ching line to draw in each of the positions (see diagram on previous page).

3. Draw the lines starting from the base of the trigram/hexagram, using the moving yang and yin signs when necessary.

4. As before, count the total number of change lines to indicate the speed of the change in the first trigram or hexagram.

5. Then reread the trigram/hexagram, counting a moving yin as a yin and a moving yang as a yang.

6. Draw a third trigram/hexagram, substituting a yang for a moving yin and a yin for a moving yang.

7. Read the new trigram/hexagram if there is one.

Sample Reading Using a Changing Trigram

Ben was in his first job as a radio presenter on a local radio station and found that he received all the worst jobs: recording the advertisements after his all-night show; being expected to attend bazaars and minor supermarket events over weekends on behalf of the radio station; being on standby during the week if one of the news or weather reporters was absent. The job was playing havoc with his social life, and he wondered whether to quit and go back to his old job in advertising, which had been much better paid with none of the stress. I met Ben while I was on a publicity tour, and, initially sceptical, he became fascinated by the *I Ching*.

Ben cast this trigram:

Wind/Wood

Ben saw that he had three change lines, and so the situation was eminently unstable. Therefore, the trigram was giving him a short-term strategy: not to give up but to be patient; to persist gently but firmly, inching his way along the path he had chosen, doing the extra work without complaint, because that was necessary to establish himself in a very competitive field.

He then turned over the change stones to see this:

Thunder, new life in the spring, boundless energy, enthusiasm and fertility, thunder at its most positive

Ben's efforts would lead to new opportunities if he put his heart and soul into his work. This was not a fixed prediction, but more of a bargain with the cosmos; if Ben did A, then B would follow.

I do not normally use the *I Ching* for pure prediction, but I heard that Ben was unexpectedly offered a new and much better job with a large consortium about a month after the reading.

Sample Reading Using a Changing Hexagram

Tricia was a grandmother of the modern kind, loving travel and running her own successful farmers' market stall five days a week. Her daughter, however, was desperate to get back to work and was pressuring Tricia to split the market work and child care so they both spent time at home with the children. Much as Tricia loved her grandchildren and having them visit, she was unwilling to give up her freedom and also had doubts about her daughter's commitment to working at the stall. Was Tricia being unreasonable? Tricia used coins to make this hexagram:

Thunder

Wind/Wood

There were four change lines, showing that change or the need for change was not immediate but not far away. Tricia immediately saw the hexagram as a tree (the wood) being shaken by thunder all around but remaining firm. The thunder was not threatening to destroy the tree, but nevertheless was disturbing. Tricia then looked up the hexagram and saw that it was *Heng* (Continuity), suggesting she should stand firm. This was not easy because Tricia felt guilty and also, she admitted, resentful of her daughter for continuing to make demands on her.

Tricia then turned over the three moving lines and drew a second hexagram:

Mountain

Lake/Marsh

Tricia saw this as a lake at the foot of the mountain, very far apart and set on opposing paths, herself and her daughter, and realized the question was much wider. Since her children left home, Tricia, a single parent, had become very independent and had withdrawn both inwardly (the lake) and outwardly (the mountain) from family life, seeking the independence denied her since her husband had abandoned her with no money. The idea of being at home again with children, even her grandchildren, horrified her.

The hexagram was called *Sun* (Decrease) and talked about it being better to offer two small bowls of rice (that is, a small concession) than making greater sacrifices unwillingly that would only lead to resentment. Tricia offered to look after the children one day a week while her daughter ran the stall. To her surprise, she actually enjoyed the day at home, and her daughter found that having one day in which she really made an effort was enough to break the monotony of the week.

Traditional Readings and Changing Lines

If you consult a traditional *I Ching* translation, you will see that each line of the individual hexagram is given a different or supplementary meaning according to whether it is six (a changing yin) or nine (changing yang). These are calculated according to the coin method described above. When you have learned the *I Ching* system, you may find that this information gives you useful additional understanding of your reading. However, greater complexity does not always add deeper significance, so if you do not choose to use these, your readings will be equally potent, just accessed by a more direct method.

Yarrow Stalks

The original *I Ching* divination method involves the use of forty-nine yarrow stalks, which are passed from hand to hand in quite complex calculating. Some find this process relaxing; others find it so worrying that it blocks their intuitive flow. Should you wish to explore it, I have listed books in Further Reading that explain it.

The Sixty-Four Hexagrams

	Upper Trigrams (read across)							
Lower Trigrams (read down)	Ch'ien ☰ Heaven	Chen ☳ Thunder	K'an ☵ Water	Ken ☶ Mountain	K'un ☷ Earth	Sun ☴ Wind	Li ☲ Fire	Tui ☱ Lake
Ch'ien ☰ Heaven	1	34	5	26	11	9	14	43
Chen ☳ Thunder	25	51	3	27	24	42	21	17
K'an ☵ Water	6	40	29	4	7	59	64	47
Ken ☶ Mountain	33	62	39	52	15	53	56	31
K'un ☷ Earth	12	16	8	23	2	20	35	45
Sun ☴ Wind	44	32	48	18	46	57	50	28
Li ☲ Fire	13	55	63	22	36	37	30	49
Tui ☱ Lake	10	54	60	41	19	61	38	58

HEXAGRAM 1: *CH'IEN*, THE CREATIVE

Heaven

Heaven

The Hexagram of Strength and Achievement This hexagram indicates that the time is right to aim high, because the "movement of Heaven is full of power" to be tapped. Sublime success is promised by using determination and untiring effort.

HEXAGRAM 2: *K'UN*, THE RECEPTIVE

Earth

Earth

The Hexagram of Acceptance and Patience This hexagram promises "sublime success" through "the perseverance of a mare"; not by forging ahead or taking the lead, but by following what is for now the assigned path without faltering. The person who has "breadth of character carries the outer world."

HEXAGRAM 3: *CHUN*, DIFFICULTY AT THE BEGINNING

Water

Thunder

The Hexagram of Being Undeterred by Initial Setbacks This hexagram suggests that, in the case of obstacles, it is important to obtain help and to persevere to "bring order out of confusion," rather than giving up and attempting another venture. The clouds and thunder will soon disperse and offer new impetus and enthusiasm.

HEXAGRAM 4: *MENG*, YOUTHFUL INEXPERIENCE/FOLLY

Mountain

Water

The Hexagram of Not Rushing Ahead Blindly New beginnings and enthusiasm are favored, like a spring beginning at the foot of a mountain. However, it is important not only to seek advice, whether from experts or from books, about the right direction, but also to be scrupulous about paying attention to the correct method to proceed, for it is said that the superior, that is, ideal, person "fosters his character by thoroughness in all that he does."

Hexagram 5: *HSU*, Waiting (Nourishment)

Water

Heaven

The Hexagram of Waiting for the Right Moment This hexagram promises that although waiting may seem frustrating, the right moment is coming once the rain has fallen and that it is important not to fret but to make the waiting time fruitful. As with many hexagrams, this one says that it "furthers one to cross the great water," suggesting that the change or venture will be a major one and it may be important to widen your horizons, either physically or by taking a new perspective.

Hexagram 6: *SUNG*, Conflict

Heaven

Water

The Hexagram of Conflicting Interests This hexagram talks of external factors that cause conflict and advises that "a cautious halt halfway brings good fortune." It warns that forging ahead regardless, even if you believe you are right, is disastrous and that wise counsel should be sought before acting to find a compromise. Even more important is to anticipate from the beginning the inevitable points of conflict in bringing disparate factors or people together.

Hexagram 7: *SHIH*, The Army

The Hexagram of Gathering Resources Like water in a dam, it is vital to draw together support and resources for necessary future action, especially in defense of one's position. Therefore, it is important to make connections now by showing generosity toward the people around and not to let inner resources be dissipated by using your strengths on the wrong cause or without restraint. This hexagram suggests that money be saved for a rainy day.

Earth

Water

Hexagram 8: *PI*, Holding Together (Union)

Water

Earth

The Hexagram of Strength in Unity Like rivers flowing together to form the sea, this hexagram suggests that strength comes from uniting with others to further a particular aim. However, it may be necessary for you to coordinate any action and negotiate on behalf of others, which involves a degree of maturity and altruism. It suggests the need to consult the oracle again before too long, whether the *I Ching* or another source of unconscious wisdom, as a guide and warns against becoming committed too late, as that way it is difficult to have any real influence.

Hexagram 9: *HSIAO CH'U*, The Taming Power of the Small

Wind

Heaven

The Hexagram of Gentle Persistence "Dense clouds, no rain"—this hexagram uses the image of the wind pushing clouds across the sky, but without sufficient strength to release rain. In any major venture, sometimes small steps have to be taken, using persuasion rather than force. Given gentle persistence, take small steps toward righting an injustice, bringing about a major change in others, or overcoming a seemingly insurmountable obstacle.

Hexagram 10: *LU*, Treading Carefully (Conduct)

Heaven

Lake

The Hexagram of Tactful Negotiations Often known as the hexagram of "treading upon the tail of the tiger," this suggests that the way forward in handling difficult people or intractable authority is with tact and good humor so that there can be positive if modest results. It is making protests or needs known without seeming to threaten the status quo. Heaven and lake are in their rightful places, and because the lake is a symbol of joy and grace, it is a time to soften demands with a smile.

Hexagram 11: *T'ai*, Peace

Earth

Heaven

The Hexagram of Union of Opposites This is the hexagram of peace and harmony and one of the key or anchor hexagrams that appears at a major decision time or turning point. As such, it is a very optimistic hexagram to create because it promises growth and prosperity, the overcoming of opposition, and a period of harmony. As heaven rises to meet earth descending, the yang and yin unite to recreate the *T'ai,* Peace. "The small departs, the great approaches" offers assurance that any pettiness will disappear and altruism will take its place.

Hexagram 12: *P'I*, Standstill (Stagnation)

Heaven

Earth

The Hexagram of Irreconcilability of Opposites This hexagram, in which heaven drifts upward, making no connection with the earth, is another key hexagram, occurring at an important point at which there seems to be a total stalemate. It indicates that peacemaking efforts or compromises are wasted because the other person or organization cannot or will not see your point of view. Accepting this is liberating, for you may decide to go your own way on this particular issue. There is the suggestion that you should not compromise your principles: "The superior man falls back upon his inner worth and does not permit himself to be honored with revenue."

Hexagram 13: *T'ung Jen*, Fellowship with Men

Heaven

Fire

The Hexagram of Positive Relationships and Liaisons Air causes flames to fan upward and so to have greater power. This is another hexagram in which expansion and widening horizons are advocated and it "furthers one to cross the great water." The expansion and development of all kinds of partnerships and relationships are favored. The fire is also seen as the ordered progression of the stars through the heavens, suggesting that it is important to recognize the different individual strengths and talents in a union so both parties thrive.

Hexagram 14: *Ta Yu*, Abundance, Possession In Great Measure

Fire

Heaven

The Hexagram of Maximum Potential This is the hexagram of the sun rising in the sky and achieving its maximum potential at noon and at the Summer Solstice; this is therefore a time for supreme effort in the promise of success. The influence of the sun's rays are wide-reaching, and strength and clarity are combined. It is also a hexagram that indicates financial advancement and accumulation of money.

Hexagram 15: *Ch'ien*, Modesty

Earth

Mountain

The Hexagram of Small Beginnings This hexagram depicts the mountain eroded and returned to the earth, to rise again (a natural stage) just as the dusk heralds the darkness before dawn. Modesty, whereby it was never forgotten how hard-earned a victory was or how rapidly fortune might be reversed, was much prized in the ancient Chinese world. Often appearing after a temporary reversal, this hexagram stresses the wisdom of modest aims and claims based on realistic and achievable goals. This ensures that the mountain will rise again, inch by inch.

Hexagram 16: *Yu*, Enthusiasm

Thunder

Earth

The Hexagram of New Beginnings "Thunder comes resounding out of the earth. At the beginning of the summer, new life comes bursting from the earth, in the form of thunder, son of the earth mother, bringing life and fertility." This is also associated with making music and the presence of the ancestors, and so this hexagram promises new beginnings, harmony, and success if a supreme effort is made.

Hexagram 17: *SUI*, Following

The Hexagram of Creative Withdrawal The image of thunder buried in the middle of the lake is likened to the man "who goes indoors" for rest and recuperation at nightfall. In the autumn, the thunder returns to the earth for its winter sleep as son of the earth goddess and, therefore, as in many ancient thunder traditions, dies in the autumn. This hexagram appears when it is time to let others take the lead and responsibility and when you need to concentrate on the inner world. It is not a retreat, but a deliberate decision to move back from a situation, rather like the runic Ingwaz (see page 150).

Lake

Thunder

Hexagram 18: *KU*, Work on What Has Been Spoiled (Decay)

Mountain

Wind

The Hexagram of Seeking to Salvage a Situation The significant feature of this hexagram is not that something has been spoiled and must therefore be abandoned (the Chinese character for *Ku* is a bowl filled with worms). It can be worked on, implying that whatever the circumstances, all is not lost. Often the kind of situation triggered by this hexagram is one caused through omission or ignoring warning signs. The answer is endeavor, using both the vigor of the wind in external action and the stillness of the mountain. Unlike Hexagram 12 (*P'i,* Stagnation), the stagnation is not immutable.

HexaGram 19: *LIn*, APProacH, ADVance

Earth

Lake

The Hexagram of Harnessing Opportunity before It Is Lost
This hexagram says that when the eighth month comes, or passes, there will be misfortune. This is not a prophecy of impending disaster, but rather says that the eighth month is spring and the time is approaching, so the opportunity must be seized before the time is past. The lake is deep in the valley and so the water of movement and stirring of emotion is held still, waiting. The opportunity may be an emotional one.

HexaGram 20: *Kuan*, ConteMPLatIon (VIeW)

Wind

Earth

The Hexagram of the Wider Perspective Known as the watchtower hexagram, because of its shape, it can be seen either as the wind blowing over a plain, giving an endless view, or as a wooden structure on a hill with flatness all around. "The ablution has been made, but not yet the offering. This represents a pause in the ceremony for thought, a contemplation of the significance of the sacrifice, and of the next step in life."

HexaGram 21: *SHIH HO*, BItInG THrouGH

Fire

Thunder

The Hexagram of Decisive and Just Action This is another pictorial hexagram, shown by its shape—teeth biting through an obstacle. The image of a storm reveals the forces of nature, and justice is also a strong feature of this hexagram. The clarity of the situation (fire) emphasizes that the obstruction is unjust, so immediate decisive action (thunder) is therefore necessary.

HEXAGRAM 22: *PI*, GRACE, ADORNMENT

Mountain

Fire

The Hexagram of Seeking Worth Rather Than External Luster The fire illuminates the mountain and makes it seem beautiful, but its light is neither far-reaching nor long-lasting. "Grace has success in small matters," and so the external and immediate advantages of an opportunity or person may be important in the short term. However, for deeper issues and long-term decisions, it is important to look beyond the form to the substance.

HEXAGRAM 23: *PO*, SPLITTING APART

Mountain

Earth

The Hexagram of Crumbling Foundations This is another pictorial hexagram of the mountain or achievements crumbling beneath the surface. It is a hexagram warning that you should be sure of your ground, create firm foundations for any undertaking, and take care over small details. You should ensure that those on whom you depend are in tune with you and not suffering from resentments that may undermine your position.

HEXAGRAM 24: *FU*, RETURNING (THE TURNING POINT)

Earth

Thunder

The Hexagram of Promise of Happier Times This is the hexagram of the Midwinter Solstice, when the darkest days are past and the new life in the form of the thunder waits in the earth for the moment to spill its seeds. It is, therefore, the light at the end of the tunnel, the promise of better times ahead, and it is a hexagram that may appear after a period of unrest, illness, or unhappiness. The message is to rest, not to worry, and to be optimistic.

HeXaGram 25: *wu wanG*, Innocence (THe unexpecTeD)

Heaven

Thunder

The Hexagram of Spontaneity This hexagram is associated with spring and the growth of new plants, thunder being a symbol of this regeneration. The kings of old were said to be "in harmony with the time," and so this hexagram indicates unexpected events or opportunities. It advocates following natural instincts, that will, if trusted, lead to the right course, rather than logically considering matters of self-interest and benefit.

HeXaGram 26: *Ta cH'u*, THe TamInG power oF THe GreaT

Mountain

Heaven

The Hexagram of Inner Strength The creative power is hidden in the mountain like buried treasure, ready for the time it is needed. Now the stillness of the mountain holds in check the energy and movement of the pure yang. It is a time to seek wisdom and learn, and so this hexagram favors all kinds of training, study, and recourse in traditional ways and knowledge.

"Thus the superior man acquaints himself with many sayings of antiquity—in order to strengthen his character."

HeXaGram 27: *I*, THe corners oF THe mouTH (provIDInG nourIsHmenT)

Mountain

Thunder

The Hexagram of Absorbing What Is of Worth This is another pictorial hexagram, showing the mouth. In eating and drinking, there is absorption from the outside to the inside, and so this hexagram speaks of internalizing valuable ideas and in words carefully expressing these ideas to enrich the lives of others. This hexagram offers another image of the thunder as fertilizing the land in the spring with the seeds of life-giving rain and so emphasizes the importance of nurturing any new venture or important relationships.

HEXAGRAM 28: *TA KUO*, PREPONDERANCE OF THE GREAT, EXCESS

Lake

Wind

The Hexagram of Being Overburdened This hexagram contains two concepts that convey the same significance, firstly the "ridgepole" that "sags to the breaking point." The ridgepole that supports the roof is too weak at the ends to hold the weight, perhaps of water in the floods. There is also the image of the lake rising above the trees. In either case, there is nothing you can do by getting anxious or angry. If the burdens imposed by life and others are too great, one can only wait for the floods to subside and not take on any further responsibilities— "if he has to renounce the world, he is undaunted."

HEXAGRAM 29: *K'AN*, THE ABYSMAL (WATER)

Water

Water

The Hexagram of Following the Course Offered, However Unpromising When a trigram is repeated in a hexagram, its power is doubled: "Water flows on uninterruptedly and reaches its goal." Water flows forward, not shrinking from dangerous abysses but plunging down them. This is the hexagon of the heart—not sentiment but following one's heart and being true to oneself. Trusting emotions but not being blinded by them can offer the best course of action in the situation under consideration.

HEXAGRAM 30: *LI*, THE CLINGING, FIRE

Fire

Fire

The Hexagram of Clarity This is the hexagram of the sun in all its brilliance, illuminating questions shrouded in darkness with sudden insight. There is a reminder that domestic issues must be considered, but the emphasis is on expansion of possibilities and enthusiasm to spread the new insight to "illumine the four quarters of the world, that is every aspect of life. It is a very positive answer to any question if one is prepared to act to fulfill dreams."

Hexagram 31: *Hsien*, Influence (Wooing)

Lake

Mountain

The Hexagram of Positive Encounters This hexagram, relying on the familial positions of Tui as youngest daughter and Ken as youngest son, is often taken to refer to an auspicious attraction and especially a love match. However, it can equally apply to any situation in which opposites come together and influence one another in a positive way. Thus any partnerships, especially those involving emotion or people of similar status, allowing for the fact that the ancient Chinese regarded the male as superior, will be fruitful and are seen as the way forward in influencing events.

Hexagram 32: *Heng*, Duration, Continuity

Thunder

Wind

The Hexagram of Enduring Partnership This is the hexagram of a permanent relationship, whether marriage or a business partnership, the oldest son and the oldest daughter in familial terms. Duration involves changing with circumstances but keeping the inner self intact and unchanged. And so this hexagram suggests continuing with the current situation or relationship as a long-term endeavor that will survive both highs and lows.

Hexagram 33: *Tun*, Retreat

Heaven

Mountain

The Hexagram of Limitation A mountain rises so far but then stops and can ascend no further. This hexagram is sometimes seen as a symbol of the time of darkness when hostile or inimical external forces prevent any further progress, and so retreat is called for, not flight. This retreat involves withdrawing at the right moment with dignity and refusing to be irritated or drawn into fruitless hostility with those who do not understand or who refuse to compromise. "Thus the superior man keeps the inferior man at a distance, not angrily but with reserve."

HEXAGRAM 34: TA CHUANG, THE POWER OF THE GREAT

Thunder

Heaven

The Hexagram of Being in a Strong Position This hexagram occurs when it is necessary to use a position of strength wisely so that achievements and actions are right "according to the established order," which refers to natural harmony rather than rigid traditions. You can take advantage of an upsurge of favorable forces as an opportunity for positive change, perhaps instigating conditions to which you had previously encountered opposition. However, the proviso is not to ignore the feelings of others.

HEXAGRAM 35: CHIN, PROGRESS

Fire

Earth

The Hexagram of Moving Forward This is the hexagram of the sun rising above the earth, the promise that each day is a new one and so the opportunities are present for moving forward with optimism. It is a hexagram associated with travel and opportunities to expand horizons, either physically or in perspective. The powerful prince on his journey is given many horses and three audiences a day with the great ruler, suggesting that the farther you venture, the greater the rewards.

HEXAGRAM 36: MING I, DARKENING OF THE LIGHT

Earth

Fire

The Hexagram of Keeping One's Own Counsel This is the hexagram of the setting sun that sinks beneath the earth. To try to influence others at present is not likely to be fruitful, because external circumstances may result in negative encounters and unhelpfulness. Your ideas, while right, are not in accordance with popular opinion, so it is necessary to keep faith and wait for circumstances to alter. Literally translated, this hexagram means "wounding of the bright thing."

hexagram 37: *chia je'n*, the family (the clan)

Wind

Fire

The Hexagram of Domestic Security This hexagram is often created when domestic concerns are foremost or the world seems uncaring. It is a reminder of the importance of familiar, secure relationships. Whether the image is of wind, gentle movement emanating from the fire and spreading warmth, or wood burning on the fire of the domestic hearth to give warmth, the idea is the same. It is a time to draw strength from and give strength to those close to you and to look to the root of any matter for the answer. It can also refer to house moves.

hexagram 38: *k'uei*, opposition

Fire

Lake

The Hexagram of Diverging Interests Fire and water cannot mingle, and in this hexagram, the lake flows downward and the fire upward. It may be necessary to accept fundamental differences of opinion and perspective with others and to accept that this is not necessarily bad, only if it causes bad feeling when one person tries to change another or suppress individuality.

hexagram 39: *chien*, obstruction, obstacles

Water

Mountain

The Hexagram of Choosing between Two Difficult Situations Here the choice lies between crossing the abyss, fast-flowing water, or scaling the steep mountain. Doing nothing is not a viable option. However, either obstacle is surmountable, given care and determination to move forward, and once faced, will ensure smoother times ahead. Consider the options before acting. Above all, try to understand how to avoid a similar situation in the future by forward planning.

HEXAGRAM 40: *HSIEH*, DELIVERANCE, REMOVING OBSTACLES

Thunder

Water

The Hexagram of Resolving Outstanding Matters As a thunderstorm relieves tension and brings refreshing rain, this is a hexagon heralding the relief of difficulties and obstacles. However, it suggests that you must quickly resolve any remaining issues or problems, taking advantage of the improving climate. Once matters are resolved, a return to normal life is the best course, rather than dwelling on the past.

HEXAGRAM 41: *SUN*, DECREASE

Mountain

Lake

The Hexagram of Coping with Reversals This hexagram reflects rather than predicts a period in which resources, whether material or emotional, are lessened. The lake evaporates but benefits the mountain with the moisture, suggesting that present privations may result in long-term benefit. It is also seen as essential to adapt to the new circumstances rather than bewailing them: "One may use two small bowls for the sacrifice." It is still possible to achieve goals by adapting available resources and accepting that the matter may take longer than anticipated.

HEXAGRAM 42: *I*, INCREASE

Wind

Thunder

The Hexagram of Rising to the Occasion This hexagram portrays wind and thunder increasing each other's power, so this is a good time to maximize possibilities. As with hexagrams of both good and bad times, the message is that the moment will not last forever so it is vital to act swiftly. There is also a strong need to be mentally and spiritually ready, emulating or adapting admirable strengths and trying to eradicate inner weaknesses that can cause people to defeat themselves in the most dangerous circumstances.

Hexagram 43: *KUAI*, Breakthrough, Resolution

Lake

Heaven

The Hexagram of Pent-Up Energy In this hexagram, the river is ready to burst its banks or the waters from the lake have risen so high that there will be a cloudburst. Therefore, there is a strong potential danger that good may be destroyed along with what is no longer desired. It is important that motives and consequences are discussed and any potentially destructive matters defused so the outcome is positive.

Hexagram 44: *KOU*, Coming to Meet, Temptation

Heaven

Wind

The Hexagram of Resisting Attractive but Destructive Offers This hexagram can appear when a short-term advantageous or attractive offer has been made, whether romantically or in financial affairs. The main problem is allowing others undue influence over you. There will be a price for taking the easy option, and this hexagram talks of furtive, underhand dealings that weaken the person who goes along with them. The image uses the traditional concept of a bold, unscrupulous girl seducing an older man and so having power over him, which he has surrendered.

Hexagram 45: *TS'UI*, Gathering Together (Massing)

Lake

Earth

The Hexagram of Being in Control Like Hexagram 8 (*Pi*, Holding Together), this hexagram talks of gathering together strength, whether supportive people, money, or inner resources. There the waters were less concentrated, but here the lake rises higher and higher and thus is a potential store of water. As the water rises too high, it spills over in a potentially destructive way. Therefore, "the superior man renews his weapons in order to meet the unforeseen," suggesting that it is necessary to be aware of future danger points and to store money or material resources to easily control and deploy them.

HEXAGRAM 46: *SHENG*, PUSHING UPWARD, ASCENDING

Earth

Wind

The Hexagram of Firm Foundations The tree pushes very slowly up through the soil and continues to grow skyward inch by inch. Plans can be made for the future that, if started and furthered, even in a small way, will slowly come to bear fruit. The superior man "heaps up small things, in order to achieve something great." This is a hexagram that can appear at a time when a person is planning either a career or life change in the future and wonders whether it is worth beginning a project that may take many years.

HEXAGRAM 47: *K'UN*, OPPRESSION (EXHAUSTION)

Lake

Water

The Hexagram of Having Nothing More to Give The image is of a lake drained of water. It can appear when a person is in a potentially destructive situation or relationship, in which he or she is giving everything, whether practically, financially, or emotionally, and receiving nothing in return. If the other person cannot be made to contribute more, it is vital to give to oneself and, if necessary, follow the course of water and move on.

HEXAGRAM 48: *CHING*, THE WELL

Water

Wind

The Hexagram of the Unchanging Source This is a core hexagram in that it appears when an issue is of deep personal significance. Traditionally, wells were regarded as entrances to the womb of the Mother Goddess; and wells endure over thousands of years, containing that

which sustains life and also sometimes healing properties. "The town may be changed, but the well cannot be
changed." The answer to any query is to seek deep
within oneself to find the spiritual answer. It may be
helpful to use the *I Ching* or another source of divination
to help narrow down possibilities. But, equally, the solution
may come in a dream, be carried on the wind, or be
seen in a flaming cloud formation at sunset. Trust this
message.

Hexagram 49: *KO*, Revolution (Molting)

Lake

Fire

The Hexagram of Shedding the Redundant This hexagram character originally referred to an animal's coat that
was shed at a certain season. The revolution that comes is
that of the seasons fighting and overthrowing each other
in succession. However, this is not random but regular. As
with Hexagram 38 (*K'uie,* Opposition), fire and water
are not compatible, but each is necessary and can counter
the other: fire to boil and transform water; water to put
out fire when it becomes too destructive or is not needed.
True freedom lies in recognizing the natural change
points in inner and outer life and using them to shed
the redundant.

Hexagram 50: *TING*, The Cauldron

Fire

Wind

The Hexagram of Transformation This is another pictorial
hexagram, revealing the shape of the cauldron, in itself a
powerful and very ancient spiritual symbol for transformation and nourishment. Food is cooked and transformed so it may be eaten and so nourish. We need to
take whatever we have in our lives and transform it, if
necessary through sacrifice and suffering, so we can
move forward in a meaningful way.

Hexagram 51: *Chen*, The Arousing
(Shock, Thunder)

Thunder

Thunder

The Hexagram of Sudden Change One of the most powerful images of the double thunder is that of shock—veering between laughter and anger, terror and ecstasy. Although everything around him may be changing, the superior man "does not let fall the sacrificial spoon and chalice"; he may change his life or have it changed, but is not diminished. This hexagram, which may appear at a major change point, suggests that you may need to set your life in order, not flinching from decisions that will shake the certainties of others. It may be that you have accepted one too many injustices with equanimity.

Hexagram 52: *Ken*, Keeping Still, Mountain

Mountain

Mountain

The Hexagram of Inner Stillness T. S. Eliot talks of the stillness between two waves. This hexagram refers to gaining freedom from external pressures and distractions. If a person is happy and tranquil within, he or she can make any decisions calmly and rationally and is not unduly influenced by others. This is especially true in a potential conflict situation. The key is to concentrate on the immediate issue and not be distracted by concerns about problems that might never arise.

Hexagram 53: *Chien*, Development
(Gradual Progress)

Wind

Mountain

The Hexagram of Following All the Necessary Steps This hexagram is related to the necessary ceremonial stages that underlie the commitment and permanence involved in formalizing a marriage. The tree on the mountain of necessity develops strong roots to protect it from exposure and so its growth is slower than a tree in a sheltered position. This hexagram, therefore, states the need to follow all the formalities in a situation, as shortcuts can lead to less-than-firm foundations. It can apply equally to matters of study and justice as well as all protracted undertakings.

Hexagram 54: *Kuei Mei*, The Marrying Maiden

Thunder

Lake

The Hexagram of Rights and Responsibilities This is the last of the four marriage hexagrams, which include Hexagram 31 (*Hsien,* Influence), Hexagram 32 (*Heng,* Duration), and Hexagram 53 (*Chien,* Development). After the formalities of the marriage ceremony take place, the young woman traditionally became subject to the authority of her husband in return for his taking on the responsibility of protecting her.

This hexagram, however, has a wider meaning in terms of formal contacts and in assessing obligations and advantages. The success of any commitment (personal, social, or economic) depends on partners honoring their obligation; so this hexagram says it is important to understand any future step in terms of gains and losses so that it is entered into with full understanding and with a view to maintaining long-term arrangement.

Hexagram 55: *Feng*, Abundance (Fullness)

Thunder

Fire

The Hexagram of Maximum Power This is the hexagram of the sun at noon, the Summer Solstice, when the time is right for action, to achieve ambitions and to seize opportunities with the certainty of success. As with similar hexagrams, it tells us to seize the moment: "Be not sad. Be like the sun at midday." There can be no demands of permanence, only the happiness and optimism of the present. To live in the present is to escape the burdens of the past and the need for certainties about the future.

HEXAGRAM 56: *LU*, THE WANDERER, THE TRAVELING STRANGER

Fire

Mountain

The Hexagram of Independent Action This is the hexagram of travel and impermanence. The image is of a grass fire on a mountain; it blazes brightly and travels swiftly over a great area, clearing what is redundant. This is a hexagram that can appear at a time when you are considering whether to stay in a situation, to move, or to travel. It favors short-term projects and commitments and advises against putting down roots or seeking happiness or success through others.

HEXAGRAM 57: *SUN*, THE GENTLE (THE PENETRATING, WIND)

Wind

Wind

The Hexagram of Gentle Persistence The double hexagram of the wind suggests that progress lies in gentle persistence. Wind can bend trees and so, by persuasion and constant gentle pressure, results can be achieved even in seemingly intractable people and events. The direction of the wind and approach must be consistent to obtain enduring results. Equally, the hexagram can be regarded as wood: the slow but steady growth of the tree, a firm foundation for gradual but solid achievement.

HEXAGRAM 58: *TUI*, THE JOYOUS, LAKE

Lake

Lake

The Hexagram of Happiness and Harmony The image is of two lakes joined and so replenishing each other. Happiness comes from balancing the inner and outer needs of the self. This is a hexagram of happiness from within, of peace, reconciliation, and tranquility. More specifically, it may refer to the mending of quarrels, the growth of friendship, or the cessation of worries concerning children or dependent relatives. This hexagram also indicates the development of psychic abilities.

HEXaGraM 59: *HUAN*, DISSOLUTION

Wind

Water

The Hexagram of the Dissolving of Barriers The ice of the autumn and winter are dissolved by the warmer winds of spring; in the same way, rigidity and blockages in progress are dissolved by a gentle though persistent approach. Life and love can move again. However, it is necessary that the creative energies are not randomly dispersed or frittered away, but focused on a spiritual or worthwhile goal so the achievements will be tangible.

HEXaGraM 60: *CHIEH*, LIMITATION, RESTraINT

Water

Lake

The Hexagram of Exceeding the Limits When heavy rain pours endlessly into lake, it eventually overflows, flooding the surrounding land. If, therefore, a person accepts burdens and responsibilities and imposes no limits, a point is reached at which it is no longer possible to function. It is a matter of assigning priorities to those tasks that must be performed and those that are the responsibility of others. This hexagram can also refer to financial commitments that again need streamlining.

HEXaGraM 61: *CHUNG FU*, INNER TRUTH, INNERMOST SINCERITY

Wind

Lake

The Hexagram of Insight The wind ruffles the surface of the lake. This motion is a visible sign of the invisible wind whose effects reveal its power. This is one of the most profound hexagrams, talking of the importance of understanding motive and unconscious forces of influence in oneself and others, so that compassion and insight replace coercion and criticism. This hexagram can appear at the time of a moral dilemma or when others have seemed unfair and selfish and it is tempting to seek revenge.

HEXAGRAM 62: *HSIAO KUO*, PREPONDERANCE OF THE SMALL

Thunder

Mountain

The Hexagram of Concentrating on Minor Affairs Just as thunder sounds muffled in the mountains and so has less effect, so it is important for the bird not to soar but to seek the nest and for people to pay attention to the minutiae of life. In money matters, it is necessary to be thrifty and, if there is sorrow, to pay attention to alleviating the immediate concerns. Progress can be made, but only in small ways.

HEXAGRAM 63: *CHI CHI*, COMPLETION/AFTER COMPLETION

Water

Fire

The Hexagram of Maintaining Efforts The image is of a kettle of water heating over a fire, and so this is a very propitious hexagram in that everything has fallen into place and plans can come to fruition. However, in accordance with the underlying principle of change, once there is completion, a new cycle begins. Therefore, this hexagram also contains warnings about not ceasing one's efforts because things are going well. The kettle can boil dry, or spill and extinguish the fire, unless it is tended. Order and success depend on continuing vigilance and effort and are only a stage, albeit an auspicious one, in the wider life pattern. "Thus the superior man takes thought of misfortune, and arms himself against it in advance."

HEXAGRAM 64: *WEI CHI*, BEFORE COMPLETION

Fire

Water

The Hexagram of Anticipating Success Significantly, this is the last hexagram. The previous one heralded the transition from autumn to winter. In this hexagram, it looks optimistically to spring. However, because water and fire are not compatible in their respective positions, it will be necessary to reconcile opposites and to make a supreme effort because the stakes are high, whether in the business or personal sphere. This is a major hexagram occurring at a time when it may be necessary to risk all in the hope of great future happiness and potential.

DIVINATION BY CASTING

Chapter 4

THE VIKING RUNES

THESE DISTINCTIVE, angular marks form the alphabet of the Vikings, but they are also believed to have certain magical properties and were used for divination. The harsh and brutal life of the Vikings is a world away from modern life, but the runes are still relevant because these symbols address all the concerns of humankind in any age: home, family, exploration, love, money, change and stagnation, and destiny.

The runic symbols are ideographic. Each one represents not only a sound but also a concept that may have many layers of meaning, much like a tarot card. For example, ᚾ "Uruz" stands for the sound *U* and also represents aurochs, mighty horned cattle that roamed through northern Europe until the early seventeenth century. It also has the divinatory meanings of strength and endurance, and, in magic, warriors invoked it to transfer the power of these mighty beasts to themselves.

Some of the runes resemble their equivalents in our alphabet: for example ᚱ (Raidho) makes the *R* sound and resembles our character. But the *D* sound ᛗ (Dagaz) looks nothing like the letter *D*. And some of the characters, such as ᚹ (Wunjo), are misleading. While ᚹ may look like a sharply pointed *P*, it is the phonetic equivalent of *W*.

History of the Runes

Runes were created by the Germanic peoples, that is, the English, Germans, and Scandinavians, who shared a common heritage and language that gradually split into different dialects. The legend of Odin inventing the runes probably dates from the legends of an ancient tribe known as the *Volsungr* who came from the Far North with the last Ice Age. They were a tribe of priest-magicians who were said to guard the ancient forests and trackways, helping anyone in need; and they used an early form of runes known as the *Ur Runes.*

The Volsungr spread their wisdom to other tribes, including the magical incantations associated with the magical symbols, before eventually disappearing back into the northern forests. These early runic symbols relied on basic universal images, such as the six-pointed snowflake/star, the original form of ᚺ (Hagalaz or Hail); the ancient sun wheel that evolved into the later Raidho or "Riding" (ᚱ); and holy signs from the Bronze Age associated with the Mother Goddess. These symbols, including the sacred lozenge that became ◊ (Ingwaz, the fertility rune), are found in ancient rock carvings in Sweden in great quantity; dating from 1300–1200 B.C. (the second Bronze Age) and 800–600 B.C., the transition period from the Iron Age.

The runic systems used today date from the second or third century B.C. During this period, the Germanic peoples of the Middle Danube (where the modern systems seem to have originated) came into contact with the Mediterranean Etruscan alphabet system via the Mediterranean traders who traveled across Europe as far as the Baltic (which was famed for its amber). The runes followed the trade routes, spread by the traders themselves, who cast lots to discover propitious times for journeys and negotiations.

Runes were still cast for divination by tribes and individuals until the eleventh century, and the last true runemasters and runemistresses did not die out until about three hundred years ago. They were used in the Scandinavian world as far north as Iceland, among the Anglo-Saxons on the plains of western Europe, and in those lands the Germanic peoples conquered, including Northumberland in the northeast of England, which developed an extended runic system drawing in the concepts of the ancient elements of Earth, Air, Fire, and Water.

The Vikings were great voyagers and so runes are found in many parts of the world, from Iceland (which they colonized in about 815) to America (discovered in about 992 by Leif, son of Erik the Red). In their long boats, Vikings sailed to Russia, Turkey, Greece, and even North Africa, where you can still find stone monuments, graves, and artifacts marked with runes. Runic symbols were not used for formal writing, which did not reach Scandinavia until the eleventh century (when the Christian monks recorded the legends and lays in Latin). Until then, the stories of the Nordic gods were preserved by word of mouth, the bards remembering thousands of lines of verse.

The word *rune* stems from an ancient northern European language, and means "a secret thing, a mystery." The modern German word *raunen,* "to whisper," comes from this stem, although some linguists give the meaning as "to roar," a suggestion of oracular inspirations.

In this section, I concentrate on the most popular surviving form of the runes, the twenty-four Norse runes, known as the *Elder Futhark,* which were used in Scandinavia.

The Wisdom of the Runes

Wounded I hung on Yggdrasil
For nine nights long
Pierced by a spear
Consecrated to Odin,
A sacrifice to myself
I hung upon that tree.
The wisest know not the roots
of ancient times whence it sprang.
None brought me bread,
None gave me mead.
Down to the depths I searched.
I took up the Runes
And from that Tree I fell
Screaming.

—"Sayings of the High One," from the Elder Edda

This particular version of the Odin rune legend is an adaptation of several translations of the early Icelandic legends and poems. The later Eddas date from the eleventh century, but scribes who were not immersed in the original tradition transcribed the sacred myths.

Many versions exist of the discovery of runes and their inherent wisdom by Odin, the Viking All-Father, suggesting that runes contained knowledge and wisdom beyond even that possessed by the Norse gods. This knowledge was seen stemming from the depths of time, from the roots of Yggdrasil, the Norse World Tree, in which were set the nine worlds, including those inhabited by gods and mortals. The three Norns, or Goddesses of Destiny, mentioned in the Introduction, were believed to guard the Well of Wyrd or Fate at the foot of the first root of Yggdrasil.

The first systematic Futharks or rune rows are more than two thousand years old. Just as our word *alphabet* comes from the first two letters of the Greek alphabet: *alpha* and *beta, Futhark* comes from the names of the first five runes: *Fehu, Uruz, Thurisaz, Raidho, and Kenaz* (ᚠᚢᚦᚱᚲ). The Norsemen believed that these runes engraved on an object endowed it with magical power.

Much of the rune lore of modern times is based on a series of rune poems, like the legends, written from the eleventh century onward. These reflect the influences of Christianity as well as a different world from that in which the runes were originally created, a world fraught with physical danger and hardship. Even here, different though related traditions are involved, the three main ones being the Anglo-Saxon or Old English Rune Poem, the Old Norse Rune Poem, and the Icelandic Rune Poem. The last two contain only sixteen runes; by then the original Futharks had been much reduced. I have consulted all three and filled in the gaps by referring to the old legends that not only contain references to the runes, but also recreate a world in which the runes formed a link between human beings and the gods, transmitting the greater wisdom from the roots of Yggdrasil.

How Were Runes Cast?

Runes were not used only for divination. They could also invoke higher powers that might influence the fortunes of man, and so there were runes for every aspect of life, such as fertility (◊ Ingwaz), the harvest (⬦ Jera), tides (⌐ Laguz), strength and victory in battle (∩ Uruz and ⋏ Ansuz), heading (ᛒ Berkano), and protection (ᚦ Thurisaz).

Around A.D. 98, the Roman historian Tacitus wrote *Germania* about the ancient Germanic people. He described a rune ceremony. A branch was cut from a nut-bearing tree and cut into rune-slips with markings. These were cast onto a white cloth. Either a priest or the father of the family or clan interpreted them, offered a prayer to the gods, and, looking up to the sky, picked up three strips, one at a time, and read their meaning from the signs previously scored on them.

Tacitus also recorded that women were involved in augury of all kinds. The runemasters or runemistresses (for it was often the women who learned the lore while the men were away at battle), were described by the thirteenth-century author of *The Saga of Erik the Red:*

> She wore a cloak set with stones along the hem. Around her neck and covering her head she wore a hood lined with white catkins. In one hand she carried a staff with a knob on the end and on her belt, holding together her long dress, hung a charm pouch.

Are the Runes Dangerous?

Like the tarot, the runes have unfairly acquired negative connotations. These stem from early medieval times in northern Europe when priests, unable to read runic inscriptions and magical charges, believed them to be dark spells capable of unlocking the powers of evil.

When Christianity came to Scandinavia in the eleventh century, the pagan gods became demonized, the goddesses were made into witches, and even black cats (who in Norse mythology pulled the chariot of Freyja, Goddess of Love and Fertility) were seen as witches' familiars. During the late 1930s and 1940s, the Nazis used the runes in their military insignia and propaganda and further darkened their reputation, which, like any other form of magic or indeed any form of learning, can be used for good or evil. The negative intent is inherent in the person or organization who uses it; in themselves, runes are merely symbols of our own inner experience.

Rune Meanings

Below I list the key words, mythology, and history of each rune. These form a template. As you study, draw, and use each symbol, you will find that you add to and alter the meanings. Like tea leaf symbols, they are a focus for your own inner imagery, and if you keep a psychic notebook, you may find that over time you have written several pages on each rune.

For additional background, I would recommend that you read Norse myths and legends from the world in which runes were created and used as well as the more esoteric approaches listed under Further Reading at the back of this book. The twenty-four runes of the Elder Futhark (Norse system) are traditionally divided into three sets of eight.

THE AETT OR SET OF FREYJA, GODDESS OF LOVE AND FERTILITY

Fehu (Cattle) This is the rune of wealth, money, financial prosperity, and the price we must pay for what we want. The basic meaning of Fehu is wealth in the sense of money or currency. Cattle were mobile property, a measure of one's wealth. The word *fee*, a payment, comes from this term, and so the rune has the added meaning of the price one must pay for any action or inaction. Indeed the Old Norse Rune Poem warns that "money causes strife among kinsmen."

Throughout the old Norse legends, the deities and heroes continually paid a price for their actions. Odin craved wisdom and so he went to the spring of Mimir at the root of Yggdrasil, the World Tree. Mimir demanded the payment of one of Odin's eyes for a drink from the waters of memory. Odin accepted and never regretted his sacrifice.

The eye was placed in the fountain, and each morning Odin drank of its healing waters. Odin's outer vision was replaced by an inner guide and the conscious sight in his blind eye by contact with unconscious wisdom. But his new insight was a double-edged sword, for Odin understood now that all things must pass, even the rule of the Elder Gods.

Tyr, the Spirit Warrior, God of Courage and War, paid the price of his right hand, his sword hand, to bind Fenris Wolf, who was threatening the gods. However, he too was aware, even as he made his sacrifice, that Fenris Wolf could only be bound until Ragnarok and the Last Battle.

But the price may not always involve noble sacrifice. Freyja, Goddess of Love and Fertility, was prepared to give her body to four hideous dwarves, Alfrigg, Dvalin, Berling, and Gerr, to obtain the wonderful golden necklace they fashioned that would make her even more lovely and desirable.

Uruz (Aurochs) This is the rune of strength, courage, and overcoming obstacles. The aurochs was a huge, wild, very fierce ox, much like the longhorn cow of modern times. The horns of these creatures were worn on Viking helmets, engraved with the rune to transfer, by associative magic, the strength of the aurochs to the warriors. The last aurochs roamed the plains of northern Europe in the early seventeenth century.

Uruz is also associated with the primal creative force, because in Norse mythology, Audhumla was the primal cow formed from the dripping rime produced from the union of fire and ice at the time of creation. Her milk nourished the cosmic giant Ymir. She also licked into being, out of a block of ice, Buri, the producer and grandfather of Odin and his brothers.

The Norse and Icelandic Rune Poems talk of hardship for the herdsmen and refinement by suffering, using the images of iron and also drizzle. They create an image of harsh reality and obstacles to be overcome by strength and endurance. Throughout the rune poems of the North, you find reminders of the cold, bleak world in which the Vikings lived, and this explains why so many of the runes use symbolism of the extremes of ice and fire, rough seas, mist, and darkness.

Thurisaz (Thorn) The rune of protection, challenges, secrecy, and conflicts, Thurisaz is associated with another harsh image, the thorn tree that can offer protection from intruders. Bramble or hawthorn bushes were used to hedge boundaries and were traditional in many parts of Europe around the dwellings of those who practiced magic. In the Norse and Icelandic poems, *thorn* is associated with the Thurs, a "giant" in the Old Norse. There were several groups of *rime-thurses* or frost-giants, who fought the gods and maintained the cosmic tension, for they represented the ancient rule before the Aesir came into being.

Because of this, Thurisaz is a rune of challenge to those who seek to make a change or go against outmoded tradition.

Thurisaz is also associated with Thor, God of Thunder and Courage, who sought to protect Asgard, realm of the gods, from the frost-giants. Thor had a magical hammer, Mjollnir, that always returned to his hand after it reached its target. As well as defending the gods against the frost-giants, Thor's hammer acted as a sacred symbol at marriages, births, and funerals. This is recalled in the tradition of eloping and marrying at the forge at Gretna Green in Scotland.

In pre-Christian times, the sign of the hammer was made a sacred mark of protection, and the thorn rune was drawn or signed to call on similar power.

Ansuz (A God) This is the Father Rune, the rune of Odin, the All-Father, and rune of inspiration, wisdom, aspirations, and communication. Odin was desperate to acquire the wisdom and knowledge of the older order of giants. Having traded one of his eyes for wisdom and obtained the knowledge of the runes by sacrificing himself on the World Tree, he desired the gift of divine utterance. For this he needed the mead of poetry, made from the blood of wise Kvasir, which made everyone who drank it either a wise man or a poet. Kvasir, himself a creation of the gods, was killed by the dwarves Fjalahr and Galar, who made the mead. The mead was taken by the giant Suttung as blood price—compensation—for his parents, whom the dwarves had killed.

Odin obtained the mead by seducing Gunlod, the daughter of Suttung. As Odin, traveling in the shape of an eagle, carried the mead back to Asgard, the home of the gods, he spilled a little of it. This fell to earth and inspired mortal poetry. From time to time, Odin would favor mortals or one of the deities and share a little of the poetic mead.

The gift of the mead involved the death of Kvasir, the death of two giants, and trickery by Odin. As with the Norse runes, there is often a harsh price to be paid for anything. The power of these runes is not in the stark contrast of good and evil with good always winning through, but in the struggle to reconcile opposites, to acknowledge man's own weaknesses, and to rise toward a greater understanding. What we say and how we say it can be crucial.

Raidho (Riding) This is the rune of journeys, travel, initiative, impetus, and change. It is the symbol of the wheel, portrayed in earlier symbolism as the sun-wheel as it passes through the skies in its cycles of day and night and the year. It can also represent the wheel on the wagon of the old fertility gods, as they gave new life to the fields (see also the rune Ingwaz, page 150). Equally, we can associate Raidho with the constellations of stars around the cosmic axis.

Raidho is the rune of the long and dangerous ride, "the worst for horses." The Norse poem refers also to the best sword being forged by Regin, the wise dwarf, for the young hero Sigurd. This sword was made from the pieces of Sigurd's late father Sigmund's sword and was so powerful that it could not be broken. Thus armed, Sigurd rode to avenge his father's death. Action and sometimes uncertainty are essential if we are to ride forward into life. But it is important, like Sigurd, to be well-prepared.

Kenaz (Torch) This is the rune of guidance, the inner voice, illumination, and inner strength. Kenaz is one of the fire runes and symbolizes the torch that lit the great halls as well as more humble abodes. This torch was made from pine dipped in resin. As well as giving light, it could also ignite the forge, the fire of the hearth, or even a funeral pyre. It was used to kindle the Need Fire (see the rune Naudhiz, page 143) that was lit at festivals. But, as always, the other aspect is also present: the burnishing, cleansing aspect of fire. And it is this purgative effect that is emphasized in the Norse and Icelandic poems.

This is the cosmic fire from Muspellheim in the South that met with ice from Nieflheim in the North in the creation of the Norse world. But it also brought about the destruction of the Aesir and Vanir orders of the gods. Its alter ego is Hagalaz, the rune of hail, and the second element in creation. The appearance of the combination of Kenaz and Hagalaz runes in a reading, or indeed any fire and ice runes, indicates a fusion of opposites. Without the torch there is darkness, and without the inner flame there is emptiness within.

Gebo (Gift) This is the rune of generosity and all matters relating to exchanges, including contracts, love, marriage, and sexual union. Gebo is the rune of giving to others and the union of mutual giving, whether in sexuality and love or formally in marriage. It can also indicate a gift from a higher source, including bounty or knowledge and insight, or even the exchange of favors or information.

In the Norse traditions, a gift always required one in return so there is always the question of whether one is giving too much in a situation—emotionally, practically, or materially. This rune is not mentioned in the Old Norse or Icelandic Rune Poems, but the Anglo-Saxon poem talks of the blessings of giving and also of receiving if one is in need (a Christianized version). However, there is a sense that giving must be mutual, even with those closest to you, and that the Christian and Buddhist idea of giving without any hope of reward does not always make for enriching worldly interactions.

Wunjo (Joy) This is the rune of personal happiness, success, and recognition of worth. Wunjo represents happiness through oneself and one's own efforts rather than through others and is often used as a focus for those in search of success.

To the Vikings, happiness meant having enough food, shelter, and wealth and being accepted as part of an extended family. Although this rune appears only in the Anglo-Saxon poem, the symbol is of one who knows few (sometimes translated as "a little of") troubles and who also has power and blessedness. The second translation makes more sense, suggesting that it is those who have experienced hardships who know the importance of taking happiness as it comes and, above all, of finding personal joy through one's own actions and not expecting life to provide.

THE AETT OR SET OF HAGALAZ OR HEIMDALL, WATCHER OF THE GODS

Hagalaz (Hail) This is known as the Mother Rune, and in the Futhark, it occupies the position of the sacred number nine. In its original shape, as the six-pointed snowflake, Hagalaz had a geometric shape found in the composition of many natural life-forms. *Hagalaz* means "hail" or "hailstone" and is regarded as the cosmic seed, for ice was the second main element involved in creation, and as such, it is the alter ego of Kenaz (see page 141). The Old Norse Rune Poem talks of hail as "the coldest of grains," associating Hagalaz with the harvest, for when hail melts it turns into life-giving water.

Therefore, Hagalaz has come to represent unwelcome, external change that, if used positively, can transform sorrow to happiness.

Naudhiz (Need) This rune represents needs that can be met by one's own positive reaction to external deprivation; it indicates self-reliance and the desire for achievement, and it is also the rune of passion. Naudhiz, the second fire rune, is another of the cosmic forces that shapes the fates of the world and of humankind.

It is the spindle that generates the Need Fire through friction; the fire from within that is manifest externally. Need Fires were lit from early times all over northern Europe on festivals such as Beltane (May Eve), the beginning of summer, at Samhain (Hallowe'en), and on the solstices. The custom is reflected today in the Christian Easter Eve ceremonies of burning the Judas Man in parts of Germany and Eastern Europe and rekindling the paschal candle and also in Bonfire Night. These were not only purging fires, but fires of new life and light, whose ashes fertilized the fields, and that persuaded the sun to shine again.

Naudhiz is a rune of want that produces the Need Fire that drives a man or woman to obtain that which he or she desires. Because of this, Naudhiz is associated with love magic. The Old Norse Rune Poem makes the link between fire and ice, the Need Fire being kindled against the frost, inner and outer.

Isa (Ice) This rune represents a blockage or a period of inactivity that one can use for good by preparing for the right moment. Isa is the second ice rune and the fifth element in the Norse world. The single vertical form of the rune means that it is contained in every other rune; again, a cosmic seed, described in the Norse poem as a "broad bridge" and in the Icelandic verse as "roof of the waves."

Isa can be seen as the ice of winter that even freezes the sea over and stops hunting and exploration, an external obstacle to movement that can be used positively for reflection or planning. Alternatively, we can regard Isa as a bridge between dimensions that those who are perhaps blinded by the fear of going forward need to negotiate with care. Isa is also the ice glacier flowing imperceptibly from Nieflheim, indicating progress that seems slow but nevertheless occurs beneath the surface.

Jera (Year) This is the rune of the harvest, of the results of earlier efforts, and of life crystals that can either be fruitful or repeat old mistakes. Jera represents the natural progression through the cycles of existence: from season to season or year to year; through the stages of life or a specific relationship or situation. It is invoked magically for a good season or harvest, for fertility of all kinds, and to achieve goals through hard work and nourishing. Both the Norse and Icelandic poems refer to a good harvest being for the profit of all men, and the Norse poem talks of the generosity of Frey or Ingwaz—the God of Fertility of the Land, whose symbolic wagon was driven across the fields in a ceremony of fertilizing the land.

The rune is a version of the old proverb, As you sow, so shall you reap; if the cyclic progression of existence becomes stagnant, it is important to unblock any obstacle, whether inner or outer, to progress.

Eiwaz (Yew) This is the rune of natural endings that lead to new beginnings, of the banishment of what is redundant in life, and of tradition. Eiwaz, the yew tree, represents the cycle of death and rebirth. Death was ever-present in the Nordic world, but it was confronted by the promise that the bravest warriors slain in any battle would won a place at the everlasting feast in Valhalla, to rise again to fight at the Last Battle. Warfare was considered the most glorious of occupations and Odin was worshiped as God of War above all his other functions.

Because the yew is the longest-living tree, it was adopted by the northern peoples as a symbol of longevity and eternal life and was frequently planted where ashes or bones were buried to transfer its immortality to the dead souls. Sacred to Ullr, God of Winter and Archery, who himself lived in a grove of sacred yew trees, the yew, whose resinous vapor can induce visions, was the tree of shamans and magic. It was also one of the trees burned as the sacred yule at the Midwinter Solstice to persuade the sun to return and is called in the Old Norse Rune Poem "the greenest wood in the winter."

For this reason, the Icelandic Rune Poem also associates the rune with the bow, often made from yew wood, as a symbol of new life from the old.

Perthro (Lot-Cup) This is the rune of what is not yet known or revealed, of the essential self, and of taking a chance. In modern rune sets, there is usually a blank rune that is known as the stone of destiny. This did not exist in the earlier forms so Perthro served as the rune of destiny. I do not use a blank rune as the older tradition seems more valid.

In the tradition of the early northern peoples, gambling and divination were very close, and decisions would be made as to whether to travel or remain close to home, to fight or take evasive tactics, by casting lots (sometimes runes). The fall of the dice or runes, or whatever was cast, would indicate, it was believed, the will of the gods.

However, this was not a fixed fate. The gambler or diviner was expected to read his *orlog,* or fate, and then take appropriate action to maximize his good fortune or avoid any potential pitfalls. There is a mention of Perthro only in the Anglo-Saxon Rune Poem, which speaks of "play and laughter in the beer hall among bold men."

"Testing their luck," which Vikings did, both in lot-casting and in the real world, was a way warriors discovered truths about their essential selves, their essence, the root person (with both strengths and weakness, vices and virtues), and so this, too, is an important attribute of Perthro.

Elhaz or Algiz (Elk-Sedge) This was the rune of the higher self, one's spiritual nature, duality, and the need for care in approaching important matters. In many ways, Elhaz is the most difficult rune to understand, for it is given several interpretations, perhaps because different images have been used to express a complex concept. Viking poetry is scattered with images, called *kennings,* such as "Sif's Hair" for example. This was used as a synonym for gold, as Sif, wife of Thor, was shaved bald by Loki, God of Misrule, who was then forced to give her a wig of pure gold.

The Old English name "elk-sedge" is a kenning for sword. It represents a two-edged blade, such as the two-edged sword mentioned in the Book of Revelation, coming out of the mouth of the Son of Man, signifying destruction on the one side and salvation on the other. It is easy for the user of a double-edged sword to injure himself, and yet it is a very powerful weapon, with double the power of a conventional blade. The rune shape is taken as a splayed hand held out in defense or the horns of an elk (another translation), both of which can be used in attack or defense.

The Anglo-Saxon Rune Poem, the only one to mention this rune, interprets it as "eel-grass," found on marshes, "that grimly wounds any man who tries to grasp it."

Eel-grass, however, also has many creative functions. It was used for thatching, as kindling for the fire, and as bedding for animals—again, that which is of worth and must be handled with care. In the same way, the path of spiritual growth and divination must be approached with respect and not be followed for selfish or negative ends or treated as a game.

Sowilo (Sun) This is the rune of victory, success, potential, energy, and expansion. As with most systems, the sun is seen as the most positive and potent symbol. This was especially true in the North, where the sun was so precious. It can also be seen as lightning and forms the third and most powerful fire rune, melting the ice of winter and causing the crops to grow. The sun festivals, especially the longest day or Summer Solstice, were celebrated throughout the northern world by rolling great fire wheels down hills, waving flaming tar torches over the fields, and lighting bonfires on hilltops to welcome the sun and give it power.

In the Far North and Scandinavia, the sun was female, and even today it is referred to as the White Sow. Along with Raidho ᚱ, Sowilo is the rune of the sun or the sun wheel, the sun moving through the year. The Old Norse Rune Poem describes it as "light of the lands," and refers to its holiness. The Icelandic Rune Poem talks of the sun as the "life-long destroyer of ice."

In the Elder Edda the Sun Goddess's golden beams brought forth green plants on the newly created earth. After sinking in the west in the evening, Sunna, or Sol as she was called, slept in a golden bed in Hel, the underworld. Before dawn, Sunna traveled through the underworld to emerge in the east through the *jodyrr* (the horse doors). It is said that her arrival was proclaimed by Goldcomb, the Cockerel of Morn.

THE AETT OR SET OF TIWAZ, SPIRIT WARRIOR

Tiwaz (Star) This rune represents the pole- or lodestar, justice, altruism, self-sacrifice, following a chosen path, or keeping faith even in dark times. Tiwaz, sometimes called the Spirit Warrior, is the constant pointer in the northern skies. This is the rune of Tyr or the god Tiw, the Norse god who symbolically presided over the Germanic General Assembly and over all matters of justice. He is also the God of War because court cases were often settled by combat or even full-scale battle. It was believed that Odin and Tyr would allow the "just cause" to win.

In the Norse and Icelandic poems, Tyr is called "the one-handed god," referring to the sacrifice he made of his most precious gift, his sword hand, to bind Fenris Wolf, a legend mentioned in the section on Fehu, the rune of the price (see page 138). This sacrifice was even greater than Odin's sacrifice of his eye to obtain wisdom, for it was not made for personal gain but for his fellow gods. Altruism, one of the noblest of the concepts in the northern world, is the runes' guiding principle.

The one-eyed Odin and the one-armed Tyr with his magical sword were seen as embracing imperfection so they might gain greater glory.

 Berkano (Birch) This is the rune of renewal, healing, physical or spiritual regeneration, fertility, and mothering in all aspects. Berkano is related to Nerthus, the Great Mother, the Earth Goddess, and is also linked to Hel, Goddess of the Underworld and daughter of the trickster god Loki. The original Nordic Earth Mother was Nerthus, and the tradition continued with Frigg, wife of Odin, who was associated with fertility and motherhood and was invoked by women in labor.

This rune contains the concept of birth, death, and rebirth. According to Norse legend, the birch was the first tree to recolonize the land after the retreat of the ice cap at the end of the last Ice Age. The old poems recall that the birch "puts forth shoots without seeding."

Birch trees were planted in front of dwellings in the northern countries to invoke the protection of the Earth Mother, and the custom spread to America with the early settlers.

Ehwaz (Horse) This is the rune of loyalty, harmony between people or inner and outer worlds, partnerships and friendships, moving house, or career. Ehwaz is associated with the horse, an animal sacred to the Vikings, particularly because it was so vital to carry the rider into battle. It therefore represents a harmonious relationship, as typified by that between a warrior and his horse. Mentioned only in the Anglo-Saxon Rune Poem, Ehwaz emphasizes the joy a horse brings to his rider and how it can make him feel like a prince or minor god.

If a warrior was killed in battle, his horse was often buried with him, and when a much-loved horse died, it was given an elaborate burial. Odin had an eight-footed gray steed, Sleipnir, on which he rode into battle. On Sleipnir's teeth, Odin had engraved magical runes so his mount might be invulnerable.

 **Mannaz (Man)** This rune symbolizes the power of human intelligence, the ability to see our lives as part of a wider pattern, and compassion and acceptance of the weaknesses and strengths of ourselves and others. In the ancient world of the North, Mannaz was seen as a reflection of the divinity in his three functions: warrior, farmer, and ruler/magician.

According to Norse legend, Odin and his brothers, Vili and Ve, were walking along the edge of the land where the earth met the sea and came upon two unprotected trees, an ash and an elm. These they used to create the first man and woman. Odin gave them the breath of life, Vili gave them intelligence and a loving heart, and Ve gave them their natural senses. They gave the man, named Ask (Ash), and the woman, named Embla (Elm), Midgard, the middle earth, as their home, and so began the human race.

When Ragnarok, the Destruction of the Existing Order, came, their descendants, Lif and Lifthrasir, sheltered in the World Tree and survived the holocaust to repopulate the new world. Mannaz says that although individuals may cease to be, they live on in their deeds and their descendants. Therefore, this rune is a celebration of the strength and potential of the individual and his or her connection to the human race in all times and places, the "increase" or quickening of dust into life, according to the old poems.

Laguz (Water) This is the rune of birth and beginnings; the initiation into life; emotions; of following the flow of life, unconscious wisdom, and intuition. Laguz is the rune of water or the sea, and the ancient poems tell of the hazards of "churning water" and the "brine stallion" that does not heed its bridle. To the Vikings, water was a frightening yet exciting concept. Sea journeys, although perilous, could lead to wondrous journeys, great conquests, and the discovery of new lands. In the tales of noble exploits, it is forgotten that many did not survive the voyages over stormy oceans.

The Aegir, the gods and goddesses of the sea, both gave and took life, offering fertility and wealth in return. Sailors always carried a coin with a hole in it or a gold earring so that if they drowned, they might pay Ran, wife of Aegir, the principal sea god, a tribute and then live in her coral caves under the waves. The sun shining on the waves was said to be Ran's treasure.

When the leader of an expedition approached a new shore, he would throw into the seas the *ainstafar* (huge wooden posts from the abandoned hall at home). They used these to mark the new enclosure, and where the currents carried the posts ashore, the sailors landed and marked out their new territory.

Ingwaz (The God Ing) This rune indicates a time of gestation, both human and symbolic, a time of creative withdrawal to wait for new strength and life, and the promise of better times. Like Jera and Berkano, Ingwaz is another fertility rune that is powerfully associated with protection, especially of the home. Ingwaz (or Ing) was the old Germanic Earth God, consort of Nerthus, the Earth Mother. Like many of the old earth gods, the God of the Corn died each year at harvesttime and was reborn at the Midwinter Solstice to shoot into life again as vegetation in the early spring. Ing was traditionally the God of the Hearth, and the huge old fireplaces that had seats were called Inglenooks because the members of the household were contained close to the fire.

Ing's sacred wagon made a circuit of the fields after the winter in a ritual reenactment, bringing fertility back to the land. The

Anglo-Saxon Rune Poem, the only one to mention Ing, talks of him riding his wagon eastward (or backward, as it is sometimes translated), in the opposite direction from the sun's natural progression from east to west. This led to the realm of darkness inhabited by the Etins or Giants and refers to his annual ritual death after which he was reborn, strong and renewed.

The constellation called Ursa Major, or the Great Bear, in Western astrology was known in the northern tradition as the Wagon.

 Othala (Homestead) This is the rune of the home, of domestic matters, of family and family finances, stability, responsibility, and duty. Some versions of the Futhark put Othala as the final rune. But it seems to make more sense to follow the suggestion that Dagaz, the awakening, should be the last rune. Othala is the rune of the sacred enclosure, the homeland, the village, the homestead. It is the rune of the home and family; the customs, duties, and responsibilities that go along with maintaining family ties.

In the rune poems, Othala is said to be "beloved of every human," but this domestic contentment is linked with a good harvest; that is, material comfort. Because Othala refers to land owned by several generations of a family rather than leased from a lord, it speaks of permanence and stability and so represents domestic stability, security, and living with others rather than branching out alone. Though the Norse people were great wanderers, nevertheless, the homestead was important to them, and as described under rune Laguz (see page 150), establishing the new homestead, however temporary, in a new land was a priority.

 **Dagaz (Day)** This is the rune of awakening, clear vision or awareness, light at the end of the tunnel, and optimism. Dagaz refers to the coming together of day and night at sunset, at the beginning of a new day in the northern world, and at daybreak or dawn. Therefore, it also represents the moment of fusion and transition and so has special potency. The midpoint of the northern day, a period of darkness and light, was dawn and the rising of the sun. It is a balancing of opposites

ALPHABETICAL CORRESPONDENCES

Letter	Rune	Rune Name	Rune Meaning
A	ᚨ	ANSUZ	communication
B	ᛒ	BERKANO	regeneration
C	ᚲ	KENAZ	illumination / inner wisdom
D	ᛞ	DAGAZ	integration
E	ᛖ	EHWAZ	harmony
F	ᚠ	FEHU	prosperity
G	ᚷ	GEBO	giving
H	ᚻ	HAGALAZ	change / disruption
I	ᛁ	ISA	stillness
J	ᛃ	JERA	harvest / cycles of life
K	ᚲ	KENAZ	illumination / inner wisdom
L	ᛚ	LAGUZ	life force / emotions
M	ᛗ	MANNAZ	humanity / tradition
N	ᚾ	NAUDHIZ	need
O	ᛟ	OTHALA	home
P	ᛈ	PERTHRO	essential self
R	ᚱ	RAIDHO	travel, action
S/Z	ᛋ	SOWILO	sun, potential
T	ᛏ	TIWAZ	justice, sacrifice
U	ᚢ	URUZ	primal strength
V/W	ᚹ	WUNJO	joy
W/Th	ᚦ	THURISAZ	protection
Y	ᛇ	EIWAZ	endings / mystery

and, like the World card in the tarot, represents the union of disparate forces in harmony, stillness, and movement.

The Anglo-Saxon Rune Poem, the only one to describe Dagaz, refers to it as "the Lord's messenger." This may reflect an attempt by scribes to Christianize the rune poems, but whether it is the light of day, the Sun God, or the Christian deity who offers enlightenment, the light of Dagaz is seen as shining on rich and poor alike, offering them hope.

In the Norse legends, Nott, the Goddess of Night, was the creator of this light. By her third husband, Dellinger (Dawn), she gave birth to a radiant son, Dag, whose name meant "day." As soon as the gods saw the radiance of Dag, they fashioned him a chariot, drawn by a white steed, Skin-faxi (Shining Mane). From his mane, brilliant beams of light radiated in all directions, scattering the fears of night.

Buying or Making Runes

Although many good rune sets exist, I believe the very best runes are those you make yourself. You do not need any great artistic skill. The runic characters were designed to be hewn in stone and are easy to copy. Runes you make yourself are special, because they are endowed with your unique qualities. Price has nothing to do with magic, and the best runes may be those drawn on a pebble that you have selected from a place with happy associations. I have some made from stones I found near Loch Lomond with my friends Daphne and John, who introduced me to dowsing, and when I use them, I recall that wonderful day in the rain on the misty shores of Scotland.

However, there are many excellent rune sets on the market—of wood, crystal, ceramic, stone, and metal. Usually these are based on the Elder Futhark, but you may find variations. There may be twenty-five runes including a blank, the stone of destiny. Keep your runes in a bag made, if possible, of a natural fabric.

STONE RUNES

Stone runes are probably the easiest to make. Go to a beach or woods and pick up about thirty stones (giving yourself a few spares) of similar size, color, and shape. They should be about the size of a medium-sized coin and flat on both sides. You mark only one side because the blank sides also have significance. Mark the symbols with a permanent marker, acrylic paint, or, if you are good with your hands, use a small chisel or sharp screwdriver to carve the shape of the rune and then paint the outline. Red is the traditional color, but I find black markings clearer. Rose quartz or clear quartz crystals made good runes, although the symbols do tend to wear off and need renewing frequently.

wooden runes

Wooden runes are traditionally made from ash, the World Tree, or oak, tree of Odin and Thor. Hazel, the tree of wisdom, is also suitable for runes. However, one of the best sets I ever had was made by my husband when he was infuriated by some local petty bureaucrats. Rather than sulking or raging, he sawed an old broom handle into pieces about the size of a large coin and burned the rune shapes into them with an old screwdriver heated over the gas stove. By the end of the exercise his irritation had been completely dispelled by the act of creation, and I had gained a lovely set of runes. Red-hot screwdrivers should be used with caution, and we have now invested in a pyrography tool, an instrument like a soldering iron but with a selection of tips for burning different shapes into wood. Equally effective is to paint the runes on the wood or to carve the outlines.

rune staves

Rune staves can be bought as polished engraved staves, but they are also easy to make. Find twenty-four even-sized twigs, about twelve inches (30 cm) long, scrape away a section of bark at the top, and mark the sign in black or red paint.

Casting the Runes

In the section on tarot divination, I described a number of different layouts in which the relative positions of the cards contribute to our understanding. I have come across numerous systems for reading runes, some of them intensely complicated and requiring protractors to measure the angles between the fallen runes. However, runes are such a fluid form of divination that I have found few rune spreads or layouts that are as effective as simple rune casting.

To cast the runes

1. On a square of white cloth, draw a circle with a circumference of approximately three feet (1 m) in black or red so that there is a plain area about twelve inches (30 cm) deep around the circle.

2. Spread the cloth out on a table or the floor. Reading in a grove of oak or ash trees can be especially powerful, but when you have confidence in your runes, and yourself, you can do a reading anywhere.

3. You can formulate a question or ask the person for whom you are reading to do so, but I have found that the most effective readings are those in which you allow your mind to go blank as you cast the runes.

4. Without looking, take three runes or rune staves from your bag, choosing ones that feel right. If you are reading for someone else, let him or her select and cast the runes.

5. Kneel or sit about three feet (1 m) away from the cloth, and, using the hand that feels best, throw all three runes together onto the cloth.

6. Ignore any staves or runes that fall outside the cloth. Read each rune in the circle in the order it fell, turning over any on which the blank side is faceup. If you are reading for someone else, ask him or her to turn over any runes that fell with their blank sides up.

7. After reading each rune, return it to its position on the cloth.

8. If you still do not have an answer to your question, cast three more runes. You can cast up to nine runes in total, including those that fall outside the cloth.

Interpreting the Runes

The first great difference between reading the runes and reading tarot or playing cards is that you may read anything from nine to none of the runes, depending on how many have fallen outside the circle.

Read the runes when you feel the need, but generally two readings a week at the most are sufficient, unless matters are changing from day to day or you are at a crisis time. You may go for several weeks without wanting to do a reading. Readings that are just for practice are not as fruitful as those prompted by a real situation.

* Look first at the way the initial runes have fallen, whether in a group (suggesting that there is an area of concern to which they are all linked) or scattered (which can suggest that several disparate issues exist or that you or the questioner feel pulled in many ways). This picture may change if you add more runes, and sometimes one rune knocks another out of the way or displaces it, often mirroring a situation in the outer world.

* Generally, the earlier runes cast in the circle pinpoint the issue of concern, while later ones offer a possible course of action or suggest an outcome of change. There are no definite rules on this. As you become familiar with rune readings, you will gain a natural "feel" for the purpose of each rune.

* If there is only a single rune, it may highlight an aspect you had not considered, but you need to allow your unconscious wisdom time to formulate an answer, either in your dreams or in a reading the next day.

* Use the meanings given earlier in the chapter as a guide to the reasons and possible solutions. Let each rune create images that may vary from reading to reading or, if you are reading for others, according to that person's need and personality.

* If a rune shows its blank side up, the issue or solution will not immediately change or resolve and it is time to wait rather than act.

* You may find that you need to use up to nine runes (three casts of three) for a complex question or when you have time

to deliberate. It is entirely up to you and sometimes a hastily cast three can instantly get to the heart of the matter.

* If you keep a record of your readings, you may find that certain key runes turn up time after time and so have special importance in your life.

* Occasionally, all nine runes fall outside the circle. This is not an ominous sign, merely an indication that this is not the right time for a rune reading. Perhaps you need a period of rest, a walk, or some physical work to let your inner wisdom rearrange the question and consider alternative solutions. Often the answer comes in a dream. If not, do a reading the next day.

An ALTERNATIVE METHOD

Standing or sitting close to your circle, shake all your runes out of the bag. Read all those in the circle that fall faceup, sometimes called Bright Staves. This can be a lengthy, involved process, although infinitely rewarding.

* If none of the runes fall upright, you should leave the reading until another day. The more upright runes there are in the circle, the more immediate the decision or action will be.

* You may end up reading more than half the runes, in which case read each one in turn, having noted the relative positions, and then try to group them according to meaning. For example, are there a number of element runes, talking about fire, water, and ice? This might suggest that it is important to take note of external circumstances.

* If there are sets of runes talking about consequences, the price you must pay, or sacrifices you may need to make, you might like to look at the pressures others place on you.

* If, however, you have runes of the sun, of personal joy, and harmony, then all is positive, and you can feel confident that any endeavor will succeed.

* If there is more than one meaning-linked rune, try to arrange them in a logical sequence.

* If your reading does not make sense, draw a quick sketch of the rune positions, and if possible, leave the reading undisturbed. Return to it after a night's sleep or a period of relaxation, and you will find the meaning has fallen into place.

Sample Rune Cast

Sylvia was in her thirties and pregnant for the first time. Her husband, Andy, had reacted to the news in a way she had not anticipated, by declaring that they should move to the country so he could commute and Sylvia could stay at home and raise the family. Previously, they had agreed that Sylvia would carry on working as before.

Sylvia was unwilling to leave the town, although she knew their present flat was too small for a family. She wanted to follow the original plan of buying a house near their present home and hiring a nanny, as she was in line for a promotion and her firm was anxious to keep her.

A decision had to be made in the near future, but Sylvia and Andy ended up arguing because he insisted there was no way their child was going to be brought up in the center of the town with an absentee mother.

Sylvia cast three runes into the circle, asking the question: "Should I give up my career plans?" Two of the runes, Hagalaz ᚺ (the rune of hail) and Jera ᛋ (the harvest), fell into the circle on opposite sides. Sylvia saw these as representing herself and Andy.

Rune 1 Hagalaz, Hail ᚺ

Rune 2 Jera, The Harvest ᛋ

The two runes in the circle seemed to encapsulate the problem, their seemingly incompatible views on the future in view of her husband's about-turn.

Sylvia saw her rune, hail and disruption, acknowledging her new creative potential, the grain of life in the Hagalaz. She acknowledged that although she feared the disruption, the baby was the most important thing in her life. However, she did not feel that this warranted giving up her career that was, to her, an essential part of her personality.

For Andy, Jera (harvest) reflected the effects of the pregnancy on him, changing his previously liberal views to traditional ones in which it was time to settle down with a wife and child in the country, while he took on the role of hunter, going forth and returning each night.

Sylvia decided to cast three more runes:

Rune 3 Eiwaz, Hidden Endings ᛇ

Rune 4 Fehu, the Price ᚠ

Rune 5 Raidho, Riding Forth ᚱ

The first rune of this second set, Eiwaz ᛇ, the yew tree, rune of endings leading to new beginnings, was hidden, blank side up. It landed close to her Hagalaz ᚻ rune, suggesting that she was the one who was going to have to make the compromise if she wanted the relationship to continue, which she did. Sylvia acknowledged that the country option might make more sense, for the area in which they lived was not a good place to bring up children. In that sense, the ending of her urban lifestyle was part of the answer.

The second rune, faceup, was Fehu ᚠ. The question in this case was not prosperity but, as Sylvia interpreted it, the price she had to pay for either following her wishes and possibly jeopardizing her marriage or giving up work and losing her own identity, as she saw it.

Fehu landed on top of Eiwaz. Sylvia was not prepared to give up her job and be a stay-at-home wife. Andy refused to compromise. Should she follow her own valid needs?

The final rune, Raidho ᚱ, the difficult but exciting journey, also faceup, was to the immediate right of Eiwaz. Sylvia realized that one solution was to move to the country and negotiate a phased return to work while she sorted out her own commuting and child care problems. It was not an ideal solution, because, realistically, Sylvia knew it would affect her promotion prospects. But that was the Fehu if she was to keep her career *and* give the baby a good environment in which to grow up.

Sylvia did not feel the need to cast any more runes. The test of a good rune reading is if it answers the question for the person who is having the reading. Life is less than ideal. People do end up making sacrifices and compromises—often the compromises have to be made by women when children are concerned. The runes sometimes offer the most realistic solution, given the circumstances.

In fact, Andy changed his mind after the baby was born, as the initial child care arrangements (a live-in nanny) worked so well. He was offered a job close to home and took over more of the child care and Sylvia continued commuting. However, she regrets the time she spends away from the baby and next time around plans to work more from home herself so she and Andy can share the child care.

THE SACRED GRID

Nine is a magical number, the number of perfection and completion of a cycle. It was especially sacred to the Germanic peoples because of the nine worlds on the Tree of Yggdrasil. Because the nine squares were enclosed in a larger square, the sacred grid represented complete protection and was a magical area, enclosed and safe, but also containing a great deal of power. It can be read horizontally, vertically, or diagonally and avoids many of the problems of a more constrained rune layout. There are two ways of reading the sacred grid.

Rune 7	Rune 8	Rune 9
Rune 6	Rune 5	Rune 4
Rune 1	Rune 2	Rune 3

The first and simplest method is to draw out runes one at a time from your bag and assign each to the appropriate rune position. The second method is to draw the sacred grid on a 3-foot-square piece of white card stock, and cast the runes one at a time until you fill all the spaces. Return any runes that fall either outside the grid or onto lines to the bag, and keep casting until each rune finds its own position.

Some people assign the three horizontal rows to the three Norns or Fates: runes one to three are in the domain of Urdhr, the Norn concerned with the past, and indicate the factors that contributed to the present situation. Runes four to six are in the domain of Verdhandi, the Norn concerned with the present, and symbolize the factors that maintain the present situation. Runes seven to nine are in the domain of Skuld, the Norn concerned with what will come to pass, and represent the future possibilities, given the intricate web formed by the interaction of the past and present. Our future *orlog* constantly changes as each new day adds another strand to the web.

You can also read the sacred grid as a collection of nine separate runes that make up a whole truth, generally about a life path or change, that is different from the sum of the separate parts.

Sample Sacred Grid Reading

Nathan was a healer in his late sixties who worked for the same healing group for more than twenty years. Lately he had taken over much of the administrative work. However, over the previous five years, the group changed radically, with younger people joining and very different methods coming to the fore. Nathan felt increasingly isolated and found that his healing work suffered as a result of the resentment he felt toward the new order that seemed to disregard the ways that had worked over the previous years. He formed a sacred grid with these runes.

Rune 7: Berkano	Rune 8: Ansuz	Rune 9: Wunjo
Rune 6: Elhaz	Rune 5: Naudhiz	Rune 4: Mannaz
Rune 1: Gebo	Rune 2: Ingwaz	Rune 3: Thurisaz

Runes 1 to 3: The Domain of Urdhr

* Gebo ✕, the rune of giving and partnerships of all kinds, seemed to Nathan to represent his healing world and the harmonious relationships in the healing group. He felt this relationship was no longer possible.

* Ingwaz ◊, the rune of withdrawal, was one that Nathan initially said belonged to the present. But he realized that he had started to become less enthusiastic about the group after the death of his wife, a fellow healer, three years earlier.

* Thurisaz ▷, the rune of the thorn and protection, Nathan said, described the way he felt—prickly. As younger people who had not known his wife joined the group the nature of the group changed, and the worse he felt. But most of all, his own vulnerability at being a widower had, he acknowledged, made him impatient of newcomers and change.

Runes 4 to 6: The Domain of Verdhandi

* Mannaz ᛗ, the rune of accepting the strengths and weaknesses of ourselves and others, seemed very significant to Nathan, because he was worried that he was no longer able to heal in the way that he had for years. Nathan said he was very tired, and because everyone seemed so self-assured, he had been reluctant to admit he had been having problems.

* Naudhiz ᚾ, the rune of need and the need to answer one's own needs, suggested to Nathan his inability to accept that it might be time to step back and address his own needs, which had previously been fulfilled through his healing work, in a different way. Perhaps the healing group was no longer the best focus for his work.

* Elhaz ᛉ, the rune of grasping the nettle and spiritual potential, reflected Nathan's fears that if he admitted that he wanted to leave the group, he would be denying his own spiritual nature. But the healing group was a double-edged sword. By evoking resentment in Nathan, it actually made him less spiritual in focus.

Runes 7 to 9: The Domain of Skuld

* Berkano ᛒ, the rune of regeneration and nurturing, said Nathan should not abandon his healing work, but carry it out in a different way. One implication of the Mother Rune is of personal care. Nathan said he had wondered about working alone, perhaps from home, so he could go back to his own special method of talking at length to those who came to be healed prior to any actual healing. This had been difficult since the group moved to purpose-built premises and adopted an appointment system.

* Ansuz ᚨ is the rune of communication and inspiration. At first sight, it seemed to be a strange rune to turn up for someone moving into a more private situation. But Nathan said he had been asked several times by a spiritualist organization to write an account of the development of healing in the movement so more traditional methods would not be forgotten. He had always declined because he had been too busy organizing the group.

* Wunjo ᛈ is the route of personal joy and success. What would make Nathan happy? Wunjo is not the rune of happiness through others, and so it implies something outside his work. Nathan wanted to visit his son in Australia, but had been reluctant to do so, again because he felt obliged to stay and work with the group. This, he now admitted, was a limitation he had imposed on himself, because he was afraid they would manage too well without him. Now that he was free, he decided to go away before embarking on his new beginning.

The sacred grid works just as well without the past, present, and future divisions, but reading the runes in groups of three seems a natural division. Choose the method that feels most natural to you.

Chapter 5

CRYSTAL DIVINATION

*So much is true, that gems have fine spirits, and may operate, by
consent, on the spirits of men, to strengthen and exhilarate them.*

—FRANCIS BACON, 1561–1626

THE WORD CRYSTAL is rooted in
the Greek word *krystallos* from *krysos* ("icy cold"), because it was
thought that crystals were made from ice so cold it would never melt.
From the earliest times, crystals and gems have been regarded as precious. Buddhists refer to clear crystal quartz as "visible nothingness."
The ancient Greeks believed that all quartz crystals found on earth
were fragments of the archetypal crystal of truth, dropped by Hercules
from Mount Olympus, home of the gods. Hence polished crystal
spheres are used in divination because it is said they will never lie.

The Greek philosopher Plato (427–347 B.C.) claimed that stars
and planets converted decayed and decaying material into the most
perfect gemstones that then came under the rule of those planets
and stars.

The Chaldeans, who lived in Mesopotamia in 4000 B.C. and
studied the stars for divinatory purposes, claimed that certain planets
were linked to crystals that were said to reflect their energies and
characteristics. These correspondences have changed over time, especially since the discovery of the planets Uranus, Neptune, and Pluto.

The planetary correspondences form the basis of the system for crystal divination in this section. In *The Complete Guide to Psychic Development* (The Crossing Press, 2003), I described a method of crystal divination that relied on colors, and it is one I have used for some years. However, the planetary system adds an extra dimension. There are eleven crystals in the system, each aligned to the energies of one of the planets and the sun and the moon.

Divinatory Crystals

You can create a beautiful and relatively inexpensive crystal divinatory set that you can also use as a focus for personal rituals and crystal gazing. The individual crystals in your set form personal talismans, evoking both energizing and protective powers.

CRYSTAL COLORS

The hot colors—red, yellow, orange, and sparkling white—contain a great deal of creative power even in their gentler shades. Any crystal in these colors has natural energizing forces and, in divination, indicates that a degree of action is desirable. They are the colors of the outer world.

The cooler colors—green, blue, pink, purple, and gentle translucent white—reflect thoughts, emotions, and spiritual desires. They are the colors of the inner world. Even black, which is not really a color but the lack of one, has a place in the spectrum of experience as a marker of time and earthly limitations.

CRYSTAL ENERGIES

Although color forms an integral part of crystal divination, the individual crystals you select have their own subtle strengths. You can use this system with any crystal of the right color or indeed with glass nuggets, painted stones, or buttons. But choosing a crystal that has a special significance may help you build a unique energy system that is right for you. By each crystal type I list its special properties.

Choosing Your Divinatory Crystals

Buy flat, oval-shaped crystals of constant size and shape about the size of a medium coin. These are on sale in New Age shops and mineral stores almost everywhere. Crystals need not be expensive, but it is better if possible to choose from a large selection, taking your time so that each crystal feels right for you. Sometimes people buy a "holding stone," a crystal that will do as a substitute until they find the right one for their personal collection.

In time, you may build up two sets, one for your personal use and one for giving readings, because there is no doubt that crystals tend to be the most requested form of divination.

I have listed alternative stones. Some "appear" naturally on shores or hillsides, suddenly glinting in the sunlight, or are washed up by a wave at your feet. Even pebbles of the right color can hold great power, especially if you have found them on a happy occasion.

You need a bag in which to keep your crystals and from which to select them for casting. You might choose a bag with silver and gold threads for the sun and moon. I have heard time after time that "the right bag" and "the right crystals" turned up for someone in an unexpected place, usually somewhere they had no intention of visiting. My original set of crystals is somewhere in North Hollywood, lost as I fled the earthquake of 1995, so I hope it is being put to good use. I found my first replacement crystal in Seattle on a much-diverted flight home.

STONE 1

The sun is associated with sparkling clear **crystal quartz**. Traditionally, the sun was associated with diamonds.
Crystal color: sparkling white

All cultures have worshiped the sun. In ancient Greece, the solar god Helios was praised each dawn as he emerged in the east and drove his chariot of winged horses around the sky before plunging into the ocean in the west at sunset.

Clear crystal quartz, like the sun, represents pure energy, the masculine power or animus that men and women need to succeed in important aspects of their lives. It is the crystal of action, individuality, and potential. When a sun crystal appears in a reading, you know it is time to develop your talents, to fulfill your ambitions (whether to grow beautiful sunflowers or be president of a merchant bank). Joy, confidence, and enthusiasm abound and you can soar high.

The only danger with sun crystals is that you may find yourself so driven that you never get to enjoy the fruits of your labors.

Carry your sun crystal when you need a new beginning but doubt yourself or when you are tired and need a sudden boost of energy.

Crystal quartz is also a powerful healer when the sun's rays are reflected through it.

Because crystal quartz is so easily obtainable, I only list the following other sun crystal.

Colorless zircon This protective stone, for clarity of thought and sexual energy, was originally carried by merchants against lightning and thieves.

STOne 2

 The moon is associated with the translucent **moonstone**, especially the white ones. Crystal color: translucent or cloudy white

The moon has traditionally been regarded as the consort of the sun, her silver to his gold, Queen Luna to King Sol in alchemy. The classical Goddess Diana (sister of the Sun God Apollo) was worshiped as the moon in all her aspects.

Moonstones are believed to absorb the powers of the moon, becoming deeper in color, more translucent, and more powerful as the moon waxes until it reaches full moon. As the moon wanes, so a moonstone becomes paler and releases its gentler intuitive energies. It is the stone of travelers, especially by night or at sea, whose tides the moon governs.

Moonstones represent the anima in men and women—deep, unconscious, intuitive gifts and wisdom from ages past. When you cast your moon crystal, it tells you to trust your inner wisdom, your intuitive hunches, and the promptings of your inner voice. Look to your inner world for fulfillment, and accept what you cannot change in your life or in others.

The only weakness of your moonstone is a tendency to inhabit the world of dreams and forget that the outside world exists.

Carry your moonstone if you need to get in touch with your inner self, or sleep with it to ensure creative dreams.

Other moonstones include the following.

Mother-of-pearl This protective power, especially for newborn babies, is associated also with money-making rituals.

Rutilated quartz Believed to be quartz containing angels or guardian spirits, its inner gold threads represent hidden treasure of both the spiritual and earthly kind.

STONE 3

The earth is associated with the gleaming golden-brown **tigereye.** Crystal color: brown

Since the earliest times, the earth has been associated with the Mother Goddess and all her bounties. Demeter, the Greek Corn Goddess, was a symbol of the fertility of the land. Roman women called her Ceres and held a weeklong spring festival in her honor. Men were excluded from the festival, during which the participants ate only products directly harvested from the earth. Demeter is often pictured as rosy-cheeked, carrying a hoe or sickle, and surrounded by baskets of apples, sheaves of corn, garlands of flowers, and grapes.

Throughout the ages, tigereye was regarded as a talisman against the evil eye, and Roman soldiers would wear engraved stones to protect them from an enemy. It was also a symbol for attracting money. Tigereye represents all money matters and practical issues such as home and property; it also represents fertility in the widest sense and the natural senses, not forgetting common sense.

When you cast your earth crystal, you should concentrate on practical matters and approaches, being aware of what is possible. Trust the evidence of your eyes and ears rather than relying on the opinions of others or your own idealistic view.

The only danger of the earth stone is that you may become overwhelmed by practical responsibilities.

Carry your earth stone when you need to keep in touch with the real world or have financial negotiations to make.

Other earth stones include the following.

Brown jasper Used for stability in turbulent times and as an "earthing stone" in magical rituals, its association with rain spells makes it a symbol of increase in all aspects.

Petrified wood (polished) For long life and for recalling past lives, it is a barrier against negativity.

STONe 4

Mercury is associated with sparkling yellow **citrine**. Crystal color: yellow

Mercury, the Roman winged messenger of the gods (known as Hermes to the Greeks), was the son of Jupiter.

Carrying a rod entwined with two serpents that could induce sleep, he delivered messages between the heavens, the earth, and the underworld. Through his skill and dexterity, he came to rule over commerce and medicine and also became patron of tricksters and thieves.

Citrine is a stone of clarity. Its sparkling transparency can filter what is of worth and transform, with its golden warmth, negative thoughts into positive action. Throughout the ancient world, citrine was placed in sleeping areas to banish nightmares and to promote peaceful sleep. It forms a bridge between thought and feeling, intuition and logic.

Citrines represent communication, travel, mental ability, and matters of health.

When you cast your citrine, you are eager for wider experiences and meaningful interactions, whether through clear communication with those around you, a chance to spread your wings, or by attempts to banish negative influences from your life.

The only danger of citrine is that it can sometimes encourage less-than-open action, albeit for the best motives.

Carry your Mercury stone when you need to communicate clearly, either verbally or in writing, or when you need to make an instant decision.

Other Mercury stones include the following.

Topaz Worn by royalty and nobles throughout the ages as a sign of wealth, the topaz is a stone of astral travel and invisibility in magic. The topaz increases in power with the moon, being at its greatest potency at the time of the full moon.

Yellow jasper Used as seals and on mosaics throughout the ancient world, yellow jasper acts as a filter for resentment and negative feelings that might otherwise accumulate; it protects against deceit.

stone 5

Venus has, as her special crystal, **jade.** Crystal color: green/pink

Venus is traditionally associated with emeralds. Venus, whose Greek name was Aphrodite (born of the foam), was beauty incarnate, the Roman Goddess of Love and Seduction. Her most famous offspring was Cupid (or Eros as the Greeks called him), son of Mars, so uniting love and war.

Jade has long been used as a symbol of love and also of the life force. In the Orient, jade was believed to contain the life force. In China, jade, carved in the shape of a butterfly, is used as a talisman to attract love. It is given as a love token to those who are the object of love and on the occasion of a formal betrothal. Jade pendants are also worn by Oriental children to ward off illness and harm.

Jade represents love, marriage, friendships, family, children, and all affairs of the heart.

When you cast a jade crystal, it is a time to use your heart and not your head. Relationships, whether seeking new friends, a love match, or developing an existing relationship, are well favored. Children or family members may need extra attention, but this will be worthwhile.

The only problem with jade is becoming awash with sentiment or giving way to emotional blackmail. Carry your Venus stone to find or nurture love or when you seek reconciliation.

Other Venus crystals include the following.

Rose quartz Wear rose quartz to attract love, to heal broken hearts, and for mending quarrels, especially with lovers and family members.

Tourmaline (green/pink) Green attracts money; pink promotes sympathy and friendship. The watermelon variety green and pink tourmaline contains both creative and receptive energies and is therefore the perfect stone of balance; it is also associated with rebirth and renewal.

Coral This is an organic gem; according to Plato (400 B.C.), coral was tied on babies' cradles and around their necks for protection. An amulet found worldwide, of a partly closed hand carved on coral, was said to protect against bewitchment. Coral symbolizes innocence and is good for any matter concerning babies and children; it offers protection when the owner (old or young) of the coral feels vulnerable.

STOne 6

Mars is associated with red or **blood agate** and **rubies**. Crystal color: red

Mars, God of War, who was called Ares in the Greek tradition, was the legendary father of Romulus and Remus, the founders of Rome. As God of both agriculture and war, he represented the ideal Roman, first as a farmer and then as a conqueror. To his quality of courage is added a nobility of spirit when his anger and warlike nature are directed against injustice and inertia.

The red or blood agate is a stone of strength and courage, worn in battle and used by the Vikings and Anglo-Saxons in a form of divination called *axinomancy*. This psychic skill was aimed at finding buried treasure and hidden spoils of war. A double-edged axe was heated until it glowed red, secured in a vertical position, and then a blood agate was balanced on the upright axe head. The direction in which the agate rolled and rested indicated the location of the treasure. If the agate stuck to the molten axe, the treasure was not in the immediate vicinity, and they would move the axe to another spot, where the divination was repeated.

Red agate represents the power of the battle, justifiable anger, and fearlessness in the face of opposition.

If you cast a blood agate, you may feel angry but helpless at unfair treatment or frustrated by apathy in others. Take courage and insist on fair treatment. Initiate the chance you desire, even if it means upsetting the status quo.

The only danger with the red agate is directing anger at the wrong source or dissipating frustration in irritability and spite.

Carry your Mars stone for courage when you feel under threat or when you need to make an unpopular change.

Other Mars stones include the following.

Bloodstone This mottled deep green and red opaque stone has red spots, formed first, according to myth, from the blood of Christ as it fell on green jasper at the crucifixion. It is therefore used for any crusades or campaigns against injustices and for moral stands or noble gestures.

Red jasper This formed the seal ring of the Roman Mark Antony and was used for seals as a stone of honor and honesty. It was also considered a defense against negativity.

Red carnelian Known in ancient Egypt as the blood of Isis, the Mother Goddess, this was used to offer protection through the underworld after death; a symbol of immortality and courage.

STONE 7

Jupiter has as his stone **lapis lazuli,** eye of the gods, a dense rich purple/blue stone with flecks of iron pyrites (fool's gold). Crystal colors: deep, rich blue and purple

Jupiter, known as the Sky-Father, was the supreme Roman god, ruler of the universe. Like his Greek counterpart Zeus, he controlled the thunderbolts, which were carried by his eagle, the king of the birds. He ruled not despotically but as the chief of a triumvirate of gods; the others were Juno, his consort, and Minerva, Goddess of Wisdom. Before using his third avenging thunderbolt, Jupiter consulted with the superior or hidden gods. In time, Jupiter was regarded as the heavenly form of the earthly Roman emperor.

Lapis lazuli, or lazulite, is often called the heavenly stone or the "eye of wisdom" and has been used for over six thousand years. The ancient Sumerians believed lapis lazuli contained the souls of their deities and, if worn, would endow them with magical powers.

The stone is considered powerful in giving access to sources of traditional wisdom and in guiding its owner to noble and just leadership in whatever field he or she chooses.

It is a stone in which the horizons of possibility are expanded, in both a material and spiritual sense.

When lapis lazuli is cast in a reading, it is time to use your head and not your heart and to follow a traditional path, consulting with others who may have expert knowledge or experience. It concerns all matters of career, justice, wisdom, idealism, and altruism.

The only danger with lapis lazuli is a tendency to be dogmatic and unwilling to compromise.

Carry your Jupiter stone when you need wisdom to make the right decision or need to apply yourself to learning a new skill or gaining deeper knowledge of a subject.

Other Jupiter stones include the following.

Turquoise Another "sky god" stone of great antiquity, this symbol of courage and wisdom is sacred to Native American Indians, where, in some tribes, it could only be worn by men; it is also considered proof against uncertainty.

Sodalite A deep blue or indigo stone with white flecks, this stone is used in meditation, placed in the center of the brow to open the Third Eye to promote wisdom from the deepest recesses of our being; it is also a healing stone, especially for stress or anxiety.

Purple Sugalite Although only in recent years used in magic, this stone encourages inner wisdom when placed on the Third Eye; it balances conscious and unconscious power, logic, and intuition.

STONE 8

Saturn is associated with **obsidian (Apache Tear)**. Crystal color: Black

In mythology, Saturnus (the Roman form of Chronos, God of Time) was Jupiter's father, who was deposed by his son. Saturnus had devoured all his children except for Jupiter (air), Neptune (water), and Pluto (the underworld), the three powers it is said time cannot destroy. Saturnus, therefore, had to bow to the inevitable. Time and progress cannot be held back, and the old order must give way to the new. Saturnus was sent to Italy, where he taught the farmers agriculture and engineering and established a Golden Age of peace and plenty.

Apache Tears, small globules of obsidian, are so named after a tragic incident in Arizona. A group of Apaches were ambushed by soldiers. Many were killed and the rest threw themselves over a cliff rather than be taken. The women and maidens of the tribe wept at the base of the cliff for a whole moon cycle, and their tears became embedded in obsidian crystals. Those who carry obsidian will never, it is said, know deep sorrow. When you hold your obsidian to the light, you can see new hope and life glimmering through.

Apache Tear is the shadow stone, just as Saturnus was the shadow side of Jupiter. It represents the limitations and inevitable progression of time that mean that actions and relationships have to take account of reality. The hand of fate can turn triumph into reversal in an instant, but can also turn challenge into opportunity, as Saturn found in Italy after his dethronement. Effort and perseverance can move mountains.

When you cast your Apache Tear, plans may be frustrated or there may be a limit to the influence you can exert over an issue that affects you. If you can use the setbacks or obstacles as an impetus for a different course, you may find in time that the change was a positive one. Accept, however, that sometimes you can only wait for the right time and for the tide to turn.

The danger with the Apache Tear is that you may feel unduly pessimistic over delays caused by others and not make the best of what is in your reach.

Carry your Saturn stone when you feel at the mercy of blind fate or when life seems like an uphill struggle but you know you have to make a great effort.

Other Saturn crystals include the following.

Onyx Even in Christian times, the head of Mars for courage or Hercules for strength would be engraved on black onyx. This crystal also offers protection against foes of all kinds and quells anger and spite in conflict situations.

Jet This organic gem is fossilized wood that has been turned into a dense form of coal over millions of years. Sacred to Cybele, mother of the Gods in classical mythology, jet is found in graves dating from the Bronze Age; it is regarded as a doorway into other dimensions.

STONE 9

Uranus has as its crystal **amber,** an organic gem of fossilized tree resin, millions of years old. Crystal color: orange

Uranus, the original Sky God, was the son and husband of Gaia, the Earth, in Greek mythology. He was called "the sky crowned with stars." He and Gaia in turn created the twelve Titans, one of whom was Cronus (another name for Saturn), and various monsters including the Cyclops. However, Uranus shut his children in the earth so they might not overthrow him. And Cronus helped his mother defeat his father to relieve her agony at having her children locked within her. Cronus castrated his father with a sickle, which became, after his own dethronement, the tool with which he taught the farmers to cultivate the land. Change can be cruel, but it is necessary for progress—and like the sickle, any instrument or action can be used for good or ill.

Because of amber's great antiquity and soft, warm touch, it is said to contain the power of many suns, of untapped potential within, a kernel of possibility. In the Chinese tradition, the souls of tigers passed into amber when they died, and so it is a stone of courage and concentrated power for change. Amber melts emotional or physical rigidity. Amber therefore represents the potential for change, for increased independence and individuality. It is another crystal concerned with good health.

When you cast your amber stone, its glowing center is a reminder that you can and should make changes that establish your own unique identity and acknowledge your innovative approach to the world and life's problems. You may feel impatient with the status quo or frustrated that others do not share your vision. Press ahead, using your natural ingenuity and creativity, for the time is ripe for change in whatever field you desire it and for your inner sun and the courage of the tiger to emerge.

The only problem with amber is if you cannot see a way ahead and turn your frustrated energy on yourself in a destructive way.

Carry your Uranus stone when you encounter a period of stagnation or you have an original idea that you wish to put into practice.

Other Uranus crystals include the following.

Orange carnelian Stone of leaders and potential leaders, especially when worn around the neck or in a ring, orange carnelian acts as a protection against envy, surrounding the wearer with a magical circle through which jealous thoughts cannot penetrate; when held to the light, carnelian promotes astral travel and inspired ideas.

Orange calcite Known as the doubling stone, because it has the quality of double refraction whereby a line viewed through it appears doubled, it is used for increasing power and doubling determination and energy, especially for change.

Banded orange agate Woven into horses' manes, banded orange agates prevented a horse from stumbling; it was also used on horses plowing fields to promote the fertility of the land and encourage the sun to shine on the crops as they grew; this energizing crystal induces optimism and fertility in every way.

STONE 10

Neptune is linked to **aquamarine**. Crystal color: turquoise, the green-blue of the sea

After Saturnus was dethroned, Jupiter gave his brother Neptune (the Greek Poseidon) the sea as his dominion.

Neptune's symbol of power was the trident or three-pronged spear that he used to shatter rocks, summon up or banish storms, and raise or sink whole countries. These he would cast at the mainland to cause earthquakes when he was angered by the sins of humankind. Neptune was unpredictable, sometimes offering safe passage to ships and filling fishing nets with fish, at other times hurling waves heavenward in defiance of Jupiter and eroding the shores.

Aquamarine means "water of the sea" in Latin and has traditionally been the stone of sailors and fishermen, used as a talisman for journeys by water and as an antidote for seasickness. The Nereids, the sea nymphs of Greek legend, and the mermaids claimed this stone as their own, and it is sometimes associated with Aphrodite, Goddess of Love, who thereby made it a symbol of harmonious marriages.

Aquamarine is the stone of emotions. Like the sea, it is sometimes harmonious, occasionally turbulent, and offers a focus for getting in touch with and harmonizing feelings. Feelings are an important indicator of the right course of action as well as the unvoiced intentions of others, in work and formal situations as well as relationships. You may need to be especially sympathetic to the problems of others. If in doubt, trust your instincts and listen to your inner voice. Follow what seems to be the most natural course rather than going against the flow. Even if an opportunity is not the one you sought, it may hold hidden advantages.

The only problem with aquamarine is when emotions become so strong that they drown the intuitive senses. Strive for harmony in personal emotions.

Carry your Neptune stone when others are being overemotional or there are confusing signals about intentions.

Other Neptune stones include the following.

Malachite Known as "the sleep stone" because of its hypnotic effect when gazed at, it also calms troubled emotions; in the work sphere, it promotes money-making and advantageous deals.

Labradorite A stone of mystery and spirituality, it is used for clearing confused emotions and illusions.

Amazonite A stress-reducer, it is also good for any form of speculation by tapping intuitive channels.

STONE 11

Pluto is associated with **amethyst**, especially the softer, more transparent shades. Crystal colors: all soft muted colors

Pluto (Dis or Hades to the Greeks) became the God of the Underworld after the overthrow of his father Saturn. He took Proserpina, Goddess of Spring, into the underworld, and so brought winter into the world as her mother, Ceres, grieved. He let Proserpina go because he loved her, but because she ate a single pomegranate seed, she had to return to the underworld for six months of each year. These became the winter months. Carry your Pluto stone when you need to withdraw from the world for a while or when you are closing a door.

Amethyst is a healing stone, especially for ills caused by fear. Ancient Egyptian soldiers wore amethyst in battle so they would not be afraid in dangerous situations. Amethysts absorb negativity and are a powerful stone in banishing magic, if they are then returned to Mother Earth or cast away with a primal scream to release all the negativity into the cosmos. The amethyst is a stone of mystery and of all things psychic and, in this way, links with the mysteries of Pluto.

Amethyst represents the mystery and the psychic aspects of Pluto and talks of the cycles of decay and regeneration, endings and beginnings, destruction and creation.

When you cast your amethyst, you may be reaching the end or beginning of a cycle and need to shed what is redundant, to close certain doors, and to open others. It may be a time of extremes, which makes the healing amethyst valuable in transforming any negative feelings or energies into positive ones and translating endings into beginnings. Alternatively, your psychic and spiritual abilities may be evolving quickly, and your dreams and divination could hold the key to a new level of understanding.

Other Pluto crystals include the following.

Smoky quartz This crystal overcomes depression and negative emotions by absorbing them, which can make it darker. You should then wash it in running water and wrap it in black silk to rest.

Blue lace agate A promoter of peace and reconciliation, in the home it prevents the rerun of old quarrels that have no resolution and the acceptance of inevitability and human weakness.

Kunzite A relatively expensive stone, in lilac or pink, that has strong antianxiety properties and, as a modern stone, is good in avoiding road rage and traffic accidents. A promoter of peace, kunzite can ease the transition from one stage of life to another.

Casting Your Crystals

Crystals, runes, and other forms of stones are usually thrown into a circle, a magical shape for containing creative energies and a shield against negative feelings. You can read crystals either for yourself or for others, and you can cast crystals into any circle, whether drawn on fabric or paper, or with a stick in an area of sand or in a special box of sand or earth kept for this purpose. The circle should be 1½ to 2 feet (45 to 60 cm) across.

To cast crystals

* Draw the circle beginning from the symbolic or actual north, with a clockwise, unbroken movement.

* If it is not a permanent circle, reverse the process when you finish your reading, beginning in the north and moving in a counter-clockwise direction, erasing the line that you etched in sand or earth.

* The advantage of using sand is that the crystals sometimes become embedded, indicating that a core issue is encapsulated in the crystal meaning. It is also easy to draw lines in sand to show connections between crystals as you read.

* Place your crystals in a drawstring bag or purse.

* Rather than thinking of a specific question, let your mind go blank. Once you cast three crystals, you will see quite clearly to which aspect of your life they refer.

* Stand or kneel about 2 feet (60 cm) away from the circle.

* Pick a single crystal, without looking, from your bag of eleven crystals. You may find your hand drawn to a particular crystal instinctively, but take your time choosing.

* This first crystal is the "crystal of self" and represents your current situation, hopes, fears, opportunities, and obstacles.

* Cast it into the circle. The nearer to the center the crystal lands, the sooner any change will take place. As crystals fall farther from the center the timescale increases.

* If the "crystal of self" falls outside the circle, the time is not right for action or change, or there are factors you have not considered.

* After you cast a crystal, hold it and let its energies speak to you before returning it to the position in which it landed in the circle.

* Take another stone from the bag without looking and cast it. This is the "crystal of others" and represents the influence of other people on your plans and dreams. If it falls close to the first crystal, other people are exerting a strong influence on the situation or on your life generally.

* If this crystal falls outside the circle, the messages or demands of others are conflicting and you should listen to yourself.

* Choose a third crystal and cast it.

* This is the "crystal of happiness to come" and encapsulates the future direction that will lead to happiness, with reference to the area highlighted in the reading.

* If this crystal falls outside the circle, results may be delayed, but you will succeed if you persevere.

* If you are reading for someone else, allow him or her to cast the crystals and to hold each one in turn as you interpret the basic meaning of the stone. Many people who have never used crystals before can pick up remarkably accurate perceptions just from handling the chosen stones.

Sample Crystal Reading

> Marian was offered a nursing job with a very high salary in the Far East for two years. But Rod, her partner, had a permanent job in Britain and could not go with her. It was a major career move for Marian, but Rod insisted that their relationship would not survive two years apart, even if they met for holidays. Marian felt she might never get another opportunity like this, but she loved Rod and did not want to lose him. All three crystals fell in the circle.

Crystal 1: The Crystal of Self The first was a clear crystal quartz, the stone of the sun. New beginnings, opportunities to fulfill her potential, and boundless energy and enthusiasm seemed to literally pull Marian toward sunnier climes and fulfilling ambitions. The crystal fell almost in the center of the circle, indicating that she would have to make a decision very soon. Marian had only a week to make up her mind.

Crystal 2: The Crystal of Others The second, the Venus crystal of love and relationships, was very close to the crystal quartz. Rod was saying that Marian had a clear choice, her love for him or the job offer. Was it not possible for Marian to have both? The jade slightly overlapped and covered the clear crystal—did Marian feel that if she turned down the job she would lose part of herself?

Marian replied that she was afraid that if she did not retain her independence, she would end up like her mother, a housewife who had lived only through her children. In contrast, Rod's mother had been a very successful businesswoman but had left Rod with a succession of nannies and au pairs as a child. Marian felt that Rod feared that she was acting like his mother.

Crystal 3: The Crystal of Happiness to Come The third stone was citrine, the Mercury crystal of clear communication. Neither Marian nor Rod were talking about the real issues (their fears at having experienced their parents' unsatisfactory marriages), nor were they expressing what they really wanted from their relationship. Citrine also talks about travel and versatility. What did Marian really desire? It wasn't necessarily the job in the Far East, but the chance to see new places, have new experiences, and to discover more about herself and the world before she settled down.

Marian decided to turn the job down. However, she suggested to Rod that they take their annual leave together and go on a holiday to the Far East, so they could see whether they might both enjoy working abroad at some time in the future. In the meantime, Rod encouraged Marian to complete a nursing degree so she could branch out into more challenging work in the United Kingdom, possibly connected with her interest, tropical diseases.

It was not a perfect solution, because Marian would have loved to take the job. But the urgent reason for moving away, feeling stifled by Rod, had lessened as they talked through the past and each saw clearly that their relationship did not have to be a rerun of their parents' failures. Last time I met Marian, she and Rod were exploring the possibility of going on an extended working holiday abroad.

Chapter 6

Tree Divination

*To dwellers in a wood almost every species of tree has
its voice as well as its feature. At the passing of the
breeze the fir-trees sob and moan no less distinctly than
they rock; the holly whistles as it battles with itself; the
ash hisses amid its quiverings; the beech rustles while
its flat boughs rise and fall. And winter, which
modifies the note of such trees as shed their leaves, does
not destroy its individuality.*

—THOMAS HARDY, *Under the Greenwood Tree*

THE OPENING LINES of Hardy's
novel conjure up a lost age, one that was vanishing even when he
wrote these words in the nineteenth century. Now, in a world of
increasing urbanization and technology, trees are too often regarded
merely as ornaments or a source of fuel or building material. The
deforestation of large parts of the world reflects humankind's increasing
indifference to trees, while mass-produced wood veneer furniture,
cheap and replaceable with changing fashion, has usurped the scratched
masterpieces of oak or pine handed down through the generations.

Few men or women now make their own marriage bed from living wood. Yet this simple ceremony was once the first act of love.

But walk in a forest or wooded area of a park, with the sun filtering through the branches and the breeze rustling the leaves, and the magic of trees remains. Go to a furniture workshop or an old manor house, and rub your hand across the smooth polished or rough woods. They are still living. And so we touch wood, half-jokingly, for luck; the power flows from primitive man who touched the trees, hoping to appease the tree spirits. The spirits are still there, essences of the different qualities inherent in the trees and, as such, touch a primitive core of wisdom.

Throughout history, the belief in magical trees, with their protective, healing, and empowering forces, has persisted. Many early cultures had sacred groves, and individual trees of particular species have traditionally been revered according to the divine force represented in the wood. Oak and cedar are, for example, father symbols, and willow and hazel are mother emblems.

The Origins of Tree Divination

What comes down to us has been passed through the traditions of the Celts. During the last half of the first millennium B.C., they occupied huge tracts of western and central Europe, extending—at the height of their power—from the British Isles to Turkey in the east.

The Celts were famed for their metalwork, road building, and chariot making and their agriculture and rich cultural life. The Celts were not united either politically or linguistically, but shared the same mythology and the same very strong religious beliefs. They were also the fierce Gauls of Caesar's Gallic Wars, the *barbari* who sacked Rome in 290 B.C. However, the systematic extension of the Roman Empire, and the Anglo-Saxon and Norse invasions, gradually destroyed the separate identity of the Celts, whose influence nevertheless has pervaded many aspects of religious, cultural, and magical life throughout the Western world.

WHO were THe DruIDS?

The Druids were the Celtic priesthood who held the secrets of magic and healing. There is historical evidence of Druids in Ireland, England, Wales, and Gaul. Although there is less documented evidence of Druids in the Celtic settlements of Spain, Italy, Galatia, and the Danube Valley, it would seem probable that they existed there. The Druids traveled to other tribes and held great meetings in which the different nations joined in kinship. Some experts believe that Druidism had its origins west of the Celtic countries, among those people whom the Celts found already established in the west of Europe, the builders of the megalithic monuments.

Being a Druid involved lifelong training that began when a boy was selected for his spiritual nature or early wisdom. It took twelve years or more to reach the first level, that of a Bard. The Bards were said to be "the memory of the tribe," as they preserved its history by learning hundreds of poems, stories, and the secret Tree Alphabet and created new songs and poetry to record new events.

The next stage in the training was that of the Ovate, which took a further ten years or more. The Ovate studied natural medicine, divination, and prophecy and passed between the dimensions. It was he who contacted the Otherworld, especially at Samhain (celebrated at the time we now call Halloween) and traveled to the Realm of the Ancestors to seek their wisdom.

Finally, after a further ten years of study, the Ovate became a Druid: adviser to kings, judge, philosopher, and high priest of the tribe.

Druidism offered resistance to the Romans in Gaul and Britain; Roman generals mounted attacks against the main Druid sanctuaries in Britain, particularly that at Anglesey. After the formal Druidic religion was wiped out in Wales by Julius Caesar during his conquest of Britain, the wisdom went underground and traveling minstrels carried this knowledge, passing it on to secret converts as they sang the old songs for entertainment. Legends, such as "The Battle of the Trees," carried the hidden traditions of the Celtic gods and heroes and of the White Goddess herself (Celtic symbol of poetry, the moon, and all creative knowledge and magic).

The Tree Alphabet

Like the runes, the Tree Alphabet provided a method of passing on secret messages and was also used for divination. The Celtic Tree Alphabet consists of angular markings, signed out using different joints of the fingers and incorporating a complex grammar for transmitting secret wisdom and lore. It was not used in formal writing.

The Tree Alphabet has largely survived orally. For this reason, many disagreements exist about the definitive form of the symbols and even which trees are included. The version I use is one that has consistent features with several forms. The capitals were carved upright (the way I use them for the staves), but were signed or etched horizontally for lowercase letters and were sometimes joined.

The Tree Alphabet was also used for magical purposes and for divination. The wooden sticks on which the magical symbols are etched are called the Ogham Staves. There are twenty symbols that were cast, much as the runes were, on the ground or a white cloth. Beneath an ancient oak at sunset, which was the beginning of the new Celtic day, was considered the most magical time and place for tree divination.

The staves were named after Ogma, a warrior god, deity of wisdom, and champion of the gods at the Battle of Moytura. Ogma was one of the original Tuatha de Danaan, the mythical gods of Ireland.

He is said to have invented Ogham writing in the fourth century A.D., having discovered the wisdom by inspiration (as Odin in the Norse tradition discovered the runes as he hung from the World Tree). But the Ogham Staves are not just alternative runes. They originate from a different culture—of hills, bubbling streams, and green groves. Whereas the runes came from the world of winter, ice, and snow, the tree staves are born of the spring, of hope and rising sap, of new life and optimism.

The Ogham Staves

The Ogham alphabet originally had only twenty letters in groups of five. Five more complex letters were added later, but the original form consists of straight lines incised across a straight stave of wood and so could easily be created in a grove for instant divination.

THE OGHAM STAVES

Beith	Birch	B	├
Luis	Rowan / mountain ash	L	╞
Fearn	Alder	F	╞
Saille	Willow	S	╞
Nuinn	Ash	N	╞
Huathe	Hawthorn / whitethorn	H	┤
Duir	Oak	D	╡
Tinne	Holly	T	╡
Coll	Hazel	C	╡
Quert	Apple tree	Q	╡
Muinn	Vine / bramble	M	┼
Gort	Ivy	G	╪
Ngetal	Fern / bracken / reeds	NG	╪
Straif	Blackthorn	STR	╪
Ruis	Elder	R	╪
Ailm	Pine / silverfir	A	┼
Onn	Furze / gorse	O	╪
Ur	Heather	U	╪
Edhadh	White poplar / aspen	E	╪
Ido	Yew	I	╪

Therefore, because these later staves depart from the tradition, I do not include them. Each of the twenty staves has two sides: a sun, or marked side, and a moon, or blank side, thus giving forty variations of meaning, which you can combine in many different computations of significance.

Ogham Staves were also associated with colors, birds, animals, and kings and so served as transmitters of tradition.

MAKING THE OGHAM STAVES

You need twenty sticks of similar size, wide enough to carve a symbol at the top by scraping away an area of bark. Mark the top of the stave with a small Celtic cross, as some of the symbols are quite similar. Alternatively, follow the old method of making the twigs rounded at the top and pointed at the bottom to differentiate those that were thrown upright from those upside-down, which would give a different symbol. Traditionally, the twigs were as thick as the end of the diviner's little finger, but these may be unwieldy.

Pick your twigs from a forest or grove of oak (the sacred tree of the Druids), hazel (the ancient tree of wisdom), or the healing ash (tree of the All-Father). Alternatively, you can make the individual staves from each of the named wood types or use wooden discs, as long as you clearly mark the top, so you can easily identify the correct symbol. Keep the staves in a wooden box or a pouch or bag of any natural fabric.

Making a Tree Circle

Cast the staves in a circle about 2 feet (60 cm) in diameter, drawn either with a stick in the dust of a forest clearing or onto an Ogham circle marked on a cloth of any natural substance. The cloth can be hessian, cotton, or silk, about 2 feet (60 cm) square, and the circle can be drawn in ink, paint, or permanent marker with the following four segment divisions:

The transition point of the Celtic day was at sunset, so the times when two periods meet are very magical.

SEGMENT 1: THE SHADOW TIME
(OCTOBER 31–FEBRUARY 2)

Shadow time runs from Samhain, the beginning of the Celtic winter and New Year, when the cattle were brought from the hills by the herdsmen and it was believed that the family ghosts also came shivering home from the fields to be welcomed by their families. In the middle of this season, on about December 21, falls the Midwinter Solstice, the shortest day, when blazing logs were burned to persuade the sun to shine again, and evergreens were hung about the house to encourage the vegetation to grow.

After this turning point, the days slowly became longer until the season ended at Imbolc, the festival of the maiden aspect of the Goddess Bride, when the first ewe's milk was available. This was the festival of early spring when snowdrop plants were pushing through the frozen earth and life was stirring again.

Staves that fall in this area indicate that there may be a period of waiting that should be creative, rather than stagnant, and in which plans can be made for the future, strength gathered, and old regrets and sorrows left behind. It is a time for domestic concerns, older family members, and issues of mortality, natural cycles, endings that clear the way for beginnings, tradition, and secrets.

This area can also represent the past.

SEGMENT 2: THE TIME OF THE DAWNING
(FEBRUARY 2–APRIL 30)

The time of the dawning runs from Imbolc to Beltane. In the middle of this segment falls the Spring Equinox, equal day and night, when hens began to lay after the dark of the winter and the first eggs were painted and offered on the altar of Ostara, Goddess of Spring, whose familiar was the mad March hare (later tamed as the Easter Bunny).

The beginning of the Celtic summer, April 30, May Eve, was when the great twin fires burned and the cattle were driven between them to purify them after the winter, when young couples gathered hawthorn blossoms and coupled in the fields to make the crops grow.

Staves that fall here indicate that it is a time for new beginnings, a return of hope, trust, and the awakening of dormant energies. New projects, travel, house moves, matters concerning babies, animals, and children, friendships, and changes of any kind can be undertaken with confidence, although results may not be immediate.

This area can represent the present.

SEGMENT 3: THE TIME OF THE LIGHT
(APRIL 30–JULY 31)

The time of the light runs from Beltane to Lughnasadh. In the middle of this segment, on around June 21, falls the Summer Solstice or longest day, when the sun is at its height and blazing sun-wheels were hurled down slopes. Bonfires were lit on top of hills to give potency to the sun. At Lughnasadh, the Corn God was symbolically sacrificed in the last sheaf of corn cut, so the seeds might be scattered for the next year's growth. A loaf was made with the last sheaf as a symbol of abundance.

Staves that fall here indicate that it is a time for maximum effort to bring dreams to reality. Focused plans will bear fruit; optimism and clear communication will clear any blockages; and relationships will flourish. Matters concerning young people, love, and partnerships are especially favored, as are health issues. It is a period for maximizing existing opportunities.

This area can also represent the immediate future.

SEGMENT 4: THE TIME OF HARVEST
(JULY 31–OCTOBER 31)

The time of harvest runs from Lughnasadh to Samhain. In the middle of this period falls the Autumn Equinox, on about September 21. This is the time of the second harvest of vegetables, fruit, and remaining crops, the harvest home. The harvest supper predates Christianity. On the day when equal night and day heralded winter, the feast formed a sympathetic magical gesture to ensure there would be enough food during the winter, by displaying and consuming the finest of the harvest.

Staves that fall here indicate money matters, questions concerning mature people and relationships, property affairs, and long-term planning. It is a period of abundance, consolidating gains, and storing up resources for any symbolic winter ahead. Good for assessment and for caution, it also offers an opportunity for mending old quarrels and strengthening ties.

This area can indicate the long-term future.

Reading the Staves

You can read Ogham Staves for yourself or for others, either to seek help with a specific question or to gain a major perspective on life. They are a potent personal tool, so if you do read for others it is important that they cast, hold, and interpret the staves from the basic meanings of circle and stave.

* Draw your circle, most potently of all between two oaks, in a natural circle (whether a fairy ring of toadstools or a circle of flowers and shrubs). Alternatively, place your tree cloth either on the ground or on the floor so you can kneel or stoop about 1 foot (30 cm) away from the cloth to cast your staves.

* Take out six staves and, holding them between thumb and forefinger of the hand with which you write, cast them all together toward the circle. Only read those that land in one of the quadrants. If none do, cast another six until at least one falls in the circle. Ogham Staves do not lend themselves easily to layouts.

* The side with the symbol facing up is sometimes called the sun-stave, representing the quality of the tree at its most positive and dynamic. Sun-staves usually reflect an actual situation and the best course of action or a dormant quality in the questioner, rather than other people.

* The blank side of the stave is called the moon-stave. Moon-staves may speak of problems from the outside world that, unless resolved, can form obstacles to success or happiness. Moon-staves can also reflect shadow aspects of oneself or others.

* See first whether you have more sun- or moon-aspected staves. Sun-staves indicate that it is primarily a time of opportunity when happiness or tranquility can be enjoyed or goals attained. Moon-staves suggest that it may be a period mainly of challenges and potential obstacles that can act as an impetus for great achievement or shedding of old burdens.

* The area in which the staves fall may accentuate the sun or moon aspect, or a clear division may exist in which some staves refer to a new beginning or dawning phase and others to a waiting or Shadow Time. It is quite possible to have sun-staves even in the time of shadow, for there may be particularly positive aspects that will come to fruition after a period of preparation. Equally, at the Time of Light, there may be negative feelings or people that need to be dealt with to achieve happiness or success.

* Let the stave and segment meanings act as a guide, but allow your intuition to put together the overall impression. If the reading does not make sense, hold each stave that has been cast in turn and see it, not as cut wood but as a living branch. Visualize it at the door of spring, at first light, and feel the sap rising golden through the warm wood and life flooding into it.

* Now place your stave in your mind's eye either in sunlight if it is a sun-aspected stave or in soft silvery moonlight. Look at the reading again and then, if possible, go for a walk where you can touch trees in their natural habitat, and let the deeper answers to the unspoken questions come to you.

The Talking Twig Method

This requires a long wooden or metal container and involves shaking the container nine times and tipping the twigs above the circle, reading those that land inside. The sound of the rattling twigs is said to echo the question. You may end up with a number of staves to read, so this is really a method to use when you have a great deal of time and the issue is a life assessment or change.

STAVE 1: BEITH (BIRCH), BEGINNINGS/REGENERATION

With the exception of the mysterious elder, the birch is the earliest of the forest trees, associated with the Mother Goddess and the moon. It is often the first tree used to create a new forest, because it grows easily and seeds itself. It is also symbolic of the novice stage of Druidic wisdom.

The birch symbolizes the rebirth of spring and is used extensively in cleansing rituals. A relic of this early Goddess worship is found in remote parts of Russia where, at Whitsun, a birch is dressed in female clothing to represent the coming of summer. Throughout Europe, birch twigs are still used in rituals to expel evil spirits, in ancient ceremonies of beating the bounds or marking out territories, and in New Year celebrations throughout the northern hemisphere to drive out the spirits of the old year.

Sun-stave Beith, which means "shining," indicates birth, new beginnings, opportunities, and the purging of what is redundant or destructive. It indicates that, even if life has recently seemed disappointing or unfair, a new beginning is at hand, made richer because of the experience and wisdom gained through previous setbacks. It is a good time to branch out or initiate new ventures, to travel, and to experiment with novel approaches or fields that had previously seemed out of reach. More generally, this is the stave of the innovator and the pioneer and may indicate that this aspect of your personality is currently very strong.

Moon-stave The blank side of Beith suggests that it is important not to initiate change for its own sake or to reject the familiar in favor of the novel. Nor can there be new beginnings if old problems and burdens are not faced and left behind. The moon aspect also sometimes indicates a slower beginning, based on inner rather than outer change.

STAVE 2: LUIS (ROWAN OR MOUNTAIN ASH), PROTECTION

The rowan tree, sacred to the moon, is known as mountain ash, quick-beam, the Tree of Life, the Witch, or Witch Wand. A rowan dowsing rod is used for detecting metals. It protects households and ventures, great and small, from doubt and harm. It is the tree most used against lightning and psychic attack.

Rowan berries healed the wounded and, according to Irish myth, added a year to a man's life.

Traditionally, a rowan twig was removed from a tree without a knife, fastened with red twine in the shape of a cross, and used as a protective device for stables, cowsheds, and outhouses. In ancient Ireland, the Druids of opposing armies would kindle a fire of rowan and chant an incantation over it to summon spirits to take part in the battle and protect them. A rowan twig would be tied around a cow's tail or placed in a milk churn to prevent witches from stealing the milk or turning it sour.

The rowan is also an oracular tree, found around ancient stone circles, again partly as protection.

Sun-stave The rowan stave may appear when you undertake an important venture or delicate negotiations or doubt your own abilities, perhaps because of unfair criticism. Luis is especially associated with protection of the home, so the matter may be a family one. It indicates the importance of giving and encouraging loyalty and the ability to overcome any difficulties, not by force, but by intuition and by making advance preparations to avoid any possible hazards. It is a stave that says you have much support, some of it from unexpected sources, and that you should go ahead with any venture and not fear the opposition of others. More generally, it speaks of great intuitive abilities and inner resources to turn obstacles to advantage, qualities that are to the fore in your personality at present.

Moon-stave The rowan indicates a need to protect yourself or those close to you from barbs and potential malice, usually unjustified, from a particular quarter. It can be small unfair accusations or sarcasm building up that leave you feeling vulnerable, so deal with each minor irritation as it occurs, and do not let anyone diminish your confidence. Above all, be cautious of fair-weather friends who may encourage gossip and indiscretion.

STAVE 3: Fearn (ALDER), FIRM FOUNDATIONS/SECURITY

The alder is the Tree of Fire, known as the tree of Bran, the Blessed (eldest son of Llyr, the Oak Father). Bran was a mighty giant who, in Celtic tradition, ordered his own beheading as he lay mortally wounded. His severed head is said to be under the White Mount or Tower Hill in London as protection so that his beloved land would never be invaded. His head symbolically offers security.

Because of its resistance to water, alder was used to make the piles on which early houses were built over lakes; and cities such as Amsterdam have foundations of alder. It was also used for clogs.

Whistles made of this wood were traditionally used to summon and control the four winds, offering security against seemingly uncontainable elements. In some versions of the Tree Alphabet, Nuinn or Nion (the ash) appears in this position, and Fearn is the fourth stave.

Sun-stave Fearn, the stave, represents secure foundations and so offers reassurance that any venture or relationships under question can withstand temporary buffeting. In terms of money or property, matters should be subject to caution and realistic targets. Security, whether material, practical, or emotional, may be a central concern, but every reason exists for optimism, so long as matters are not left to chance. Attention to detail and small steps can lead to long-term lasting success and happiness. There is underlying power but this must, for now, operate within boundaries. On a general level, Fearn talks of your ability to turn ideas into realistic action and your reliability and levelheadedness.

Moon-stave Avoid shortcuts or less-than-straightforward dealings and offers that promise quick returns. Whether in relationships or work, permanence is of more value than excitement at present. Risks, over-ambitious plans, reckless words, procrastination, and extravagance, by yourself or others, may lead to longer-term problems.

Stave 4: Saille (WILLOW), Intuition/Dreams

The willow is said to be the tree that loves water most and is sacred to the Moon Goddess, who is the giver of dew and moisture. The willow is also the tree of enchantment and of the Crone or Wise Woman aspect of the Celtic Triple Goddess (whose stages of life mirror the waxing or maiden phase, full or mother, and waning moon). Willow wands are said to make dreams and wishes come true.

Because its cut staves sprout leaves and shoots, the willow is often associated with rebirth, regeneration, and the renewal of inspiration after a stagnant period.

Emotions lie under its sway, feelings flowing like water that can be a guide to right action as much as logic.

Sun-stave Saille talks of the need to trust your intuitions and hunches, to follow your heart, and to flow with the stream of life. It may be a period when emotional concerns are to the fore or when answers or directions are not clear-cut and yet you can feel stirrings within. Listen to your dreams, especially those that recur or seem especially vivid. Generally, Saille may indicate that your imaginative faculties are a strength that you do not always use or value.

Moon-stave This represents the illusory aspects of the imagination, inaction, hopes of magical solutions, and an unwillingness to look at the world the way it is. Once you acknowledge reality, then your imaginative faculties can be called into play to find creative solutions and to open wider vistas of possibility. Even the most prophetic dreams can only be of value if used in the external world as an impetus for action.

STAVE 5: NUINN (ASH), EXPANSION

Ash is another Father Tree, the Tree of the World Axis (for example, Yggdrasil in the Norse tradition), and such Father Gods as Odin of the Vikings and Gwidion of the Celts.

Nuinn is the tree of the traveler (whether the Father Gods seeking the expansion of knowledge or the spirit in the realms of wisdom or the physical traveler who explores far-off lands). The ash was a very sacred tree to the Celts, and as late as the nineteenth century in Killura, in Ireland, a descendant of the original sacred ash of Creevna was used as a charm against drowning. After the Irish potato famine, emigrants carried the tree to the United States to protect them in their new home.

The ash was used for Druidical magic wands, especially for astral travel. The ash became the tree of seafaring throughout the northern hemisphere, being associated with Poseidon-type deities of the sea. In ancient Wales and Ireland, all coracles and oars were made of ash, as were rods for urging horses on.

Sun-stave Nuinn is the power of the seafarer, of the seeker of the truth, the explorer of new territories and opportunities. This stave can indicate an inner hunger or restlessness or, alternatively, powerful ambitions that evoke courage and confidence. As a general characteristic, Nuinn indicates a pioneer with a thirst for knowledge and new experiences and an open mind.

Moon-stave Nuinn can indicate impatience with the present situation and difficulties with people with a more limited perspective. Bureaucracy and pettiness can also prove obstructive, but they cannot be ignored. Moving away from problems does not necessarily resolve them.

STAVE 6: HUATHE (HAWTHORN/WHITETHORN), RESILIENCE/COURAGE

The hawthorn, whitethorn, or may tree has an unfounded association with ill luck. It is considered unlucky to bring hawthorn blossoms indoors except on May mornings. This tree is sacred to Mars and other northern thunder gods. Huathe is believed to act as a shield against physical and psychic harm. In pre-Christian times, it was planted around sacred boundaries to resist evil.

The whitethorn, the most common form of hawthorn, was also the tree of the White Goddess (under the name Cardea), who used it to cast spells. The Glastonbury thorn, or Holy Thorn, blossoms twice a year, once around the Midwinter Solstice. Legend says that when Joseph of Arimathea arrived on the west coast of England on January 5 in about A.D. 63, bearing the Holy Grail from Jerusalem, he landed on the Isle of Avalon. Weary and despairing, he planted his staff, which had been cut years before from a hawthorn tree. Instantly, the staff began to bud and flower and has done so every year since.

Clumps of hawthorns were used on hilltops as markers of the old traders' paths and ley lines that date back to Neolithic times or even earlier. Such trees were chosen because they were resistant to inclement weather and secret guardians tended them.

Hawthorn twigs gathered on Ascension Day are believed to have exceptional power.

Sun-stave Huathe may appear if you feel discouraged or need extra impetus to press ahead. Unbowed by wind or weather, presenting sharp thorns to all who attack it, and yet a symbol of courage rewarded at Glastonbury, Huathe is an assurance that it is possible to resist any hardships, face obstacles with courage, and emerge strong and triumphant. As a general characteristic, hawthorn represents the power to fight for what is right and determination to achieve objectives, no matter what the cost.

Moon-stave Hawthorn can be negative if the sharpness and irritability become a characteristic response even where there is no threat. Courage can tip over into aggressiveness or be swallowed as self-hatred if the real threat is not identified and confronted. Equally, constantly critical, carping people should be ignored and their barbs turned back on them.

STave 7: DUIr (oaK), STrenGTH/power

To the Druids the oak was their special tree. The word *Druid* is said by some scholars to mean "knowledge of the oak," from *dru* ("oak") and *wid* ("knowledge"). He who has knowledge of the oak is said to have power to command the elements for his own use and to control storms.

The oak is the tree of endurance and power, and as a meeting-place over hundreds of years, it became a repository of accumulated wisdom. The oak was king of the waxing year from the Midwinter Solstice (December 21) to the longest day (June 21). The midsummer fire is always oak, and the ceremonial Need Fire, lit at the great festivals, is kindled in an oak log, thus symbolically fueling the power of the sun.

Duir means "the door," and the oak's roots are believed to extend as far underground as its branches reach up to the sky, so embracing the three realms of the underworld, earth, and heavens. The space between two oaks was said to be the doorway to unseen realms where fairies lived.

Sun-stave Duir is perhaps the most potent tree stave of all, indicating pure masculine power, strength, and assertiveness, but tempered with nobility, idealism, and altruism. Given determination, patience, strength of purpose, and persistence on the part of the questioner, success will follow and ambitions (especially in career and personal happiness) will be fulfilled. As a general characteristic, Duir represents leadership, knowledge, authority, and a noble spirit.

Moon-stave Used unwisely or for less-than-noble ends, Duir can be manifest in yourself or others as stubbornness in the face of reason and determination to force through issues or override others in the pursuit of personal ambitions. However, the moon-stave can also appear when tradition is stifling and the strength can be channeled into breaking away from a preestablished path.

STave 8: TINNE (HOLLY), FaTe

The Holly King rules the waning year from midsummer to the Midwinter Solstice, and each year, according to Welsh legend, the Oak and Holly Kings fought for supremacy on May 1. The original holly tree of the Celts was probably the twin brother of the common oak tree (the evergreen scarlet oak, holm oak, or holly oak).

Holly was sacred to the Celtic god Taranis, a thunder god/giant who carried a club made of holly. He was also the Green Knight referred to in the old Irish legend of "Sir Gawain and the Green Knight." The masculine aspect of the female evergreen, the ivy, holly is a symbol of the Christmas promise of the renewal of life after the shortest day on the Midwinter Solstice. Though the reign of the Holly King ended, the evergreen was a reminder that in six months, his reign would return. Hence, a holly wreath was hung on doors to shelter dispossessed tree spirits and attract their good fortune to the home at Christmas. It is also a very protective tree; and both holly blossoms and the wood, when used on lintels and window frames, offer protection from harm to the household. Holly is sometimes used as a symbol of Christ.

Holly represents the message that there is a time for action and a time for withdrawal, a time to work and a time to rest, a time when fortunes increase and decline and rise again. It is one of the most profound staves, for whatever is happening in the present is part of the wider cycle of experience; good or bad, it is a vital stage.

Sun-stave Whether you have faced or are facing an advantage or reversal, the Tinne stave says it is a stage that you should enjoy or endure and use as a building block for a long-term future plan. You should not worry about guarantees of permanence or fear that present sorrows will last. Accept whatever is of benefit, or wait for the tide to turn if times are less settled. As a general characteristic, holly is the stave of the person who is in tune with life's ebbs and flows.

Moon-stave Tinne is destructive only if a person swims against the tide of inevitability and refuses to accept that external events or fate can influence life and this may not be fair. A positive reaction to events beyond our personal control can maximize "luck" and minimize "ill-fortune."

STave 9: COLL (HaZeL), WISDom

The hazel is the Celtic Tree of Wisdom, especially during the season when it brings forth nuts (symbolic of kernels of wise thoughts). It is associated with the sacred number nine, because the hazel takes nine years to produce nuts and because there was a sacred well called Connla's Well in Tipperary over which hung the nine hazels of poetic art.

The Druids carried a hazel rod as a symbol of authority. In ancient courts, a hazel rod was held by the accused to ensure a fair hearing. Hazel was also used to mark the boundaries of a court of justice, and so it can represent boundaries as a subsidiary meaning.

In modern times, as in the past, a hazel rod is used in divining for water and buried treasure. In Wales, it is said that one can wear a cap woven from hazel twigs to make wishes come true. Hazel rods were also taken by Irish settlers to the United States to keep away snakes.

Sun-stave Coll represents intelligence, justice, and recourse to traditional knowledge, especially the creative arts. Therefore, when a matter of justice is involved or decisions must be made, the hazel stave indicates that any response should be considered carefully and impartially, using the expertise of those best qualified to offer advice. When principles are at stake or an issue is controversial, Coll advises that a measured response (using facts and figures, as well as idealism) may be more effective than an instant reaction. As a quality, Coll is the stave of the naturally wise person.

Moon-stave In excess, hazel can mean that spontaneity and natural human feelings are repressed, and the questioner (or more usually, someone close to them) can appear cold, calculating, and intolerant of human weakness. Equally, knowledge can be used destructively, so secrets should not be revealed unwisely, and injustice should not be tolerated, however lofty or authoritative the perpetrator.

STave 10: QUerT (APPLe Tree), FerTILITY/ABUNDance

This is the Celtic Tree of Life and of the sacred Isle of Avalon. According to Celtic legend, the apple tree was created by the Triple or Trefoil God, Trefuil Tre-Eochair, who became associated with St. Patrick. He was known as the Triple Bearer of the Triple Key and, as such, was the male fertility principle associated with the Triple Goddess.

Orchards have always been considered sacred ground, and apple trees were "wassailed" (drenched in cider) to encourage a fruitful crop, not only of the orchard, but also of the local land and community. Traditionally, apple wood was used for wands to cast magic circles, especially for love and fertility magic; and apple bobbing is an old form of Druidic love divination to discover who of a group of young maidens would first be married. In the modern world, fertility is not only of the soil and of people but also extends to any aspect of life that needs renewing, especially health.

Sun-stave Quert says that this is a propitious time to initiate or nurture any projects that may bear fruit over a period of months or even years, rather than yielding immediate gain. It can refer to an addition to a family, not only by birth, but through new friendships or people coming into your life who may be of importance. Giving freely, being open-minded and generous in words as well as materially, and showing enthusiasm for new ideas or interests creates a sense of abundance and well-being. Positive sexual liaisons are favored. As a characteristic, Quert demonstrates a generous, outgoing nature and an abundance of enthusiasm that attracts positive people and opportunities.

Moon-stave The apple tree's negative aspect can reflect the fact that relationships may suffer from a lack of communication and that a fresh approach is needed to give new life, whether to love, flagging health, or a seemingly unprofitable venture. Generosity should be restricted to those who are appreciative.

STAVE 11: MUINN (VINE/BRAMBLE), JOY

The vine was imported into Britain during the Bronze Age and grew on south-facing slopes, although the native bramble or blackberry, viewed as a magical plant, was used more frequently for wine making, because it grew wild. The imagery for both plants signifies the releasing of inhibitions, symbolically through intoxication, but in reality through the joys of life, health, and beauty. Unlike ivy, this is unbridled joy, embracing the whole spectrum of happiness, from physical ecstasy to a peak experience of spirituality.

Mythologically, the origin of the vine dates from the Fall of Man. When Adam and Eve were banished from the Garden of Eden, the banishing angel, pitying them, gave them the vine and told them to seed it through the earth. Noah planted a vineyard as soon as the ark reached dry land and began the first wine production.

The vine has always been associated with spiritual as well as physical succor. In the Gospel of St. John, Christ spoke of himself as the vine and the apostles as the branches. Constantine the Great, the first Christian emperor of Rome, made the vine an official symbol of the Christian faith.

Sun-stave When Muinn appears in a reading, it indicates that personal happiness, rather than success, is the most important factor. Few caring people ask what would make them happy as opposed to what would please those around them. Yet only if we are happy in ourselves can we make others happy. The vine, therefore, is a very positive stave to cast, promising that happiness will come, not through selfishness, but through self-love and valuing our own strengths and unique qualities. As a characteristic, Muinn belongs to the natural joy bringer.

Moon-stave The vine's negative aspect lies in a tendency to seek happiness through escape into overindulgence in physical pleasures. Beware of those whose excesses, however endearing, are enjoyed at the cost of the happiness of others.

STAVE 12: GORT (IVY), RELATIONSHIPS/LOYALTY

Ivy was traditionally regarded as the harbinger of death; it was perceived to choke the trees around which it grew. Yet it was also seen as being bound to those trees. It remained evergreen, a symbol of hope throughout the winter, the female queen and counterpart of the Holly King, traditional ruler of winter. Houses covered with ivy were believed to be safe from psychic attack, and ivy was regarded as a prime source of pagan sexual power. Ivy was worn as a crown at the winter feast of Saturnalia or Misrule in Rome, but goes back in the mists of time as the green womb of the mother.

Because the ivy blossomed in October, it was associated with the last harvest sheaf, which was bound with ivy.

The ivy came to be associated primarily with fidelity and was worn in bridal headdresses long before the adoption of orange blossom. Ivy is a symbol of married love and loyalty. Its symbolism can be extended to all stable relationships and to any family connections, emphasizing the deep bonds that transcend any surface disagreements.

Sun-stave In a reading, Gort is indicative of the need or desire to concentrate on love, enduring friendship, or family commitments rather than work or less-binding ties. It promises hope and stable happiness, rather than unbridled joy, and sometimes appears when a person is considering a new commitment or change in a relationship. For an uncommitted person, Gort can mean that a relationship may develop in the near future and that this will bring happiness of a different kind. In general, Gort belongs to a loyal, loving person whose relationships are or will be essentially supportive but not stifling.

Moon-stave This aspect of Gort is that of the strangling ivy and warns about possessiveness, jealousy, and overdependence in a close relationship.

STAVE 13: NGETAL (FERN/BRACKEN/REEDS), RICHES/PROSPERITY

One of the very old tree staves, ferns and bracken are said to bloom golden on Midsummer Eve between eleven and midnight and produce their flowers immediately afterward.

It was said that if the seeds were gathered on a white cloth, a pewter dish, or a Bible and then shaken with a hazel rod, they gave the power of invisibility. If scattered, the places they fell would indicate buried gold. Thereafter, they were said to attract prosperity.

The reed was originally an ancient Egyptian symbol of royalty and of learning. In Ireland, a house was not established until the reed roof was in place, so that prosperity would visit the home. The reed's association with the height of the sun's power at midsummer made it a symbol of gold and riches. Ngetal is therefore an auspicious stave to cast for all money-making endeavors and questions.

Sun-stave Ngetal assures the success of any financial matters and money-making schemes. It does not promise automatic wealth, but indicates that ventures will prosper, given concentrated effort. If the sun-stave appears, it is therefore a good time to initiate projects concerned with finance, business, and property, to deal with financial questions and problems, and to consolidate any gains with further schemes, rather than holding back and waiting.

As a general characteristic, Ngetal represents someone with a shrewd business head and also the vision to devise ingenious ways of increasing profitability.

Moon-stave The negative side of the fern only comes into play if speculation and outlay are not followed by positive action or if others prove a great drain on finances.

stave 14: straif (blackthorn), effort/persistence

 Straif, an old Breton word, comes from the same root as "to strive," as well as "strife." Its fruit, the sloe from which sloe gin is made, comes from the same stem as "to slay" in early English.

Because Straif blooms when the bitter northeast winds are at their height, a harsh winter is called a blackthorn winter. Therefore, effort and persistence, especially under duress, are intrinsic to the blackthorn, as to the other thorn trees.

The blackthorn produces white blossoms on an almost black branch and is said to bloom at midnight on Christmas Eve. It, therefore, has a holy meaning to counter the often unfairly negative perceptions of the thorn, especially this tree (the darkest and most impenetrable of the species). Its thorny, shrublike trees are incredibly hardy and form a barrier associated with both physical and magical protection. Made into a plaited crown and burned and scattered over the fields on New Year's morning, the blackthorn ensures a good crop. The blackthorn crown is also sometimes merely scorched and then kept in the home as a bringer of luck.

Sun-stave Although seen as a tree of hardship, Straif is a source of tightly knotted energy and so represents concentrated supreme will and persistence in the face of any challenge. The spiritual aspect of the blackthorn suggests that nobility of spirit will win through and that opposition and obstacles can be overcome. Often there is no ideal time to begin a venture. But less-than-optimum conditions can trigger energies and determination that provide a strong impetus to action. If other people are involved, stay united and your defenses will be impenetrable. As a general characteristic, the blackthorn belongs to a person who perhaps has not had an easy life but, as a result, has developed incredible willpower and energy.

Moon-stave The doubts and negative views of others can weaken the impenetrable strength of the blackthorn, causing vulnerability, division, and hesitance in pressing single-mindedly toward a goal.

STAVE 15: RUIS (ELDER), SECOND SIGHT/THE UNEXPECTED

The elder is the ultimate fairy tree. It is said that if you wear a crown of elder twigs on May Eve (April 30) you can see magical creatures and ghosts. Native American Indians call the elder the "Tree of Music." So potent is the elder whistle that nature spirits dance to its tune. The Rollright Stones, ancient standing stones in Oxfordshire, are, according to legend, an invading king and his army whom the local witch, known as the Hag of Rollright, turned to stone. She then turned herself into an elder tree, close to the stone, to stand guard throughout the centuries in case the enchantment was broken. On midsummer eve, a feast was for many years held near the king-stone, and the elder tree was ceremonially cut. (Elder trees were one of the guises assumed by witches.)

A waterside tree, the elder has white flowers that bloom at their peak in midsummer, like the rowan, thus making the elder another aspect of the White Goddess. It is often referred to as Lady Elder.

Ruis is the stave of the divinatory arts and second sight and adds a prophetic note to other staves cast with it. It talks of the unseen world and our most spiritual and magical nature.

Sun-stave When logic and even intuition have failed, the elder offers a magical solution that may come suddenly in a dream or waking moment of insight. It presages an unexpected upturn of fortune, whose form you can gather from studying the patterns in the clouds, the embers in the fire, sunlight or water, or the dregs in the bottom of a teacup. Let life come to you for once, carry on with your everyday world, and believe. As a characteristic, the elder is the stave of the natural psychic, the dreamer and visionary who is as comfortable in other dimensions as in the material world.

Moon-stave Wholly magical solutions are rare; it is important not to suspend life and effort until the right job, person, or opportunity comes along. Magic works best when you are active. If you wait for perfection, you can miss lesser but still real possibilities of happiness.

STaVe 16: AILM (PIne/SILVer FIr), CLarITY/creaTIon

The pine is one of the few trees that is androgynous. It was worshiped by the Celts as a symbol of fire because of its resemblance to a spiral of flame. Pine was used in the resin torches that lit the halls throughout northern Europe, and so it has become associated with the torch that flames in the darkness.

The silver fir is the tree of Druantia, the Gallic Fir Goddess, and it is a potent symbol of birth and creation. In the Isles of Orkney, it was the custom to whirl a flaming fir torch around the head of a mother and her newly delivered child to purify them.

Ailm, therefore, represents the inner creation moving into the outer world, the new idea being put into practice, just as the pine torch casts its fire to illuminate the darkness in the hall or dwelling. It is a stave involving communication, insight, and illumination.

Sun-stave Ailm is a stave to be welcomed, for it represents the moment when matters become clear and when there seems a way forward, perhaps after doubt or uncertainty. Be prepared to use persuasion to get what you want, for you are definitely on the right track. Creative energies are all around you, and you may find that your natural talents take new, unexpected directions.

Moon-stave Others may seem difficult or uncommunicative. Listen to what people really say to avoid misunderstandings.

STAVE 17: ONN (FURZE/GORSE), TRANSFORMATION/CHANGE

Onn is named after the Gallic goddess On-niona, a goddess of Spring, whom the Gauls worshiped in groves of ash trees. Gorse blooms golden with its flowers and prickles at the Spring Equinox, and so is a symbol of the early sun. At this time the gorse is burned and so the hills are aflame with gold. Tender shoots grow to replace the burned ones and are eaten by sheep. The destruction of the gorse encourages the grass to grow. Gorse gives the first blossoms for the bees as the ivy provides the last, and so it heralds the first riches of spring. As the fern represents gold, so the gorse is said to indicate hidden silver. It was formerly used as fuel, food for livestock, and even in roofs.

Just as spring transforms the dead world of winter and burning transforms the gorse into food, so the energies of the Onn stave stand for change, whereby one stage of life is transformed into another by "grasping the nettle."

Sun-stave When Onn appears in a reading, it is like the stirring of spring, and you can anticipate a change for the better. As with all transformations, this may involve disruption and even loss of the status quo, but also promises excitement and renewal. You may receive a sudden opportunity that you previously would not have considered. Perhaps a secure path seems suddenly to lead nowhere.

The gorse is the first flower bees use, so this will be a busy period. As a characteristic, Onn represents a mind that is always open to new possibilities with a strong vein of adaptability, so that change is welcomed and not feared.

Moon-stave This indicates that you may be in danger of missing the moment through uncertainty about your own abilities and versatility. Sometimes the narrow horizons created by others can hold in check your natural urge to take a chance. Listen to the call of spring, and brush away the cobwebs is the message of this moon-stave.

STave 18: Ur (HeaTHer), STronG EMOTIONS/PaSSIONaTe FeeLInGS

The Gallic Heather Goddess was called Uroica, portrayed sometimes as a queen bee, an early symbol of the Mother Goddess. Heather is linked with the images of both mountains and bees, for it is a plant of midsummer and so the bees swarm around it. Another ancient myth associated heather with an Irish giantess called Garbh Ogh. She was many centuries old and was said to hunt the mountain deer with a pack of seventy dogs, all of whom had the names of different birds. When Garbh Ogh chose to die, she piled around herself stones in a single cairn, "set her chair in the womb of the hills at the season of the heather-bloom," and breathed no more.

The heather bloomed scarlet at midsummer and so came to be associated with passion. White heather, being rarer, is considered especially lucky, and if a person comes upon white heather growing naturally, he or she can pick it and any wish made will come true.

In Celtic legend, when Oscar (son of Ossian, the renowned third-century Irish Bard and warrior hero) lay dying on the battlefield at Ulster, slain by Cairbar, he sent his true love Malvina a sprig of purple heather. As she heard the message of love carried by a faithful messenger, her tears fell on the flower, which turned pure white. Since that time, white heather has represented eternal love.

Sun-stave Heather is the stave of passion, not only in love, but any strong feelings and desires (typified by the height of the sun at midsummer). It appears when feelings are strong, whether of love, devotion, desire, or even, as with the ancient Goddess Garbh Ogh, the desire for an ending. The emotions may be deep and unacknowledged, but whatever it is you desire (success, love, happiness, an ending), now is the time to follow your heart and to use the energies of your personal midsummer that rapidly approaches. It is a time to speak out, to ask or to demand, to listen to your heart and not your head. As a characteristic, Onn is the stave of the person who feels deeply and is in tune with the emotions of others.

Moon-stave When devotion to another person or cause is causing pain, you may not be listening to your heart but to the demands of an emotional leech. You may be vulnerable to emotional blackmail because your heart is naturally filled with love.

STAVE 19: EDHADH (WHITE POPLAR/ASPEN), MATURITY/HEALING

The white poplar is the tree of the Autumn Equinox, the late harvest, maturity, and old age. It is very similar to the aspen. Both are known as "the shiver-tree," partly because they were believed to have the power to cure fevers and agues. This was because their leaves shook even when there was apparently no breeze (it was believed that "like cures like").

An old rhyme said, "Aspen tree, Aspen tree, I pray thee shiver instead of me." One explanation for the aspen tree shivering is that it was the wood used in the crucifixion, and thereafter it has shaken at the thought of the agony it caused. Poplar leaves had magical powers attributed to them and were used in ancient flying potions.

Because the white poplar is associated with the last harvest and the autumn of life, it is a stave that stands for fruition (whether of a project or relationship) and also with reconciling whatever is unfair or lost and cannot be regained. It offers genuine hope for the future, based not on unrealistic dreams but rooted in what is possible. The black poplar represented loss of hope, and the two trees were used in an early form of yes/no divination.

Sun-stave In a reading, Edhadh represents the fruition of past efforts. Now is a time for balancing the books, for assessing gains and losses, mending old quarrels, tying up loose ends, calling in and repaying accumulated favors, and accepting the reality of the world and people as they are. Healing can be both physical and mental. As a characteristic, Edhadh is the stave of the natural healer and peacemaker, indicating a mature and balanced worldview, however young the person.

Moon-stave Regrets and recriminations for losses and past injustices can mask real achievements and gains. Others may act in an immature way, but only by remaining detached and accepting that some debts will never be repaid can personal harmony be maintained.

STAVE 20: IDO (YEW), IMMORTALITY/REBIRTH

The yew is known as the Death Tree in all European countries. Its use in England is recalled in *Macbeth,* in which Hecate's cauldron contained "Slips of Yew, silvered in the moon eclipse."

The silver fir of birth (Ailm) and the yew of death are sisters. They stand next to each other in the circle of the year, and their foliage is almost identical. Yew spikes are poisonous. As an evergreen, the yew tree stands in graveyards as a symbol of immortality, for it can live two thousand years or more. Its branches grow downward to form new but interconnected stems. In the old Irish tale, "Naoise and Deirdre," stakes of yew were driven through the dead bodies of the hero and heroine, so they would remain apart. However, the stakes grew and joined at the top over Armagh Cathedral.

Associated with the Wheel of the Year, and the death aspect of the Triple Goddess, Ido is the stave of endings, transformation, and rebirth. As an old trunk decays, it is replaced by a new one inside.

Sun-stave Ido is a stave that may appear at the time of a natural point of change or ending of a phase. Because it so strongly symbolizes rebirth and immortality, the ending is almost always a positive one, leading to new opportunities and new enthusiasm and life. That is not to say it will be without regrets. If there have been separations or isolation, the yew indicates the coming together of people in a more permanent and satisfying way. As a characteristic, the yew does not indicate pessimism, but rather an awareness of the finite nature of existence and so a leaning toward those situations and relationships that offer a deeper significance.

Moon-stave This can appear when a situation is allowed to run beyond its natural course and there is stagnation. Fear of the unknown can be worse than the actual experience. If others hold you back, it may be because they are afraid of being left behind and so may need reassurance.

Sample Reading Using the Ogham Staves

Samantha was a single parent who suddenly found she needed to raise money urgently because she was in dire financial straits. She had worked as a healer and a psychic counselor in her spare time, but had refused to take money for her gifts. A new contact offered her work at a number of mind/body/spirit festivals that would alleviate her immediate crisis and enable her to feed her children. But was it morally wrong to take money in view of her previously strong convictions?

Samantha cast six staves, all of which fell in the circle:

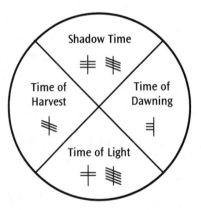

Stave 1: Sun-Stave Ur (Heather)—Strong Emotions/Passionate Feelings This fell in segment 1 (the Shadow Time). It suggested that Samantha's passionate feeling that she should not use her gifts for money resided in the segment of the past. This feeling had been valid before her current crisis hit. As the segment of endings, the Shadow Time says that some of our ideas may be redundant as we move toward the spring and new challenges.

Stave 2: Sun-Stave Ngetal (Fern/Bracken/Reeds)—Riches/Prosperity This fell in segment 4 (the Time of Harvest). Ngetal in the sun-stave was prompting Samantha to put money-making schemes into action and promised prosperity for her long-term future. This was not in any way telling her to sell out her principles or charge extortionate fees, but to put her talents to use profitably, as a person would do with any other talent. If Samantha was worried, she could charge for her time as any other consultant would do—and, as most workers in spiritual fields do, charge the poor and desperate nothing.

Stave 3: Sun-Stave Tinne (Holly—Fate This fell in segment 2 (the Time of the Dawning). How Samantha would respond to what fate cast her way was a current and urgent issue. Hence, this stave was in the segment of spring. It was a time for new beginnings and for putting ventures into practice. Holly talks of meeting the demands of the moment in the best way—Samantha might decide, when times are better, to revert to giving free psychic advice, but for now survival was the priority.

Stave 4: Moon-Stave Straif (Blackthorn)—Effort/Persistence This fell in segment 1 (the Shadow Time). *Straif* comes from *strive,* but Samantha was holding back the knotted concentrated energy of this tree of hardship and allowing doubts to penetrate. Her sister, who was wealthy but unwilling to help, said Samantha was cheapening herself and should earn her living in an honest way. Such advice is not helpful and should be treated for what it is worth. A voice from the past? Samantha's sister had been ultracritical of whatever Samantha did.

Stave 5: Moon-Stave Onn (Furze/Gorse)—Transformation/ Change This fell in segment 3 (the Time of Light). The second moon-stave was in the time of maximum power and pointed to the immediate future. Onn was the stirring of spring and, as a moon-stave, warned of missing the moment of transformation. Samantha had the opportunity to establish a new way of life, and she could try it to see where it led. Samantha was very gifted, but had never reached a wider audience. Perhaps this was the next step she needed to take if her gifts were to be of use to more people.

Stave 6: Sun-Stave Ruis (Elder)—Second Sight/The Unexpected This fell in segment 3 (the Time of Light). The final sun-stave augured psychic development as an immediate short-term goal for the future. But it also promised the unexpected. If Samantha followed the path toward which fate was pushing her, she might well have found there were advantages she could not anticipate. This is always a stave for taking a chance, and there is a hint that hidden benefits that may affect one's whole life may follow and that the sun will shine if a supreme effort is made now.

Samantha decided to go ahead and has found that her sincerity and desire not to exploit anyone have given her a great deal of instant success. She can now afford to heal people without charge, because her psychic counseling is proving so popular, and as her worries about money recede, her powers have developed even more.

DIVINATION THROUGH IMAGES

Chapter 7

Tea Leaf Divination

WHAT DO the following shapes that appeared in the bottom of a teacup represent to you?

Alison, an advertising executive in her early thirties, interpreted this image as a plane, taking her away from her current unprofitable love relationship to a holiday in the sun. She had been deliberating about whether or not to book the trip. Alison decided to go ahead with the holiday, although her boyfriend warned her he would not be faithful if she went away.

Fiona, who was seventeen and studying to be a dancer, saw the shape as a dragonfly that represented her own fragile hopes as she flitted from audition to audition in the hope of winning a full-time position in a touring ballet company. Although Fiona had wondered about taking a secretarial course, she felt the dragonfly was telling her to keep trying.

Anne, who was about to retire, saw this as a monkey clinging to a branch, about to leap. This mirrored her own need to adapt to her new lifestyle and to explore new fields rather than settling down into a rut of bridge games and art classes, as had many of her newly retired friends. Anne determined to use the lump sum she would get for retirement to go and see squirrel monkeys in their natural habitat—she had always been fascinated by monkeys—and find out about voluntary conservation work with animals.

 Phil, who was in his forties and ran a haulage business, interpreted the same pattern as a cricket singing cheerfully, although its future was precarious. Phil had to decide whether to invest the last of his capital in new vans (which would enable him to take advantage of the long-haul market) or sit tight and hope that business would look up. He interpreted the optimism of the cricket as an indication that he should go ahead and invest.

Such interpretations are very different from fixed, conventional tea leaf meanings. The symbols acted as a focus for deep-seated wisdom for the best course available, information that was not accessible to the conscious, decision-making mind. Magic? Yes, in the sense that the tea leaf image aided decision making by triggering different responses to the same image in different individuals, so it answered a personal question, perhaps unvoiced or not fully formulated, on which future action would be based. None of the four made their decisions solely on the basis of a single tea leaf image: it was the culmination of many other methods of exploration, psychic and logical. As with all forms of divination, tea leaf reading can play a vital role in planning, but logic and common sense are also part of the process.

Tea leaf reading is the simplest of the psychic arts. Our grandmothers and great-grandmothers, and their mothers and grandmothers, who passed down the craft, usually through the female line, did not use complicated books with hundreds of meanings. They instinctively interpreted pictures in the clouds, in the suds as they stood at the washtub, in the embers of the fire, or in a candle as they sat beside the bed of a sick child. So, too, as the matriarchs presided over gold-embossed china or a Brown Betty earthenware teapot, they listened to what their children, grandchildren, neighbors, or friends said with their hearts and not their lips and read their fortunes in the leaves. In industrial areas of Britain, the Brown Betty—a plain dark brown pot—is the traditional teapot used for tea leaf reading. You may find one in an old-fashioned hardware shop or even a flea market.

Tea leaf reading is also a very intimate process. While you can easily read your own leaves or those of others from a plastic cup at work or in a crowded café, at its best, tasseography takes place in a quiet, warm room, with tea, hot scones, and lashings of intimate talk, gossip, and laughter.

The Origins of Tea Leaf Reading

In Chinese tradition, tea was used as early as 3000 B.C. as one of the elixirs of long life. It was said to have come out of an egg when the Divine Artisan was creating the world. According to Buddhist legend, the first tea leaves came from the eyelids of the holy one, who cut them off to prevent himself from falling asleep while he was meditating.

Tea was used for divination in the Orient almost from the beginning of its use as a drink. The tea ceremonies still practiced in Japan today have their roots in meditation and creating that quiet space in which insight can come spontaneously. From China, the secrets of tea cultivation and divination spread to India and Sri Lanka (the former Ceylon). From India, the Romany Gypsies brought the magical art to Europe.

Tea did not arrive in England much before the middle of the seventeenth century and was very expensive, costing from $10 to $15 per pound in the prices of that period. It was not until 1885 that tea from India and Sri Lanka reached England in any quantity, and so even in Victorian times, tea was a great luxury, kept in a locked wooden box by the lady of the house.

But the art of divination from the dregs left behind in a cup or glass was practiced in Europe much earlier. Wine dregs were consulted (a craft known as *olinomancy*). From early times, too, peasant women made herbal brews for minor ailments and to preserve good health and afterward, the family matriarch would us leaves from the brews to discover the root cause of the distress.

Tasseography has remained primarily an art of the Romany Gypsy or the home rather than the professional clairvoyant. It can be accompanied by varying rituals as to the kind of cup and methods used, but, in essence, tea leaf reading should be learned by practice rather than by rote, and the questioner's interpretation of a symbol is invariably the right one.

To read tea leaves

* Use a traditional tea, such as Earl Grey or Darjeeling, with firm, separate leaves.

* Warm the teapot with water that has not quite boiled and rinse it out. As you do this, concentrate on the question you would like to ask.

* Put a spoonful of tea in the pot for each person, plus one for the pot. Let the rest of the water reach a boiling point, add it to the pot, and leave for three to four minutes, unstirred (longer for a stronger brew).

* As you do so, ask the questioner if there are any special areas or issues. This is not cheating. Psychic guessing games waste time, and the whole point of any reading is a dialogue, using the tea leaves or indeed any form of divination as a problem-solving tool and indicator of potential paths. Tea leaf pictures may not be precise, but they usually suggest an image or an overall impression.

* At the end of this section, there are two hundred symbols. Read through them, changing any that do not seem to fit the significance you attach to a particular symbol. You can refer to this list in the unlikely event that a symbol in a teacup reading does not evoke any response in you.

* Learning symbols by heart is counterproductive. Trust the magic invoked as you read the leaves, not only for but with a friend in the powerful psychic space where your two intuitions join.

Using a Tea Strainer

The easiest way to become comfortable with tea leaf reading is initially to use a tea strainer and read the leaves that are caught in it as you pour your tea. This way, you can practice interpreting a variety of symbols, and such readings are very effective. Use either a traditional metal tea strainer or a cheap plastic mesh one, as long as it is quite deep.

To use a tea strainer

1. Pour a cup full of tea through the strainer, and shake the leaves before they have time to settle.

2. Holding the handle of the strainer nearest to you, close your eyes, open them, blink, and see if the leaves make a picture. Use this overall impression to give yourself the feel of the reading, whether it represents a positive situation or a challenge or obstacle, which may contain a built-in solution. Any symbol has both positive and negative connotations that will become evident from the overall "feel" and context of the leaves.

3. Ask the questioner if he or she can identify any particular images and, if so, what they mean in a personal context. We all have a unique image system, though rooted in a universal one. If no images spring to your questioner's mind, suggest what you see, and ask how he or she would interpret that image. At this stage the questioner usually disagrees with your idea of the symbol, and the real psychic dialogue can begin.

4. If you have problems interpreting the leaves, add some more tea. Alternatively, if they are clumped, pour plain boiling water over the strainer into a dish to disperse the tea leaves more evenly within the strainer. You can even use a magnifying glass to examine each symbol closely.

5. Finally, draw together all the strands of the reading and different images (you may have one major symbol and a few minor ones). In this way, not only will you clarify the issue, but you can also determine possible courses of action and likely results from the leaves.

Sample Reading Using a Tea Strainer

Jane was in her early twenties and engaged to be married, but had potential mother-in-law trouble. Adam was an only child and his mother interfered in every aspect of their life, provoking arguments between Jane and Adam. These invariably ended with the mother-in-law-to-be as the "wronged angel" and the ungrateful son and wicked daughter-in-law-to-be on the side of the demons. Adam stood by helplessly and usually placated his mother.

Jane poured a cup of tea through a strainer and produced two very definite images in the wire mesh. One was near the rim (which is said to augur the present and immediate future) and one at the bottom (a few years hence). Both were close to the handle of the strainer, which, according to tradition, places the issues close to home.

 Jane saw the uppermost image as a horse, suggesting that she and Adam should gallop away into the sunset, for while they were so close to his mother, she felt they would never have a chance to establish an independent life. Adam worked for the Civil Service and might have been able to get a transfer, but he always felt guilty about leaving his mother, who had been divorced for ten years, although she had many friends and a job as a nursing administrator.

 Jane saw the second image as a black widow spider—no prizes for guessing its identity! This highlighted Jane's underlying fear that Adam's mother would not disappear even if she and Adam did move away. Running away was not the answer. Jane realized she had to tackle the problem now, or it would haunt them in the future. The black widow is said to sting its mate to death, and Jane had a sudden insight that Adam actually encouraged his mother's possessiveness, as he enjoyed two women fighting for his love. Jane had to attack the problem on two fronts, and if neither mother nor son would give up their stifling relationship, Jane realized she might have to accept it or walk away.

Teacup Reading

Once you are confident about interpreting the tea leaf images, use a teacup. Take a large, shallow cup; plain white on the inside is preferable. A clear, glass, heat-resistant cup is very effective, because you can see your reading from both sides.

1. Pour the tea into the cup without using a strainer. If you are reading for someone else, allow them to pour, as this concentrates their unconscious powers while their hand is occupied with conscious repetitive action.

2. After you or the questioner drinks the tea, leave just enough liquid in the bottom of the cup so the leaves are still floating.

3. Ask the questioner to swirl the remaining tea three times round the cup, clockwise for a man and counterclockwise for a woman, using the left hand.

4. The questioner should then place the cup upside-down on the saucer. A wide one is best.

5. Twist the cup around three more times, this time counterclockwise for a man and clockwise for a woman, again using the left hand.

6. If you know the person well, put your hand on top of his or hers and turn the cup upright again, so the handle is facing toward you.

7. If the questioner is a stranger, you can turn the cup yourself.

8. Keeping the handle toward you, twist the cup in all directions until you can see images in the leaves. Hold the cup in your left, intuitive, hand and support it with the right.

9. Aim for an overall picture or impression, closing your eyes, opening them, and blinking if you feel uncertain of any instant pattern.

10. If there is a dominant image, in terms of size or clarity, read this first.

11. Read individual images in the cup from left to right, noting any groupings or connections.

12. Refloat the leaves in boiling water and drain them again if you can make no sense of the images or want a further reading on the same question.

Areas of the Cup

Divide your cup into imaginary quarters around the circumference. Keep the handle closer to you as your marker point.

The Handle Quadrant This represents the questioner; therefore, leaves in this area concern him or her, his or her home, and those close to him or her. If this area is crowded, the person may be overwhelmed by responsibility for those close or, more positively, may enjoy a rich home and personal life. This will become clear from the images.

The Opposite Side from the Handle This is the realm of strangers, acquaintances, colleagues, and matters away from the home, including work and travel. A crowd here can suggest either that this is currently the most dominant area of life or that there are concerns with the outer world.

The Quadrant to the Left of the Handle Images here represent the past or people moving out of the questioner's life. Any large or very dark images here can suggest unresolved matters from the past that are affecting the current issue, especially if this area is crowded.

The Quadrant to the Right of the Handle Symbols here are indicative of people and events moving into your life. You may find these images more shadowy and incomplete, suggesting that present actions are making one particular set of events more likely than another. If this area is blank, it does not mean there is no future, merely that energies are concentrated on present or even past endeavors.

Images Close to the Rim These indicate the present or immediate future—days or weeks away. Some people use numbers that appear as indicators of precise timings, but I am convinced that the future can be affected by so many factors that not only are the times usually inaccurate but they can encourage unconscious waiting for a fixed destiny to unravel. Neither do I equate the rim of the cup with joys and the bottom with sorrows, as many traditional readers do. The significance of a symbol depends on how it is perceived in relation to the whole reading and the potential it offers for action.

Images Farther Down These can indicate events some months ahead and the bottom of the cup years ahead, a more distant future. However, you may find that you seem to get contradictory messages—for example, an image at the bottom of the cup in the quadrant of the past. This might indicate that past events will still influence you for years, unless you decide to put them behind you. If this all seems too complex, read your teacup as a whole, and you will find that the answers are quite clear, even if you disregard timescales.

Two Hundred Tea Leaf Symbols

I include the Sun Sign symbols as these may be unfamiliar to some readers. If your personal Sun Sign comes up, it is an auspicious sign and indicates that you will have a chance to use your own particular strength in the near future to special effect.

More generalized signs, such as dots and stalks, are included with the specific symbols for ease of reference. For numbers, I have given their more general significance—for example, "one" indicates a new beginning or striking out alone. Individual letters can refer to a person. If the identity is not clear, gather extra information from other images in the same area of the cup. Symbols can apply to specific people, situations, or qualities in oneself. The general tenor of the reading will reveal this.

Acorn Health and plenty.

Airplane Distant travel; rising above difficulties.

Anchor Successful completion of a journey; a stabilizing force in a difficult patch.

Ant Hard work; joining with other people to complete a task.

Apple Fertility or love; a sign of good or improving health.

Aquarius, the Water Carrier ≈ Independence, idealism, detachment.

Arch/Bridge Joining together in marriage or a long-term relationship; reconciliation of quarrels.

Aries, the Ram ♈ Assertiveness, individuality, impulsiveness.

Arrow Attack. If pointing toward the handle, an attack on the questioner; pointing away, an attack by the questioner that may be necessary to defend a position.

Ball Bouncing back from any difficulties; being alert to a constantly changing situation.

Ball and Chain Being held back by obligations that are not easy to shed, but need discarding.

Basket A full basket indicates a gift or welcome addition to the family or immediate circle. An empty basket suggests giving too much.

Bear A strong and protective ally or the need for strength to resolve a situation.

Bees A swarm of bees indicates news on its way about changes in the immediate family or close circle of friends.

Bell A celebration, marriage, or surprise announcement by someone close.

Bird/Flock of Birds If flying away from the handle, birds indicate departure, perhaps for a set period or a natural spreading of wings. If coming toward the handle, the birds bring new opportunities or announce the arrival of someone new.

Book A closed book says secrets exist that you need to know. An open book represents a new opportunity through learning or in legal matters.

Bottle If full, you should pour your energies and talents into a particular challenge or avenue; if empty, you may feel exhausted and need to take care of your health.

Butterfly Regeneration; a chance to assume a new role or position.

Cage/Prison Real restrictions are holding you back. Wait for the right time when you are free to move ahead.

Cancer, the Crab ♋ Secretiveness; vulnerability behind a tough exterior; strength and love in domestic matters.

Capricorn, the Goat ♑ Caution; concern with following convention; efforts that will be rewarded.

Cat Aloofness; stealth; a hint of treachery in others, especially if the cat is pouncing.

Chain Links with others promote strength.

Chessboard/Chessmen Maneuvers are being made all around, so concentration and deliberation before acting are vital.

Child/Baby Children will bring pleasure. If none are on the horizon, someone may act childishly.

Chimney With smoke, a chimney indicates comfort at home. Rising smoke suggests success; horizontal smoke, a smokescreen; while an absence of smoke can mean a need for attention exists at home.

Circle or Ring A single circle or ring means a relationship or partnership being made more permanent or the impending successful completion of a project. Interlinked circles are a sign of harmony with others.

Clock The time is coming when you can fulfill an important need or wish.

Clouds Doubts or obstacles should clear soon.

Clown Someone close may be hiding unhappiness; a danger of acting foolishly.

Clubs ♣ Bright ideas, creativity, curiosity, and a desire for adventure.

Comet A sudden unexpected opportunity to shine that may be short-lived and so should be seized.

Cow Tranquility; also a gradual increase in prosperity.

Crescent Moon If waxing, this is a time for wishes and new beginnings; if waning, it is a time to rest and wait.

Cross This suggests limitations and obstacles to overcome.

Crown An elevation in status, finances, or recognition of worth.

Cup/Goblet Emotions and hidden desires.

Dashes Enterprises and gains are afoot, but they will take time to mature.

Deer/Stag Arguments should be deflected, as there is no clear right or wrong in this case. Deer can be seen as gentle; a stag as an amorous male.

Diamonds ♦ Financial and practical matters are to the fore; slow steps ensure success.

Dice Time to take a gamble.

Dinosaur Ideas may be outdated and need rethinking.

Dog A loyal friend. A dog running toward the cup handle indicates a reunion.

Door If open, a step into the unknown that can be potentially exciting; if closed, an avenue that is not yet open.

Dots Money or money-making opportunities; small dots are small but lucrative openings.

Dragon In the face of fierce opposition, you must find the opponent's vulnerable spot. The more traditional meaning is that a change of home is in the offing.

Drum Rumors, disagreements, and a call to action.

Duck Travel by water or opportunities from abroad; finding a natural niche in life.

Eagle Aspirations and ambitions, broad horizons.

Ear Be aware of what is being said, but do not take gossip seriously.

Egg Fertility; ideas at any embryonic stage can successfully be put into practice.

Eight Caution; material security; following convention.

Elephant Wisdom and strength; a slow but determined approach is the best.

Envelope/Letter Good news is on the way; respond to any urgent mail, especially if it is official.

Eye Trust the evidence of your eyes and not what people tell you; read any small print.

Face A happy face indicates new friendship; an angry face, a confrontation.

Fan Beware flattery and sweet words that may mask malice.

Feather Inconsistency, unpredictability, and possibly cowardice on the part of others.

Fence If high, protection; if broken, a need to mend quarrels.

Fish Speculation and increasing fortunes; foreign travel.

Five Clear communication, versatility, and restlessness.

Flag A need to show courage and rally resources.

Flower A single flower indicates love; a bouquet, tribute or praise; success in examinations or interviews.

Foot Swiftness is needed to succeed; venturing farther afield in search of opportunity.

Fortress You can breach a seemingly impenetrable institution or authority with logic and perseverance; personal barriers.

Fountain A source of inspiration; sexual love or passion.

Four Working in the limits of available resources or the current situation.

Fox Use subtlety and stealth to get what you cannot by persuasion; beware of people not telling the truth.

Frog Transformation; moving; ability to move in different worlds.

Gallows/Noose Feeling constricted and needing to break out of a potentially destructive situation; can also be a good luck symbol of better health.

Garland Recognition or promotion.

Gate If open, new pasture; if closed, a need to watch possessions and finances.

Gemini, the Heavenly Twins ♊ A current or forthcoming problem will need skills of communication and adaptability to solve it.

Giant Great steps forward are presaged; or a person with a dominant personality will enter your life.

Goose/Geese Warnings are coming that, if heeded, can save a situation.

Grapes Good health, a time to indulge your desires (this can be a good thing sometimes).

Grass Discontent with a present situation is looming. This may reflect inner restlessness.

Guitar/Violin Harmony, romance; in some circumstances, vanity and irritability with those less talented.

Gun/Cannon Aggression that may burst out if not acknowledged and properly directed against the real cause; a time to blast away the inertia of others.

Hammock This heralds a desire to opt out and be unconventional.

Hand If outstretched, this presages a new friendship, perhaps from an unexpected source; if closed, it warns of meanness from an unexpected quarter.

Hat A visitor or formal occasion may be imminent; traditionally, a rival may appear.

Heart/Hearts ♥ You will find new or greater love or deep affection; also a family situation in which sympathy and sensitivity is required.

Hen This indicates the arrival or increasing influence of a nurturing, motherly presence; a fussy person.

Hill/Mountain A time for furthering long-term ambitions, dreams, journeys; if covered in mist, it indicates an uncertainty about which path to take.

Holly Family gatherings; significant personal events close to Christmas; joy.

Horn Symbol of plenty, peace, and magical strength.

Horse Expect to encounter unselfishness and reliability; travels, especially if the horse is in full gallop.

Horse and Cart Movement and a change of work or home. If the cart is full, the move is an advantageous one.

Horseshoe Good fortune, happy marriage; protection against hostility.

Hourglass, Egg Timer Time is important and perhaps limited for the completion of a task.

House Domestic matters and security are to the fore. It may be necessary to devote extra time to the home and those in it.

Iceberg Hidden depths to a person or situation that can be hazardous if not recognized.

Igloo A temporary refuge against inhospitable conditions that should not be regarded as permanent.

Inkpot/Spilled Ink An inkpot indicates important matters to be communicated in writing, perhaps legal or official matters. Spilled ink suggests areas of doubt that you should clarify before committing pen to paper.

Insect Small, irritating worries that should be brushed aside.

Island Holidays or pleasurable retreats, but also signifies a feeling of isolation.

Judge The need to weigh the pros and cons of a situation; an authority figure being unnecessarily judgmental.

Jug A full jug is a sign of good health; empty jugs indicate that money may be trickling away.

Juggler A time of trying to balance different priorities and meet conflicting demands; if balls are in the air, balancing them successfully.

Kangaroo Happy family affairs, especially involving children and young people; leaping in at the deep end.

Kettle Domestic discussions and family gatherings that bring satisfaction.

Key A puzzling matter will soon clear up; a sign of increasing independence.

King A male authority figure, father, or older person who may be high-handed; a powerful ally.

Knife/Crossed Knives Arguments and disagreements; beware of false friends.

Ladder Promotion, advancement or spiritual development; a time to aim high.

Lamp Finding a lost possession; sudden illumination about a troublesome issue; light at the end of the tunnel.

Leaves An indication of happiness, prosperity, success; falling leaves herald a natural change point or happiness in the autumn.

Leo, the Lion ♌ Courage, loyalty, leadership; craving the approval of others.

Libra, the Scales ♎ Peace-loving nature, harmony, indecisiveness.

Lighthouse Warnings of potential obstacles or dangers that can be averted if recognized.

Lines, Straight A direct course, a straightforward journey or enterprise.

Lines, Wavy or Broken Uneven progress; the need to take detours to achieve an aim.

Lizard Carefully check, as the source may not be reliable; a primitive instinct.

Loom/Spinning Wheel Plots and machinations behind the scenes; industrious and consistent efforts bring tangible rewards, according to plan.

Loop A roundabout route; pointless disagreements; impulsive decisions that could be unwise.

Luggage Holidays; can also indicate unnecessary emotional or physical burdens that a person carries.

Magnet Sudden irresistible attraction, either romantic or sexual; a new interest that will become important.

Map Travel or a desire to travel; finding the way after a period of uncertainty; careful plans that will lead to a new destination in life.

Maypole An ancient fertility symbol, indicating the stirring of life, whether a pregnancy, a new project, or happiness in the spring.

Mermaid Illusion of beauty and worth; temptation, infidelity, or short-lived passions.

Mirror Vanity; a feeling of life passing one by; also significant dreams.

Mole Secrets soon to be revealed; a seeming friend who is undermining a person's position.

Monk/Nun A wise friend; seeking a spiritual path; a desire to withdraw from life for a while; forgiveness.

Monkey A mischief-maker or fickle friend; also ingenuity and enterprise in solving problems; a curious child.

Moon (see also **Crescent Moon**) A full moon indicates a month hence for an anticipated event; magical activities and psychic development; a love affair or unrequited love.

Mouse Timidity; the need to take the initiative, especially to improve finances.

Nail Fingernail—unfair accusations; metal nail—a keen sense of injustice; points that strongly need emphasizing to get what is rightly owed or promised.

Necklace Admiration, perhaps a secret admirer; bonds of love or deep friendship. A broken necklace indicates an estrangement that should be approached with care.

Needle Mending a quarrel; teasing or criticism based in jealousy that should be ignored; making do with a less-than-satisfactory situation in the hope that it will improve, rather than giving up.

Nest Homemaking and domesticity; alternatively, a desire to flee the nest and be more independent or adventurous.

Net Feeling trapped or a safety net in a new venture; gaining what has long been sought.

Nine The number of completion and perfection; also self-interest.

Oars A need to seek one's own remedy rather than waiting for help; moving farther afield.

Octopus Becoming involved in too many ventures or with too many people whose needs may conflict; may also represent a person with many talents.

One The number of creation, pure energy, and initiative; new beginnings.

Ostrich A person who ignores a real threat or an unpleasant situation in the hope that it will go away.

Owl A person of immense wisdom; also a warning of tasks neglected.

Oyster Hidden treasure, resources, or strengths that, if developed, you can use at the right time.

Padlock If open, an opportunity to escape from an unwanted encounter or to extricate oneself from a difficult situation; if closed, unvoiced worries about security of one's job or property.

Palace/Castle An improvement in circumstances; a desire for more luxurious accommodation; a feeling of being intruded on at home by outside concerns or interfering visitors.

Palm Tree A desire for, or the possibility of, exotic travel; achieving recognition or tangible success or prosperity; a need to be cherished.

Parachute Help at a time of vulnerability; unfounded fears of failure or disaster.

Parrot Chatter and triviality that mask the real issue; a need to avoid passing on gossip; a desire for more solitude in work or domestic spheres.

Peacock A promise of a more opulent lifestyle; a vain friend; justifiable pride in achievements.

Pendulum A need to harmonize with those around one; looking beneath the surface for the real meaning of a situation; changing course.

Pickax/Ax Determination to cut through bureaucracy or pettiness; powerful action.

Pig Overindulgence in any way; a person who is generous, especially with hospitality.

Pigeon A trustworthy messenger or arbitrator; unexpected communication from afar.

Pipe A comforting presence; deliberation and consultation with all involved before making a decision.

Pisces, the Fish ♓ Intuition; being pulled in two directions; imagination and sensitivity.

Precipice Warning of walking into danger or discord; however, can also be the need to take a chance.

Purse Unexpected expenses; can also indicate a person who is cautious with money.

Pyramid Healing; psychic powers; a need to look to the past for the answer.

Queen A female authority figure, a mother, or an overdose of nurturing others.

Question Mark A question must be answered before you can make a major decision or commitment.

Rabbit Speed is of the essence; fertility; happiness at Easter; also the need to confront foes.

Rainbow Wishes can soon be fulfilled; but can also mean waiting for unrealistic dreams to be fulfilled.

Rat A warning to beware a deceitful or vindictive person; more positively, can also be a suggestion to try stealth and cunning when force or persuasion fails.

Raven/Crow A wise warning that may not be welcome; beware of revealing the confidence of others.

Rectangle Rigid attitudes on the part of others may reduce the scope for immediate action. Progress can, however, be made, if constraints are recognized.

Rider A new positive influence coming into the home. If facing the handle, a new work colleague or friend in the workplace or social sphere. If facing away from the handle, a need for a cooperative effort to achieve success.

Road A new path may open; if there is a fork in the road, a choice must be made.

Rocket A very ambitious plan that will need tremendous impetus to launch, but may have far-reaching effects.

Rocks Potential hazards. With care, these can be surmounted and used to scale greater heights.

Ruins (especially Ruined Buildings) The need to rebuild and learn from the past; also connections with ancestors and a deep sense of family tradition and history.

Sagittarius, the Archer ♐ Focused action, optimism, vision, and tactlessness.

Scorpio, the Scorpion ♏ Mystery, psychic development, commitment, and revenge.

Seesaw Fluctuations in circumstances or opinions mean it is important to keep the balance; mood swings in others may be difficult to gauge.

Seven The unconscious world, inner wisdom, a long-term perspective.

Shark Unexpected attacks can be repelled if you are sufficiently forceful.

Shell The inner voice that speaks the truth; intuitive wisdom.

Signpost The need to check alternatives before acting; a changing point when you can see indications of the relative merits of each path in advance.

Six Harmony, peace, and reconciliation.

Snake Regeneration; shedding old responsibilities and burdens.

Spades ♠ Logic, calculation, challenges, and changes, often promoted by difficulties.

Spider Persistence and ingenuity; fate; the strong link between past, present, and future.

Square Protection, rather than restriction; a time of preparation; material security.

Squirrel Saving for the future; the hoarding instinct.

Stalks/Sticks These represent people who feature prominently in your life. Two or three are a family; a large group can represent an organization. Straight stalks indicate reliability; wavy indicate those who vary their opinions according to mood and situation.

Star Wishes and dreams; hope, a chance to achieve prominence; single-mindedly following a particular pursuit or goal. A five-pointed star indicates magic and psychic development.

Stork Pregnancy, birth, an addition to the family circle; good fortune at home.

Sun Talents, achievements, success, ambition; traveling to sunny climes; happiness in the summer.

Taurus, the Bull ♉ Patience, material security, possessions, property, possessiveness.

Telescope Answers or opportunities that lie beyond the immediate environment or in the future; mysteries soon to be revealed.

Tiger Luck in money and speculation; ferocity and aggression.

Tortoise/Turtle Longevity; anything to do with the past or tradition; success you achieve slowly.

Tower If with steps, an ascent financially or in status; feelings of restrictions; a half-finished tower indicates unfinished plans.

Tree Health; strength; protection; gradual growth in the area of life that is most significant.

Triangle Mystical symbol; unexpected possibilities or undeveloped talents that can lead to success. If the apex points downward or away from the handle, opportunities must be seized before they are missed.

Tunnel Temporary confusion or setback that will soon clear; the need to probe to clear up uncertainty.

Two Duality—either two separate facets of life or two people who may be rivals; a betrothal; integrating two conflicting factors or people.

Unicorn A rare opportunity or unusual experience; magical insights.

Volcano Simmering anger or passion that needs channeling; an angry person who hides his or her feelings.

Weathervane An inconstant person; indecisiveness; the need to watch for signs of change to act at the right moment.

Whale A huge undertaking that can be successfully fulfilled; traditionally, commercial or administrative success; nurturing others.

Wheel Travels and change; the Wheel of Fortune may bring new opportunities or challenges; an end to a period of stagnation.

Window A new insight or chance for freedom; a curtained window can indicate narrow horizons in others.

Wolf Protection, defensiveness; mother love; loyalty to a group or organization.

Sample Teacup Reading

Maria was widowed and in her forties with a son who, although he lived away from home, always asked for help and money. Maria only had a part-time job and her son Tony had, yet again, asked for a loan that she knew would never be repaid. Tony said that if Maria would buy him a car, he would be able to get work at a late-night pizza parlor in a town ten miles away, with the prospect of the next permanent position if he did well. Work was scarce in the area, and Maria was eager for Tony to obtain employment.

Her cup had several very clear signs. The first three formed a definite cluster near the rim and the handle, indicating that the matters were close to home and occupying present thoughts.

 Snowflake Maria interpreted this as her son coming home yet again, when life was cold, for her to sort out his problems.

 Scissors The time had come, Maria said, to cut the apron strings, as Tony was in his late twenties and she had helped him since he left school, with very little result. But how could she turn her back on her son?

 Window Maria said the window was closed, and she felt that her own life was passing her by. She suddenly had a strong desire to go out into the world and do something for herself; to spread her wings.

The next two signs were also close together, to the right and halfway down the cup, therefore coming into Maria's life during the next few months.

 Star Maria felt she had concentrated on her son's happiness for so long that she had not fulfilled her own dreams. Her sister in Australia recently asked her to visit there for three months, but Maria had been worried about leaving her son.

Egg A new beginning or plan that could bring happiness if developed. But should Maria spend her savings on a car for her son or an airplane ticket?

The final two symbols were to the left and near the rim—factors to be moved out of her life to clear the way for the new beginning.

Pickax Maria needed to be determined and a lot less understanding if Tony was ever to stand on his own two feet.

Bull Maria needed to act decisively if she was to make a life of her own. Taking the bull by the horns, she decided to go Australia.

But what about her son? Maria could at least give Tony a start. She offered to lend him her own small car while she was abroad, so he could take his job and, without Mother's helping hand to save him, he had a real incentive to succeed.

PERSONAL
DIVINATION SYSTEMS

Chapter 8

Numerology

"I AM NOT a number, I am a free man!" was the defiant cry of Patrick McGoohan at the start of every episode of *The Prisoner,* the television series about a man trapped in a nightmare world in which unseen and incredibly powerful forces tried to reduce him to a cipher.

Numerology takes the view that we can reduce everybody to a number—but it does not seek to rob us of our individuality. Rather, numerology helps to realize our own unique potential. It describes the paths that change according to the way we react to the opportunities fate offers and the doors life closes, sometimes apparently without reason.

In the section on runes, I described how each letter of the rune alphabet was associated with a certain power. The Hebraic and Egyptian alphabets also have these connotations. But our alphabet, inherited from the practical Romans, has lost such meanings. We might use *X* to signify the unknown, but that is as far as it goes. Numerology seeks to remedy this deficiency by linking each letter to a number that does have magical significance. In this way, you can discover your weaknesses and strengths by finding your unique combination of numbers, deduced from your name and birth date. If you can tap into these underlying vibrations, you can understand what holds you back—or what may unconsciously drive you to react in certain ways. You can also discover auspicious days, years, and even places where your "personal number vibrations" are in harmony with the movement of the wider world.

If you accept the principle of synchronicity, then your name in its many forms, as well as your birth date, assume significance and mirror not only what you are, but what you could be.

Our names are immensely important in influencing how the world perceives us and how we view ourselves. Birth names may cause pride or immense embarrassment; a nickname may endear or diminish us. In the different roles we play in the world, we are addressed in ways that reflect diverse aspects of our personality: from Mum and Dad to the name used on a passport, on a name badge at work, among friends or neighbors, and by loved ones. In changing a name, you change more than your image. You alter your relationship with the world. The individual letters that make up names each have a numerical significance, so we can reduce a name or birth date to a single or master number to give information about hidden talents and future paths to success and happiness.

Origins of Numerology

The ancient Egyptians and Chinese used numbers for divination. However, it was mainly the Greeks and the Hebrews who developed the systems used in modern numerology. In the sixth century B.C., the philosopher and mathematician Pythagoras wrote: "Numbers are the first things of all of Nature." He regarded numbers as not just having mathematical significance, but as being central to all religious and philosophical wisdom. Each of the primary numbers, he said, had different vibrations, and the vibrations echoed throughout heaven and earth, including humankind. "The Music of the Spheres" expressed the harmony of the heavenly bodies, each of which had their own numerical vibration.

The meaning of a number is universal, although varying symbols may be used in different cultures. The Pythagorean system, based on the nine primary numbers, is most commonly used for basic numerology, although the "master numbers" of 11 and 22 are sometimes added in certain aspects of numerological divination.

According to Pythagorean theory, the letters *A, J,* and *S* equal 1; *B, K,* and *T* equal 2, and so on. The following table shows how the alphabet breaks down into numbers.

1	2	3	4	5	6	7	8	9
A	B	C	D	E	F	G	H	I
J	K	L	M	N	O	P	Q	R
S	T	U	V	W	X	Y	Z	

Numbers of Power

There are four main personal numbers that reflect the different facets of a person. They do not usually coincide, for if we were the same in all situations and at all times, we would be either incredibly spiritually evolved or remarkably impervious to life's slings and arrows. I use the example of Amelia Susan Jones, a divorced teacher in her forties.

BIRTH OR LIFE PLAN NUMBER

This is the number of possibility that unfolds throughout life. It provides an excellent indicator of what could or should be your predominant traits, strengths, and weaknesses, some as yet undeveloped. These traits may be most apparent at creative or change points in your life. Ideally, this number is the same as your Destiny or Fate Number, which reflects the attributes that have been manifest in your life so far.

But people's lives rarely unfold spontaneously in a perfect way, and it can take many false starts, obstacles, changes of direction, and conscious decisions to develop our potential to its full.

As with astrology, the Birth or Life Plan Number is a symbolic or synchronistic number. With changes in the calendar and times over the centuries and in different parts of the world, and the fact that the birth of Christ did not occur on 1/1/00, there is no absolute point of reference. Even the current practice of using C.E. or Common Era rather than A.D. does not fully resolve this issue, for changes such as daylight saving time are just one example of how a person's birth date can vary by a day. Nevertheless, in practice, the Birth Number does offer an unchanging marker for the individual.

This number offers the most scope for long-term divination of futures yet to be made, as different challenges (unexpected, as well as planned) call different facets of personality into play. A sudden promotion or layoff, a birth or bereavement, falling in love or out of it, a windfall or financial loss, or even waking up one morning and deciding that the chosen path is no longer the right one—any of these can bring to the fore a strength that has never been utilized or eradicate a weakness when survival or thriving is an issue.

CALCULATING THE BIRTH OR LIFE PLAN NUMBER

Add together all the digits of the date of birth, expressed numerically, and then reduce them by again adding the sum together until the result is a number between 1 and 9.

In the case of Amelia Susan Jones, who was born on 11/21/1957, we have the following:

$1 + 1 + 2 + 1 + 1 + 9 + 5 + 7$
which equals 27.
27 gives us $2 + 7 = 9$.
The Birth Number is 9.

The only numbers we do not reduce to single digits are 11 and 22. These last two numbers are sometimes called the master numbers, because they symbolize evolved states of awareness.

When calculating your Life Plan Number, you also don't count 0, so 20, for example, would become 2. Zero in a birth date is a mystical symbol. One or more noughts in a birth date suggests that the possessor has a deep core of spirituality that may manifest itself as concern for others or as enhanced psychic ability.

THE DESTINY or FATE NUMBER

We make our own destinies in the way we tackle the opportunities or challenges that present themselves, and so the Destiny Number represents all we have achieved in both work and our personal world. A number derived from all the letters in the complete birth name make up the Destiny Number.

The Destiny Number is also indicative of change and so is important for divination. It indicates the most likely course your future will take, given the present trends and direction. This, in itself, offers alternatives to the conscious mind and the possibility of changing what seems like a set path.

Using the Pythagorean table gives us the following Destiny Number for Amelia Susan Jones:

A M E L I A	S U S A N	J O N E S
1 4 5 3 9 1	1 3 1 1 5	1 6 5 5 1

1+4+5+3+9+1+1+3+1+1+5+1+6+5+5+1
which equals 52.
52 gives us 5 + 2 = 7.
So Amelia's Destiny Number is 7.

ACQUIRED FATE NUMBER

This is your full name, taking into account any variations of name changes, whether legal, informal, or by marriage. This reflects the new persona (if any) you acquire and can replace the birth name as a benchmark of achievement, as any star of film or music who has changed their name, and soared upward, will verify. Calculate this name separately from your birth name. If there is a variation, you can see how you, perhaps unconsciously, change the direction of your life by something as simple as using your middle name and dropping your first one. This, then, is the number of life change and new directions and refers to a permanent alteration in the full name. For example, names by marriage, nicknames, and terms of endearment are calculated separately under Personality Numbers, explained later in the section.

As with the birth name, this is calculated by adding together all the letters in the new full name, as used in the world. For example, when Amelia started work she dropped the name Amelia. When she married in her late twenties, she took the name of Green. She has kept the name of Green at work for the sake of continuity with the children and staff but calls herself Susan Jones on all official correspondence.

Her Acquired Fate Number is therefore:

S	U	S	A	N		G	R	E	E	N
1	3	1	1	5		7	9	5	5	5

1+3+1+1+5+7+9+5+5+5
which equals 42.
42 gives us 4 + 2 = 6.
So Susan Green's Acquired Fate Number is 6.

THE Heart or soul Number

Find this by adding together the vowels of your full birth name. It reveals the inner private person; the secret hopes, fears, and dreams; the longings of the soul; the underlying and often unconscious motivations in life. It can be very valuable in understanding what sometimes seem to be impulses or drives.

The Soul Urge or, as it is sometimes called, the Heart's Desire, is an important core influence in numerology.

As well as *A, E, I, O,* and *U, W* and *Y* also count as vowels when used in a full name. *Y* is a vowel when no other vowel exists in a syllable—for example, Lynn or Marilyn—and when it is preceded by a vowel and sounded as one sound—as in Rayner. *W* is a vowel when it is preceded by a vowel and sounded as one sound—for example, Crowley. The sum of all these letters, converted to numbers and reduced to a single number or a master number, gives the Heart Number.

Amelia Susan Jones would be the following:

A	E	I	A	U	A	O	E
1	5	9	1	3	1	6	5

1+5+9+1+3+1+6+5
which equals 31.
31 gives us 3 + 1 = 4.
So Amelia Susan Jones's Heart Number is 4.

THE PERSONALITY NUMBER

The Expression or Personality Number, obtained by adding all the consonants, represents the persona or face you show the world, the traits that others see most readily. This is the point at which to consider all the different names by which you are known. For example, I am Mrs. Eason in formal situations, Cassandra to some people who know me slightly, and Cassie or Cass to others. It is important to realize how a subtle change to our names can affect our relationships. Notice the way a salesman begins using your first name in an attempt to create a feeling of intimacy.

List the different names by which you are known in a variety of situations, and see not only how the numbers vary, but how the image you create, consciously or not, puts forward certain characteristics.

Amelia listed three main names, each of which were added separately and reduced to a single digit. Though this can be time-consuming, it is very worthwhile because you can see how your different facets link and whether any of the numbers formed present a different persona from the one you had thought you were conveying. Some of these names will be a full name, as worn on a name badge; Susan's new official name was the one she was called at work, but because she was a teacher of young children, she was most frequently referred to as Mrs. Green. Titles become relevant if they are used verbally or written as part of your daily work role (for example, Dr. Smith) but would not otherwise be counted.

Susan was called the following names:

"Emma" by her mother
"Sue" by colleagues at work and friends
"Mrs. Green" by the pupils and adults in the children's hearing

Emma = M + M = 4 + 4 = 8
Sue = S = 1
Mrs. Green = M + R + S + G + R + N = 4 + 9 + 1 + 7 + 9 + 5 = 35 = 8

So her Personality Numbers are:

Family: 8
Friends and colleagues: 1
Work/pupils: 8

Her family and official work numbers coincided.

Later in this section, I analyze the significance of these numbers in relation to Amelia Susan Jones's life.

Keywords and Potential for Each Number

The meanings of the individual numbers vary from system to system and also according to the context in which the numbers are used. The following system is one that is closely associated with traditional numerology. It was not one I had tried until quite recently, but I find it works remarkably well. However, if you find that other number associations make more sense to you, substitute those meanings.

1: The Number of the Innovator

Initiator of action, creative inspiration, a pioneer, a leader, independence, personal attainment, individuality, enthusiasm, drive, assertiveness, strength, boundless energy, originality

The 1 person always has the potential for greatness as a leader, but may falter as a follower.

2: THE NUMBER OF THE NEGOTIATOR

Cooperation, adaptability, consideration of others, skills in partnerships of all kinds, mediator, balanced opinions, desire for justice, ability to see both sides of any question

The 2 person has the capacity to become a great mediator, but may find it hard to make decisions or choices.

3: THE NUMBER OF THE CREATOR

Expression, verbalization, communication (both written and verbal), charisma, persuasiveness, sociability, creativity (especially in the arts), entertainment, the joy of living, optimism, expansion of horizons, fertility of ideas, generosity

The 3 person is a great communicator and joy-bringer, but may spread their abilities and interests too widely.

4: THE NUMBER OF THE REALIST

Stability and common sense, practical foundation for ideas, skilled planner, loyalty, trustworthiness, ability to carry through projects, dedication to duty, excellent organizational skills, ability to work within constraints, steady growth, firm understanding of reality

The 4 person has patience and perseverance in abundance, but can be dogmatic and get bogged down in routine.

5: THE NUMBER OF THE VOYAGER

Expansiveness, visionary, love of adventure, the constructive use of freedom, ability to appraise an entire situation at a glance, wide horizons, open-mindedness, eagerness for new knowledge and experiences, versatility

The 5 person is one of life's natural travelers (both physically and in breadth of vision), but can find it hard to persevere when difficulties arise or boredom sets in.

6: THE NUMBER OF THE PROTECTOR OF THE WEAK

Altruism, protection of the vulnerable, skill in nurturing both those close and the world in general, community, sympathy, idealism, sacrifice, compassion, generosity with personal and material resources and time, acceptance of others' weaknesses, wisdom (especially concerning people)

The 6 person cares for stranger and friend alike and has a remarkable understanding of people; however, he or she may suffer the loss of personal identity through worrying too much about others' needs and becoming overwhelmed by responsibility.

7: THE NUMBER OF THE WISE ONE

Understanding, knowledge, awareness of tradition, thirst for knowledge and the acquired wisdom of ages, deep and profound thought, spiritual nature, introspection, secrecy, religions, mysticism, healing, sensitivity, love of beauty and harmony, seeker after truth

The 7 person has a font of knowledge and wisdom acquired through painstaking research, but can be oversecretive and divorced from the real world.

8: THE NUMBER OF THE ENTREPRENEUR

Status-oriented, power-seeking, high material goals, ambitions, confidence, focused aims and energy, success with business and money, efficiency and proficiency, competence in any chosen field, logic and analytical powers

The 8 person is endowed with tremendous potential for conceiving far-reaching schemes and ideas and has the tenacity to follow them through to completion; he or she can be materialistic and concerned with success to the detriment of emotions and relationships.

9: THE NUMBER OF THE CRUSADER

Courage, desire for perfection, humanitarianism, selflessness, crusader, impulsiveness, intolerance of prejudice or inaction, honesty, campaigner, a refusal to be deterred no matter what the obstacle, forcefulness in the defense of principles, outspokenness

The *9* person is fearless in pursuit of a worthwhile cause, but can be impatient and even aggressive with those who do not share his or her vision.

11: THE NUMBER OF THE DREAMER

Intuition, imagination, ingenuity, psychic awareness, illumination, idealism, a dreamer whose night- and daytime visions may prove prophetic, inspiration, insight into the unspoken motives and intentions of others, seeker of the secrets of the cosmos

The *11* person is equally at home in the past, present, or future, but can be led off course by illusion and an inability to turn dreams into reality.

22: THE NUMBER OF THE EAGLE

A master builder of society, a shaper of policy, global thinking, nobility of thought and action, the coming together of reason and intuition, logic and feeling, vision and practicality, energy and compassion; the greatest of the numbers, it offers potential for achievement either in the world's terms or in spiritual evolution

The *22* person has the capacity to succeed in any field, but can fall prey to depression or disillusionment.

Amelia Susan Jones: A Numerological Appraisal

Here's a closer look at one person's numerological appraisal.

THE BIRTH OR LIFE PLAN NUMBER OR NUMBER OF POTENTIAL

Amelia Susan Jones, born on 11/21/1957:
This gave $1 + 1 + 2 + 1 + 1 + 9 + 5 + 7 = 27 = 9$
Her Birth Number was 9.

Amelia was potentially a crusader and an idealist. This was probably why she spent so much of her life working with underprivileged children and devoting her holidays to inner-city volunteer work. In the future, she wanted to work with Maori children on a possible exchange visit to New Zealand.

DESTINY OR FATE NUMBER

This reveals what Amelia made of her life before she altered her name by marriage and by dropping her first name. This still forms the core of her life and influences her future plans.

Amelia Susan Jones has the following Destiny Number:

$$1 + 4 + 5 + 3 + 9 + 1 + 1 + 3 + 1 + 1 + 5 + 1 + 6 + 5 + 5 + 1 = 52$$
$$5+2 = 7$$

Seven is the number of the wise soul. Amelia had been brought up as the only child of elderly parents in an isolated village and spent her early years reading and developing her plan to become a teacher of less-privileged children. This had been opposed by her parents and Amelia found it a great shock when she discovered the reality of teaching in an inner-city area. Her *9* courage carried her through, but she married a refined man who found her idealism at odds with his own materialistic attitude.

ACQUIRED FATE NUMBER

Amelia first dropped her name *Amelia* and then changed her surname to Green. The numerals for her Acquired Fate name, by which she is still known, are as follows:

$$1 + 3 + 1 + 1 + 5 + 7 + 9 + 5 + 5 + 5 = 42 = 6$$

Susan Green's Acquired Fate Number is therefore 6.

At this point, Susan's caring side came to the fore as she took on the troubles of the world and assumed the persona her husband desired in a wife. However, she became overburdened as she took on more work to fill the increasing loneliness. When her husband told her he was leaving her for another woman, she blamed herself. After the divorce, she struggled on with this role. It might be helpful if Susan assumed her maiden name once more at work (as well as officially) now that she is divorced, as this would give her a new Acquired Fate Number:

Susan Jones
$1 + 3 + 1 + 1 + 5 + 1 + 6 + 5 + 5 + 1 = 29 = 11$

One of the master numbers, *11* calls into play entirely different qualities: intuition, imagination, ingenuity, psychic awareness, illumination, idealism, a dreamer whose night- and daytime visions may prove prophetic, inspiration, insight into the unspoken motives and intentions of others, seeker of the secrets of the cosmos. Not Susan Green, the quiet wise one who assumed the burdens of the world, whose crusading spirit was manifest through her work; Susan Jones would become the acquired destiny of the individual.

Susan admitted she was very drawn to healing and had discovered she was a natural healer. However, she had never acknowledged this side openly.

THe HearT or souL NumBer

Using the vowels only to calculate this, Amelia Susan Jones would be the following:

AEIAUAOE = $1+5+9+1+3+1+6+5 = 31$
$3+1 = 4$

Four is the number of the realist with infinite patience and perseverance. Susan's inner world was a revelation to her. Yet this practical side lay at the root of her ability to cope with her difficult job, a demanding husband, and later a failed marriage. Both Susan's parents and her husband had encouraged her to see herself as impractical and incompetent, because it suited their own purpose and gave them power over her.

This was a belief Susan carried with her, although she daily coped with crises and never panicked. All she had to do was acknowledge her own capabilities, and the lack of confidence that was holding her back from change—and ultimately happiness—would disappear.

THE Personality Number

Using the consonants to calculate this number, Susan was known as the following:

Emma by her mother, Sue by colleagues at work and friends, and Mrs. Green by the pupils and adults in children's hearing.

Emma = M + M = 4 + 4 = 8
Sue = S = 1
Mrs. Green = M + R + S + G + R + N = 4 + 9 + 1 + 7 + 9 + 5 = 35 = 8

Her Personality Numbers are as follows:

Family: 8
Friends and colleagues: 1
Work/pupils: 8

Her family and official work numbers coincide.

Her mother's choice of name was startling. Little Emma—ambitious, assertive? Emma's mother unconsciously called her daughter by an endearment that gave off threatening vibes. Was this, Susan suddenly wondered, the reason her mother always criticized her?

But what about the children at school? Authority and ambition were qualities she had never seen in regard to herself at work, but there was no reason why she should not apply for promotion. In the past, Susan had declined opportunities for advancement because she believed she could not cope. Sue (number 1) pleased her, with its connotations of an independent, energetic, original thinker. Perhaps she should think of herself as Sue and drop the Susan?

Numerology is not a static art, but a divinatory form to help us understand the undercurrents and potentials that can lead to changes in action and attitude six or twelve months down the road. Sue might even fall in love again on the new path.

Personal Year

The Personal Year is helpful in evaluating the trend of the coming calendar year. For a clue to what lies ahead in the coming year, or any particular significant year in the future, calculate your Personal Year using the following formula. Years are sometimes calculated in nine-year cycles, from beginning to completion.

Reduce the year in question to a single digit.

The year 1997 would be 8 ($1 + 9 + 9 + 7 = 26; 2 + 6 = 8$).

Now, add your month and day of birth. This time, if you make the significant numbers of 11 or 22, reduce them to 2 or 4. Then add the two numbers together.

Amelia Susan Jones's birthday was 11/21/1957.

Susan wanted to know what kind of a year 1998 would be for her, because she was hoping to go on a working exchange visit to New Zealand.

$1 + 9 + 9 + 8 = 27 = 9$

Add to this Susan's birthday and month: $11 + 21 = 32; 3 + 2 = 5$

9 [year] + 5 [birthday and month] $= 14 = 5$

Her Personal Year for 1998 is therefore a 5, the number of the Voyager. Personal Year 5 represents the perfect year for travel, as it responds to a feeling of restlessness. If this is channeled into an exciting project, Susan will not be tempted to give up her teaching work, which is integral to her life, but she can still expand her horizons.

THE NINE-YEAR CYCLE

Year 1: A New Beginning Year 1 is the beginning of a new nine-year cycle. It augurs new opportunities and challenges. This is a time to clarify your goals and initiate any changes that are necessary to move into the next phase with confidence.

Year 2: Consolidation and Waiting You may need to build bridges, network, and cooperate closely with other people. It is a time for developing new relationships at work and emotionally or to concentrate on improving existing ones. Any effort you make now will bear fruit before the next twelve months is over.

Year 3: Creativity and Communication A joyous year to be lived to the full. Creative efforts will blossom, and communication (whether spoken, written, or creative) will hold the key to success and happiness. Fulfill pressing tasks and commitments before taking on more.

Year 4: Steady Progress and Caution Hard work, persistent effort to overcome any limitations, and caution with money and resources will ensure slow but tangible achievement. Organizing for long-term objectives rather than immediate targets will avoid frustration and the squandering of energies on unrealistic aims.

Year 5: Expanding Horizons The five-year itch hits and an inner restlessness affects every aspect of life. Travel is in the cards, perhaps a house move or change of routine and new interests; innovation and wider perspectives will avoid the temptation to make major life changes for the wrong reasons.

Year 6: Love, Reconciliation, and Domestic Matters Love and family matters bring joy, but also added responsibilities, with perhaps concern over more vulnerable family members, older people, and children. It is a year for mending old quarrels. Even if you are footloose and fancy-free at the beginning of this year in the cycle, you may find as the months progress that your deeper feelings are awakened or you are motivated to create a permanent base.

Year 7: The Inner World You may feel the need to withdraw temporarily from conflict either at work or in your personal life and to cut down on responsibilities to those who may no longer need support but are unwilling to relinquish your care. This is a year to concentrate on your personal happiness, inner harmony, building up resources of strength, and paying attention to health matters (especially to any stress-related symptoms).

Year 8: Achievement and Recognition A time to aim high and to have confidence in your own abilities, this is a year to fulfill dreams and gain recognition, whether in terms of promotion, increased status, or monetary rewards. You may make major decisions that will affect your life path and have opportunities to expand in different directions. Beware of neglecting your personal life.

Year 9: Completion, Assessment, and Endings This is a time to consolidate any gains and build on successes of the past. When you evaluate your achievements, you may decide it is time to shed certain aspects of your life or that a stage in a relationship is coming to an end and you need to move on to the next if it is to flourish.

SIGNIFICANT DAYS

Use the year meanings as a guide for specific days for yourself. Take a date, such as 1/1/2000, which equals $1 + 1 + 2 = 4$, and add it to your Birth or Life Plan Number. If, for example, this was 1, you would have a Day Number of 5. This would be a good date to travel or try a new activity, but not perhaps to propose a business partnership or permanent relationship, as the number is one of restlessness and change. You can use this method to plan auspicious days for certain activities.

Other Applications of Numerology

Here are some other uses for numerology in daily life.

NEW ADDRESS OR PLACE OF WORK

To find out whether a new address at work or a change of abode accords with any of your personal spheres, add together all the numbers of the address, including post or zip code, as it would be written on a letterhead. Add to this the number correspondences of any house or company name, roads, towns, counties, or districts. Only include the state or country if you are moving from another state or abroad.

If none of your personal numbers are in accord, it does not mean that the place is wrong, merely that it will evoke different feelings and call into play untapped qualities.

You may find that at a new workplace you spontaneously acquire a new name that does harmonize. For example, in a number *1* place, people who display individualism and assertiveness would thrive, while as a home, a number *1* place would need many personal touches to make it your own. Innovations and ingenuity will overcome any idiosyncrasies that make living in a new accommodation initially uncomfortable.

COLLEAGUES, FRIENDS, AND POTENTIAL PARTNERS

See if you can discover full birth names, acquired names, and date of birth, perhaps from a driver's licence. Compare their overall numbers, either the Life Plan or Destiny numbers, and see in which areas you resonate and what their characteristics are. If you draw a blank, use the methods listed above (for example, look at vowels to see if you vibrate in harmony on a soul level). If the person is important, draw up a profile of their different aspects. This can be a good way of understanding the tactics of a rival or an unfriendly mother-in-law.

PREDICTIONS ABOUT CHILDREN

We often end up calling our children by quite unexpected names— a song heard during late pregnancy, a name that spontaneously comes into your head, a name recalled from a dream, or one that seems to fit a newborn infant can often override tried and tested family favorites. Many people insist that children "choose" their names. Often, a family's pet names arise as a result of a child's stumbling attempts to vocalize his or her own name.

To find out about your child's potential talents and maybe even future occupation, discover his or her special number by using the Christian or birth name, plus middle name, but not surname. Add to this any pet name/nicknames the child has, reducing the total of all these to a single digit. This method is far more accurate for young children under eight years old than using either the birth date or full birth name. After eight, which coincides with the decline in natural psychic ability, the ordinary methods are best.

animals

This is rather different. An animal reveals his or her personality even as a tiny kitten or puppy. You can discover the right "psychic name" by finding the number that its character most resembles and experimenting with names until you get a number with which the animal's personality resonates. This link seems to make the animal more responsive and in tune with its owner.

a new secret name?

While your birth name is always important and you may not want to change it officially, a secret name can empower you to develop characteristics that can influence both your self-image and the way you project yourself. As with animal names, choose a number that seems to embody the positive characteristics you desire (perhaps more assertive, courageous, or balanced than the person you reveal at present), and experiment with names until you find one with the right number vibration. Repeat your secret name nine times before sleep and nine times on waking, plus silently any time when you feel under stress. Before long, people will comment on the new qualities you have taken on.

Chapter 9

PENDULUM DOWSING

*Everything in the universe has its own energy and
vibrates to its frequency. This biosphere that we live
in is a primordial soup of their frequencies. We are
born into and feel it all times. It is the "stuff"
of universal consciousness. Dowsers are people who are
consciously connected to this universal flow of energy.
They feel it, code it and identify things by their
brokerage of this energy and are persons whose
spiritual journey has brought them to the knowledge
of "co-creation"*

—THE AMERICAN SOCIETY OF DOWSERS, INC., 1996

THE STATEMENT ABOVE may
sound far removed from divination. Yet pendulum dowsing for decisions operates precisely on the premise that all experience is connected. When we dowse to discover hidden feelings and needs, and to explore potentially enriching paths, we use the same technique as a dowser who searches for water, minerals, or lost objects, either by walking over a designated area with his or her hazel rod or holding a pendulum over a map to pinpoint the desired pathway by remote dowsing.

A dowsing pendulum is any weight on a string or chain, whether made of crystal quartz (which contains living energies of the earth), a ring, trinket, key, or plumb bob from the local hardware store on a chain, a cord, or a piece of string. The master dowser Tom Lethbridge once claimed to have dowsed successfully with a piece of chewing gum on a thread.

The Origins of Dowsing and Pendulum Divination

There are two suggested origins for the term *dowsing rod*. The first, and my own favorite, is from the old Cornish *dewsys* ("goddess") and *rhodl* ("tree branch"). The second and most traditional view traces the term back to the Middle English *duschen,* meaning "to strike," from early German references to dowsing rods striking down toward the ground.

The Chinese and ancient Egyptians practiced the art. However, the occult master of the divining art was said to be the demon Python of the Delphic oracular cult whom, it was claimed, could be contacted via a ritual in which a priestess offered him perfume while holding a rod of wood and reciting magical phrases. The rod-holder put her ear to the ground to receive replies said to be murmured so low they could only be heard in the mind. The mysterious source of dowsing continued to be associated with external forces as late as 1850, when the chemist Chevreul debated whether, among other theories, a pendulum's movements came from God via the angelic hierarchy or from the devil and his minions.

A form of dowsing for decisions was first recorded in the first century A.D. when Mercellinus, a Roman writer, described a tripod from which hung a ring on a thread. On the circumference of the tripod was a circle showing the letters of the Roman alphabet, and the ring swung toward different letters to spell out answers to divinatory questions.

A famous female dowser was Lady Milbanke, who so annoyed her son-in-law, the poet Lord Byron, with her hobby that he wrote after her death, "She is at last gone to a place where she can no longer dowse."

How Does Pendulum Divination Work?

Attempted scientific explanations have varied over the centuries with new discoveries, but all seem to touch on an unknown factor linked with the human psyche. Early explanations interpreted dowsing as signals from the aura of underground water or metal. Theories followed of a sympathetic attraction between specific minerals and rods cut from certain trees. The idea of magnetic or electrical influences on dowsers and their rods also held sway for a time, only recently being replaced by theories that dowsing succeeds due to radiation or waves akin to the electromagnetic waves emitted by television or radio stations.

However, no one is any nearer to accounting for the intangible power that enables people to dowse successfully for water or minerals from maps. It may be, as Tom Graves (who has written several books on pendulum dowsing) suggests, that dowsing is a technology to use and not a science to understand.

In the everyday world, people use dowsing to a high level of accuracy to find wells in areas of drought in the most unlikely places. Indeed, the Swiss pharmaceutical giant Hoffman–La Roche is said to use dowsers to find water sources for its new sites. The best dowsing involves real need, either to find something or to answer a question.

The fact that the pendulum movement is controlled by muscular response is seen as a weakness in the system, especially in dowsing for decisions, in which it is said that the dowser uses the pendulum to confirm a choice he or she wants. However, you will find that, unless someone deliberately cheats, the hand movement is unconscious and often gives an unexpected result. The principle is the same as that underlying picking certain tarot cards or casting particular runes. In all these cases, the most appropriate card, rune, or pendulum response is triggered by psychokinesis (movement of physical objects by mind-power), a power triggered by unconscious processes deep within each person.

Whether we are accessing what the psychologist Jung called "mankind's collective unconscious" outside conventional time/space limitations or touching our personal, deep inner wisdom, there is no doubt that dowsing for decisions operates with an accuracy equal to the more easily demonstrable forms of dowsing for water or minerals.

What is more, dowsing for personal decisions, because it is so strongly linked with the personal psyche, is a form that instantly succeeds with many people.

With this form of divination, practice does make perfect, in that you learn to ask the right questions and, most importantly, to trust the wisdom revealed through your crystal pendulum. The pendulum can be very helpful in confirming on the material plane what you thought you knew on the psychic level (for example, insights revealed in dreams or sudden flashes of inspiration).

However, you can only practice pendulum dowsing when you have a real question that has genuine personal significance. Physical dowsers generally have a purpose in their dowsing. Each time they succeed it adds to their confidence in their own abilities. This reduces the conscious barriers and doubts that can prevent unconscious knowledge accurately guiding the pendulum or dowsing rod.

Choosing a Pendulum

One of the cheapest and most effective conventional pendulum shapes is a plumb bob on a piece of picture cord. However, the most commonly used pendulums are pointed-ended crystals on a single ring and chain. Personal objects, such as lucky charms or medallions, also work well because we endow them with our positive feelings and so they are tuned into our emotions. You can use any object that is important to you: a ring, a childhood lucky charm, a small medallion, or a birthstone pendant. You can also change your pendulum according to circumstance—a key on a shoelace always makes an instant psychic tool.

Many people do like to have a special crystal pendulum and, after allowing another person to use it, hold it under running water, especially if the questioner has felt very depressed or angry. If you intend to read the pendulum for other people, either informally or professionally, you might prefer to keep a personal pendulum for your own work and have a second pendulum for readings. I have always used the same pendulum for both types of divination and have had no problems. So I now work on the principle that a temporary user of my pendulum, unless they feel particularly negative, will not upset the more permanent vibes.

However, if my pendulum feels heavy or looks dull after any use, I sprinkle it with salt, wash it under running water, and pass it through the smoke from a stick of frankincense for the protection of the sun, jasmine for the protection of the moon, and finally through the flame of a white or purple candle.

Some dowsers believe you must vary the length of cord on your pendulum according to the object sought and draw up complicated (and differing) tables listing the correct length for each metal or element. Some pendulums even have a hollowed-out section for placing a sample of the substance on the principle that like attracts like.

This doesn't seem to fit with the idea that the process operates on a nonmaterial level, and experts constantly argue about the correct lengths of cord. Dowsing is a personal art and experiments show that if you believe another person's measurements in conventional dowsing, they will work for you, even in cases when you have misread the charts. So use whatever length of cord feels right so that the pendulum doesn't drift aimlessly round, 6 to 8 inches (15 to 20 cm) seems to me best when dowsing over a chart, but others use longer or shorter chains. It is a matter of experimenting.

Most people find it comfortable to hold the pendulum between thumb and forefinger and wind any extra chain round the index finger, using the left hand for right brain intuition, although this is not a hard-and-fast rule.

The only other equipment you need is paper and pen to draw your grids and flow charts and record your results.

Discovering Your Pendulum's Responses

Sitting comfortably at a table, the best position for decision making, hold the pendulum still over the center of your paper, and let it move in its own time. Alternatively, give the pendulum a gentle push so it gently swings backward and forward.

A Yes Response

Frequently, a clockwise circle or ellipse forms the yes response. Although this can vary according to the user, the response usually remains consistent once established, whether the pendulum is used for questions about health, happiness, or money. To find your personal yes response, the interaction between you and the pendulum, visualize a very happy moment, a success, or a peak achievement time when you suddenly mastered a skill or reached the top of a high mountain, either actually or symbolically, and felt a surge of achievement. The pendulum will respond to the recalled positive emotion with a yes response.

A No Response

A negative pendulum response is generally the opposite of the yes response; for example, a counterclockwise circle or ellipse. But your personal pendulum's no may be entirely different. Discover this by concentrating on a moment when you were disappointed or failed to reach the peak of your particular mountain.

The Ask Again Response

Sometimes the question asked is not the real one that concerns you or it is ambiguously phrased. In this case, your pendulum may cease to move or may make a horizontal swinging movement. Practice this by thinking of a time of confusion, perhaps catching the wrong train or losing your way, and your pendulum should demonstrate this vital third movement.

Divination Using the Pendulum

Pendulum divination is very personal and works best when you carry it out for yourself. The test of time usually confirms the rightness of decisions, as the pendulum rarely gives the answers you expect, unless they are the right ones. However, you can read the pendulum for someone else or professionally. The rule is the same: the person posing the question should hold the pendulum. The method can work even if you read for someone who is not present; I have successfully used absent dowsing on TV phone-ins with success, but I always ask the person at home to repeat the question, using a pendulum, and to trust his or her own response rather than mine, if they differ.

To perform a pendulum divination

* Ask, or get the person for whom you are reading to ask, a question that prompts a yes/no reaction from the pendulum.

* Let the person for whom you are reading hold the pendulum and think of a "happy/sad" or confusing moment to establish personal "yes/no/ask again" responses. These can be established quite quickly and give the questioner an opportunity to tune into the pendulum and imprint vibrations.

* Ask the questioner to concentrate on the question, at the same time holding the pendulum in a static position. In my experience, people pick up the pendulum technique incredibly quickly, and even skeptics in demonstrations I have given on radio and television have expressed astonishment that they can feel the pendulum moving on its own in spite of conscious efforts to move it in the opposite direction.

SINGLE QUESTIONS

Sometimes a single question can provide the answer to an option or dilemma. It needs to be phrased so that yes or no is the answer, which precludes an either-or contained in the same question. With practice, even quite complex issues can be answered with a carefully phrased proposal. There is no limit to the scope of issues that you can tackle, with the proviso that it should always be a question that really needs answering and that evokes some degree of emotion in you or the questioner, whether positive or negative.

USING A FLOW CHART

An issue may not be clear-cut or may have several facets. The first question may be only a surface aspect of a deeper issue. Using a flow chart and asking six or seven questions can unravel the most obscure issue and may suggest solutions that had previously eluded you, but suddenly seem the only possible course. Again, it can work for another person and you can record the different questions and answers.

1. If a matter is a root one or seems clouded with confusion, ask a question without consciously formulating it. You may be surprised at your choice.

2. Write the question at the top of the flow chart and then concentrate on it, either silently or by repeating it until the pendulum responds.

3. Record the response in the appropriate column. If the pendulum tells you to ask again, write a new question in the central column.

4. If it answers yes or no, write your next question in the appropriate box.

5. Let the second question come spontaneously. You may find that the direction changes or brings a seemingly unrelated issue to the fore. Trust the pendulum wisdom, and the matter will become clearer.

6. Continue until you have five or six questions and answers and can see a way forward.

7. Alternatively, list your questions and write the response next to each question to form a single column.

A Sample Flow Chart Reading

> Andy desperately wanted to spend the summer sailing with his friends, but Liz, his girlfriend, had asked him to go abroad with her family. Andy had been seeing Liz for six months while he was finishing a masters degree in history, and Liz was eager for him to get to know her parents and younger brothers better.
>
> Andy drew up three columns as "yes," "ask again," and "no." His first question was: "Should I go on holiday with Liz's family?" Taking the answer as "ask again," he wrote his next question in that column and moved on. At the end of the session, his chart looked like this:

Yes	Ask again	No
	Should I go on holiday with Liz's family?	
		Do I want to go on holiday with Liz at all?
		Do I want to settle down with Liz?
		Do I want to settle down with anyone?
		Should I go back to the university in October and take my Ph.D?
	Do I want to take a year off to crew on a holiday yacht and then see?	
Will I regret it, if I do what Liz and my parents want?		

The answer to the last question was yes. Andy had fallen for Liz, but things had progressed faster than he had anticipated. Liz was pushing for a deeper commitment. Andy loved sailing and was so proficient, he had been offered a place crewing on holiday yachts for American tourists around the Greek Islands. He was lukewarm about returning to university for his doctorate, but his parents insisted he had a future as a university lecturer if he persevered.

The issue had suddenly widened from whether he should go on holiday with friends or his girlfriend to the question of what he, rather than other people, wanted to do with his life.

Andy realized he would either get the sailing bug out of his system and return to a more conventional lifestyle after his year off or perhaps develop a career in the leisure industry. At any rate, his speciality being ancient Greek history, he could double as a tour guide. But first he had to tell Liz and his parents how a key on a chain had changed his life path.

The Grid Method—Deciding between Options

If you must make a choice between several options, the grid method is a good way of discovering the relative merits of different paths. You may be able to achieve this with a single grid or you may need to draw a series of grids and gradually narrow down information in more detailed parameters until you get a specific answer. With this method, you can plan everything from where to spend a holiday to major life changes.

The Sacred Grid of Nine was an ancient northern magical device used by wise women and frequently drawn in the earth in front of the hut of a shaman of either sex. It was also drawn on a specially erected platform that acted as a protective magical area. The nine squares are contained in a larger protective square, which also concentrates the energies of time and space.

THe GraviTaTional Force OF THe PenDuLum

Just as a hazel rod pulls toward the source of water or minerals, a pendulum can be felt pulling downward toward a particular option out of several listed in a grid formation. The feeling is described as a heaviness, or a gravitational pull, and works even when a questioner uses the technique for the first time.

1. What is the issue? You need to formulate an initial question or area for which there are several options. Then you should formulate the options that can each be represented by one word, or alternatively, be as detailed as you wish.

2. You may not need all nine squares; if so, place the options at random in a number of squares. You can ask the pendulum to show you which squares to use. Block off the rest in black or red.

3. Hold the pendulum 3 to 4 inches (7.5 to 10 cm) above the paper on which you drew the squares.

4. Pass your pendulum over each row in turn, beginning in the bottom left square and moving from left to right in a continuous movement.

5. Travel right to left over the second row and, finally, left to right over the third row.

6. You may instantly feel a definite pull down over one square. If you do, you have arrived at your answer.

7. The pendulum may, however, hover over two or three squares, as if uncertain. There may be more than one likely option, and you may end up combining or reconciling two courses of action.

8. If no definite choice has been made, move backward from the top right over the three rows, firmly holding the pendulum.

Sample Grid Reading

Greg had recently married Sylvia, a younger woman with two teenage children, and was finding family life far from idyllic. Previously, he had lived on his own after a failed relationship and he had no children of his own. Since he moved in, the once-friendly children refused to cooperate in any way, and his wife resisted any attempts Greg made to impose order on the household. The situation was causing bitter quarrels between Sylvia and Greg. Increasingly, he had been staying late at work, and Susan, a sympathetic female colleague, had been very supportive and was hinting that she would be willing to become more than a friend.

Greg's question was "How can I best resolve my present unhappiness at home?" What were his options?

Move out and live alone	Begin a relationship with Susan while remaning married	Move out and begin a relationship with Susan
Accept the situation and let time and familiarity resolve the present crisis	Threaten the teenagers when Sylvia is not there	Bribe the teenagers
Insist the children go and live with their father	Try to talk to Sylvia in a nonemotive way in order to work out a joint strategy	Try to talk to the teenagers in order to come to an amicable compromise, accepting that his own ideals of family life may not be realistic

Greg moved the pendulum over the nine squares very slowly and felt it hover over several squares, reflecting the fact the he was torn between what he wanted to do and what he felt he ought to do. His impulses led him toward abandoning the situation, taking temporary refuge with Susan, or forcing his will on the children.

However, Greg acknowledged that his stepchildren were understandably very confused and resentful at an outsider taking over their home and their mother. What is more, Sylvia, who struggled for years to bring up the children with very little help from her ex-husband, who saw the children only rarely, was torn between a desire to protect them and to hold onto her own sudden chance of happiness and love.

Greg ran the pendulum over the grid a second time and it moved more steadily. On the third pass, it stopped on the line between the second and third choices: to talk to Sylvia and the children, maybe together, in a nonemotive way, and try to reach a compromise. This acknowledged Greg's own unrealistic expectations of what domestic life with a family would be. The pendulum became very heavy and, in spite of Greg's efforts to move it for a fourth time, remained settled.

The pendulum told Greg what he knew deep down was the best way forward. He went home with a bottle of wine for Sylvia and a video for the children and began the slow but potentially rewarding path. His divination promised not instant gratification or escape, but a firm foundation for the destiny Greg had chosen—a happy family life.

Chapter 10

PALMISTRY

As FINGERPRINTING has become scientifically acceptable, by implication, palmistry has also taken on a scientific authority in the eyes of many people. Some experts now say that a teaching course of a year or more is necessary before you can even begin to understand the technicalities. However, as with all methods of divination, palmistry is primarily a psychic art.

One can acquire a working knowledge of divinatory palmistry in a relatively short time by identifying where principal lines and fleshy mounds called mounts lie on a typical hand. These lines are not fixed and can deepen or change even over a relatively short period. Indeed, Chinese palmistry relies much more on interpreting transient signs in the hand than westernized forms of the art. Because the changes are relatively slow (unlike, for example, card or rune layouts), this form of divination is best practiced on others, although you can read your own palm effectively at irregular intervals.

By picking out potential paths and current strengths and weaknesses through interpreting the lines and mounts, decisions can be made and future opportunities explored. As with any other divinatory form, the questioner is not subject to a fixed fate; but when he or she takes one path rather than another, this is reflected in altered hand lines, albeit subtly, in as short a period as three months. Indeed, my own hand lines and mounts changed dramatically in what has been one of the most traumatic, but at the same time potent, periods of my life.

The ancients recognized that it was possible to pick up indications of incipient health problems in the hand: for example, liver or bile conditions from a papery feel and yellowish tinge or problems such as anemia from pitted nails. Likewise, a consistently weak Love or Heart Line might suggest emotional vulnerability that could be manifest as disease related to the stomach.

Such aspects have a place in medical palmistry, a mixture of actual observation and intuition; and indeed chirognomy studies the appearance of the hand as an indicator of character and health. A study of relative hand and finger sizes and skin texture is given in the books I list under Further Reading.

The Origins of Palmistry

Prehistoric handprints have been found inside cave walls in places as far apart as France and Africa, along with other magical markings. Palmistry is thought by many scholars to have originated in India more than forty-five hundred years ago. It is part of a vast field of esoteric wisdom, referred to as *Samudrik Shastra,* which can be translated as "the ocean of knowledge." Palmistry may have traveled from India into China via the trade routes and thence westward to Egypt and ancient Greece.

Pythagoras, the Greek philosopher and mathematician, wrote *Physiognomy and Palmistry* in about 530 B.C. It is recorded that Aristotle and the Roman emperors Julius Caesar and Augustus were skilled in palmistry.

However, some schools of thought believe that palmistry began in ancient Egypt and Sumeria. In a sense, both may be true, for once man walked upright, the hand took on universal significance as the wielder of tools. Similarly, the hand acquired a magical significance as the holder of the pen and therefore the instrument of the mind.

During the Middle Ages, palmistry was immensely popular, and Gypsies and village wise women read hands for the purpose of both fortune-telling and character assessment. By the fifteenth century, palmistry had been banned by the church, along with other psychic arts. But

276

this drove it underground rather than destroying it, because it was a divinatory form that needed no tools. The knowledge was passed on orally, usually from the matriarch of the family to the eldest daughter.

In the nineteenth and twentieth centuries, palmistry was popularized and once again given a semiscientific basis through the use of statistics and demonstrations by such psychic artists as Cheiro, an Irish fortune-teller whose real name was Count Louis Harmon. However, it has remained a domestic divinatory tool and even today is handed down through families, especially those with Gypsy roots.

How Does Palmistry Work?

The hand is traditionally considered to be the mirror of a person's past, present, and future. It is believed that both a person's potential and the achievements and failures of his or her life are imprinted on the hands. According to this theory, the lines on the left hand reveal the abilities and weaknesses present at birth that may be unraveled during life, so making a person predisposed to follow one course rather than another.

The lines on the right hand reveal the acquired self, the self molded by circumstance and by people encountered on the road, the destiny achieved so far. This assumes that your right hand is the dominant or writing hand. If a person is left-handed, the right hand is the hand of potential.

No wise or responsible palm reader would say that the future is fixed—only that certain life paths seen in the hand have been pursued and others have not. As a result of past choices, there are new options that offer a variety of possibilities.

No single point in life would reveal, on the left hand, the entire contents of the individual's book of possibilities, but merely the menu for the current set of options and the next chapter or so, forming just over the horizon. In this way, the inactive hand is the most predictive and, for this reason, should be read after the active hand of current actions and choices.

A more modern view regards the right hand as revealing the logical, intellectual, assertive, practical aspects of personality. According to this theory, the left hand represents the creative, intuitive, and imaginative spheres. This is because the left hemisphere of the brain, the logical side, controls the right hand, and the right, creative, sphere of the brain controls the left hand.

These views are not mutually exclusive, and one interpretation may make more sense to you than the other. Alternatively, you can blend the two and read the left and right hands respectively on two levels, first potential versus actual and then feeling versus thought.

Assisting the Energy Flow

Before plunging too deeply into a study of this subject, hold the hand of a trusted friend or family member. This gentle but firm tactile contact is the essence of the best palm reading, enabling you to make intuitive and telepathic connections. In our society, tactile contact is not always welcome or appropriate. With strangers, if you or the other person feel uneasy about a physical connection, you can offer a pendulum palm reading instead. This involves placing the palm to be read upright, supported by a table, then gently and slowly passing a crystal pendulum over each line and mount in turn.

To assess the energy flow

* Read the potential/feeling palm first (the left in a right-handed person) and then the current life/logical (right) palm second.

* Slowly move your fingers or pendulum over the whole palm, one hand at a time. You may find that you are not following the visible lines, but that the pendulum traces invisible energy paths that deviate from them.

* Concentrate on the energy you feel, whether it is a gentle warm tingling, a blockage, or even a lack of feeling in the line or area of the palm.

* If you use a pendulum, the yes response may indicate a clear line of energy, and a negative response may mark a blockage. If the pendulum does not respond, you may be encountering an area from which all feeling has temporarily gone.

* If the palm is crisscrossed by gently flowing tinglings of electricity, all the aspects are in harmony.

* If there are blockages, this is not necessarily a problem unless the whole hand is knotted, in which case it is more important to help the subject gently unknot the tight areas by talking. Blockages can indicate a temporary obstacle, which can sometimes be self-imposed or can indicate a period of necessary waiting. Your instinct will tell you which is correct. Knowledge is freedom, and so for the intuitive reader, a blockage is a potential source of energy for change.

* If an area feels dead or, more positively, temporarily asleep, ask the subject why. It can indicate that a particular avenue (for example, in career or love) has ended or that a bad experience has led to a lack of trust or confidence, and so talents and feelings have atrophied. This is not a once-and-for-all state and can, given encouragement, revive. These energy fluctuations are the most subtle and yet important indicators of alterations in emphasis.

* Even when you learn more about traditional meanings, you should always begin the reading of both hands with an assessment of energy flow.

The Meanings of the Specific Areas and Lines

A sensitive reader trusts the feeling of a line to mediate the meanings of the various lines and mounts. I once had my palm read by an old Romany woman who looked at my face the whole time. From my naive, psychologically biased viewpoint, she was a fraud who could not possibly be reading the palm she was so blatantly ignoring. Instead, I reasoned, she was seeking cues from my facial expressions. Yet, although the Gypsy only fingered my hand lightly as she talked, all her words were true to the core. Later, when I studied palmistry, I realized her line meanings were in rough correspondence with received wisdom.

Yet my hands were no more than a map that she read psychically, and that gift comes from trusting the inner voice and from constant practice in a variety of situations, using traditional meanings as guides rather than rules.

The areas and lines of the hand refer to the age-old issues of love, success, health, family, money, and happiness. Let the feelings flow between you and your subject in a positive, nonjudgmental way, and you may discover that palm reading is the most satisfying of all the divinatory arts.

The lines are the pathways that have been, are being, or can be trodden; the mounts are the repositories of characteristics that can be unfolded in positive or negative ways. So divinatory palmistry contains a fair amount of character assessment as a starting point for prediction.

The Mounts

These are the seven fleshy contours that appear on the palm, the high spots or mountains on the plain or side of the hand. The most prominent ones are roughly at the base of each finger and thumb. These are named after the ruling finger or other feature that they are nearest. In general, the larger the mount, the stronger the characteristic in the person.

The mounts are named after Apollo (the God of the Sun in Greek and Roman mythology), the moon, and the planets Venus, Jupiter, Saturn, Mercury, and Mars. They can be either positive or negative, according to what feels instinctively right and fits with the general trend of the palm reading. The mounts under the fingers are either directly below or may be slightly to the side.

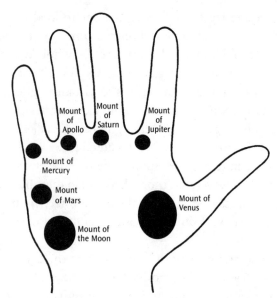

* The mounts' state of development can be seen in relation to the other mounts on the individual palm and varies between the two hands.

* If the mounts are hard to read, get your subject to cup the hand in question slightly.

* Begin by pressing the mounts gently or holding your pendulum over each in turn to see what energies you feel. A surge of power, like a mild electric shock, can suggest an excess of the quality, while a very weak energy flow or a blockage is equivalent to an underdeveloped mount.

* Trace paths between them. These may not follow the visible lines of the hand and may even follow a crisscross or circular path.

* If there is no connection between the mounts, the relevant aspects of life may be fragmented. One may link to all the others and may be the ruling principle of the subject's life.

THE MOUNT OF JUPITER
(UNDER THE INDEX OR JUPITER FINGER)

 The Mount of Jupiter is the most important for assessing strength of character. It signifies ambition, idealism, and wisdom. A well-developed mount suggests that principles have a strong influence, that justice is important, and that you would not be prepared to compromise over major issues, especially in your career.

If the mount reaches the large part of the middle finger or is very high, it can be considered overdeveloped. This might suggest a tendency to be dogmatic or overambitious in a particular area of life, or it could mean you are a natural leader who is frustrated through lack of opportunity.

A small, low, or nonexistent mount could imply a lack of confidence, a tendency to worry, or uncertainty over the right course of action. There may be too many dominant people in the subject's life.

THE MOUNT OF SATURN
(UNDER THE SECOND OR SATURN FINGER)

The Mount of Saturn is concerned with life's problems and coping with them. On the whole, this mount is relatively flat compared with the others, so any prominence suggests that limitations are viewed as challenges and as an impetus to change.

A well-developed mount heralds a life that is not free of trouble but welcomes challenges and thrives on finding solutions.

A high or overdeveloped mount can indicate feelings of helplessness in the face of problems and may result from a long period of being drained of resources and having to support others.

A flat or hollow mount can mean a tendency to avoid facing difficulties or a relatively untroubled life.

THE MOUNT OF APOLLO OR THE SUN
(UNDER THE RING OR APOLLO FINGER)

The Mount of Apollo is the area of artistic talent of all kinds: creativity, communication skills (whether written or spoken), and sensitivity. A well-developed mount is the sign of the optimist and joy-bringer; someone who utilizes their creative talents to the full, whether in communication or art, and who is at one with the natural world.

An overdeveloped mount suggests that material possessions and outward appearance may be of undue importance.

A flat or indented mount is a sign of undeveloped artistic abilities and an inability or unwillingness to communicate.

THE MOUNT OF MERCURY
(UNDER THE LITTLE OR MERCURY FINGER)

The Mount of Mercury is the area of inventiveness, desire for travel, business and sales acumen, practical skills, intelligence, versatility, and, surprisingly, psychic ability. It involves communication (in a factual, as opposed to creative sense) and persuasiveness. It is a relatively small fleshy mound at or near the base of the little finger.

A well-developed mount indicates good business sense and ingenuity in money-making ventures, scientific ability, leanings toward medicine or exploration, or a first-rate salesperson, whether of goods or ideas.

An overdeveloped or high mount suggests that the desire for professional or financial success may tempt a person to use less-than-straightforward means. It suggests restlessness and a love of travel and adventure (both physical and sexual) that can lead to an unstable lifestyle.

A flat or low mount can be a sign of difficulties with managing money and a lack of ambition and self-confidence, sometimes because earlier failures have proved a deterrent to future ventures.

THE MOUNTS OF MARS

Three areas on the palm are associated with Mars. It may be easier to regard all three areas as a unit, because the meanings are interlinked, with the lower areas moderating or accentuating the qualities of the God of War. The Mount of Mars is sometimes called Upper Mars.

The Mount of Mars (Directly under the Mount of Mercury)
The Mount of Mars represents courage, physical energy and strength, a desire for action rather than deliberation, and strong passions.

A well-developed mount represents courage in adversity, energy that is not diminished by opposition, assertiveness, and carefully focused action mingled with altruism and an industrious nature.

An overdeveloped Mount of Mars can be a sign of aggressiveness, resentment, an argumentative streak and fierce competitiveness (especially in physical matters), and sometimes thoughtlessness toward others.

An underdeveloped mount can mean a tendency to avoid confrontation and an inability to stand up against injustice whether to oneself or others.

The Plain of Mars This is situated in the area of the palm that descends from the center, at the level of the Mount of Mars, almost to the wrist. The Plain of Mars can be subdivided into Middle Mars or the Quadrangle (so-called because of its shape), and Lower Mars (also called the Triangle).

Middle Mars/the Quadrangle This lies between the heart line and head line and speaks of sincerity and altruism and their mitigation of the basic aspects of Mars. The shape and size, rather than the fleshiness, are the main criteria, but this can vary with the movement and changing form of the heart and head lines.

A large, broad Middle Mars represents honesty, openness, loyalty, and unselfishness, especially in defense of those who are weaker. This can be linked with a well-developed Mount of Jupiter.

A very large Middle Mars Quadrangle suggests tactlessness and a tendency to take risks, especially physical ones.

A narrow Quadrangle can indicate deviousness and gossip or backbiting under pressure.

Lower Mars/the Triangle This is situated above the Mount of Venus (which is under the thumb), forming an isosceles triangle pointing downward from the head line to the life line. It joins Middle Mars/the Quadrangle

This area represents intellectual achievement balancing physical energy, physical health, and vigor and generosity.

If the triangle is large and clear, the possessor manifests a balance of thought and action, assertiveness, and consideration for others. It can indicate health and vigor, both mental and physical.

If the triangle is long, stretching almost to the wrist and side of the hand, the trend is toward generosity and idealism, manifest in action, and tact and concern for the feelings of others, mitigating Mars.

A narrow triangle can stand for repressed anger, manifest in rigid attitudes that may limit thought and creativity. The triangle can widen over time if a person acts to resolve underlying conflict and resentments or acknowledge negative and often justifiable emotions in a controlled way.

THE MOUNT OF THE MOON OR LUNA
(UNDER UPPER MARS)

The Mount of the Moon is just above the wrist. It forms the second largest mount in the average hand and is often quite fleshy, extending to the edge of the hand. Its connection with the moon places it in the realms of imagination, dreams, fantasy, and intuition.

A well-developed Mount of the Moon may reach to the edge of the hand and will be well-proportioned in fleshiness to the other mounts, although larger. This indicates harmony with both the natural cycles of life and self and an intuitive awareness of the feelings, even unspoken ones, of others.

An overdeveloped mount that becomes cushionlike at the base of the hand can suggest unrealistic expectations of life and others, a tendency to prefer dreams to action, and overindulgence, but can also indicate a very rich imagination.

An underdeveloped Mount of the Moon can indicate difficulty in understanding the feelings and weaknesses of others, a need for a fixed routine, and a dislike of fantasy or frivolity. This is usually due to upbringing or circumstances in which this aspect of personality has been suppressed and this mount is readily open to development.

THE MOUNT OF VENUS (UNDER THE THUMB,
ACROSS FROM THE MOUNT OF THE MOON)

In human terms, this mount is the font of the human personality, and when there are emotional difficulties, it is the one most dramatically affected by circumstances.

This is usually the largest of the mounts, covering one of the biggest blood vessels in the hand and extending from the base of the thumb to the edge of the hand and the wrist. The Mount of Venus represents love, passion, affection, or sentimentality and is influenced over time by major changes in relationships, whether romantic, family, or more formal partnerships.

A well-developed Mount of Venus means that a person's approach to love and relationships is mature, based on genuine feeling and not dependency or possessiveness. Relationships of all kinds will be warm, based on trust and an ability to give and receive affection and approval. Commitments will be long-lasting, and the possessor of the well-developed mount will be faithful to any partner or family member.

An overdeveloped mount indicates emotional turmoil, intense passions that can lead to unwise sexual encounters or unsuitable romantic entanglements, difficulty in settling in a permanent relationship, or possessiveness and unwarranted jealousy.

An underdeveloped mount can imply coldness and selfishness, simply unawakened emotions and a fear of commitment, or a destruction of trust through the infidelity or emotional blackmail of others.

The Lines

The wrinkles on the palm are called "lines." Like the mounts, each major line has a name and a meaning, which can be positive or negative according to the application. For example, a long Line of Life does not, in spite of its name, foretell a long life, but talks about a potentially smooth passage through life, which may be ultimately less rewarding than one with many breaks and chains. Sometimes a challenge or setback can act as a spur to success, and so a lifeline with breaks can be of great advantage in offering choices and unexpected opportunities.

Like the mounts, even the major lines change and deepen, breaking and acquiring branches and marks throughout life and, as the Chinese believe, many smaller lines linking with major lines can be relatively transient in the face of major life changes.

BALANCING THE LINES

The lines are closely linked both with each other and with the mounts. For example, the inspiration for life could arise not purely from the Life Line, but out of a strong emotional need to connect with another person, reflected by an intense Heart Line or from energy pounding from the Mount of Venus. Alternatively, the life force could be driven by ambition or the desire for intellectual satisfaction, expressed by a strong Head Line that is more developed than either the Line of Life or Heart or from a powerful input from the Mount of Jupiter. Ambition could also motivate the pursuit of love.

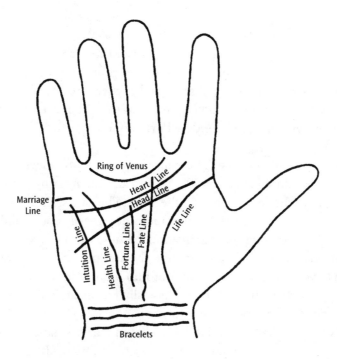

An individual may experience most harmony, if not drive, when the three major lines are equal in length and strength. A dominant Heart Line indicates that emotions are the driving force, and if the Head Line is not strong enough to harness these emotions, these creative energies may be wasted. Equally, if the Head Line is strong but the Life Line is weak, there may not be enough personal impetus to carry through plans.

The relative strengths may change at different times of life and can suggest other aspects that need to come to the fore. It can be especially helpful to compare the three major lines in both hands to use potential but perhaps undeveloped strengths to create a more balanced life.

Like the mounts, each line has positive and negative connotations revealed in the application of the trends in the real world. Dual or parallel lines indicate two alternative paths or two different strands to life; the general indication of the hand plus an intuitive pendulum examination will reveal whether this is an advantage or cause of potential conflict.

INTERPRETING THE LINES

Before you interpret the lines, you may want to repeat the energy assessment (see page 280). Once more, use your fingers or a pendulum to trace the energies and see whether there are any blockages or sudden surges that might indicate impetus to action or overreaction.

The following are considered primary lines.

The Life Line This runs in a curve from above the thumb, between the thumb and the forefinger, to below the thumb, joining the wrist. The timescale sometimes used in assessing this and other lines is not a valid way of using the information, because outside events and personal reactions to events can radically alter the course of life and lines. However, the more impetus put into life, the stronger and deeper the Life Line becomes; not only physically, but in the pulsating positive vibrations that you can sense.

A long, well-defined line with a broad curve is indicative of a powerful life force manifest both physically and mentally. The possessor is determined and focused, but also aware of the needs of others. It is the line of an achiever, but not a ruthless one.

A pale, narrow line, or one that begins and ends short of the possible span, may indicate that energy is less focused, but that, if the incentive is great enough, supreme effort and achievements are possible over shorter periods.

A broken or branching line suggests different phases or life changes. This is not necessarily bad, but simply means that the process of maturing and aging will unfold alternative pathways. A very short Life Line, joining the Line of Fate (see below) can suggest momentous changes caused by external events, which, if handled positively, can offer exciting opportunities.

Lines branching from the Life Line are called "effort lines." The mount, finger (which has the same meaning as the mount it rules), or other line that the branch joins can indicate whether this is a surge toward money, success, or love.

The Heart Line The Heart Line begins between the Mount of Mercury and the Mount of Mars and runs toward the Mount of Jupiter. It is sometimes said to represent the dilemma (or the union) of intellectual and instinctive processes. This line deals not only with love and relationships, but also with all matters concerned with emotions, the spirit, and the inner world. A great deal of disagreement exists about the meaning of the variations in this line, but a clear, deep, long line is taken to show that the possessor has emotional depths, is in tune with his or her own feelings, and is concerned about the needs and problems of others.

This is the highest line to cross the palm below the fingers. If the Heart Line is close to the fingers, it can indicate that emotions may be more restrained than in someone with a lower Heart Line.

A coarse, grainy line can be an indicator of sensuality or a particularly passionate relationship, while a pale, flat, broad line can suggest sentimentality, but—more positively—tranquil emotions.

A broken line, or one with several branches, is not a sign of broken relationships, but perhaps indicates that feelings may be initially intense but not long-lasting. This can change when the right relationship comes along as long as the possessor is aware of a tendency to be discouraged when idealism is replaced by reality.

A Heart Line that ends at the Mount or even finger of Saturn is one that indicates that happiness in life is assured, because love is an important part but not the sole purpose of life, and means that obstacles in relationships are met by patience and determination to find a solution.

 The Head Line This is the line running across the palm from the area between the thumb and the forefinger to the Mount of Mars or Moon area. This gives either an assertive or intuitive slant to intellectual activity. It is a line whose links with other mounts and lines are especially influential.

The Head Line can have several starting points: for example, from the Life Line, whose energies thereby reinforce natural determination in the Head Line. Another beginning is at the Mount of

Jupiter, which can indicate great authority and wisdom, but—on the negative side—also egoism. A Head Line beginning from the Plain of Mars can indicate irritability and impatience with others, especially those who are less gifted. An ending at the Mount of Mercury indicates added business acumen.

A strongly marked Head Line signifies intelligence and imagination, logic, determination, and application, but can—less positively—also allow a touch of ruthlessness. Often considered the most significant indicator of the outer world, the Head Line may join the Heart Line, showing that heart and head are closely in tune, although their union can occasionally lead to dilemmas between success in the world's terms and happiness.

A long, well-formed line is indicative of justice and idealism, while a pale short line can suggest timidity and diffidence in career or social dealings.

A broken Head Line can indicate the subject has many talents and options, but should not make changes out of restlessness.

Branches, too, are links to wherever they lead: to the Heart Line for intuitive decision making; to the Moon for a fusing of conscious and unconscious powers. A branch to the outer edge of the palm suggests a broadening of possibilities—traditionally said to be a sign of fame or infamy.

The following are considered secondary lines.

The Fate Line or Line of Saturn This line, running vertically down the middle of the hand, from between the Mount of the Moon and the Mount of Venus to the Mounts of Saturn and the Sun, is the Fate Line. It is often faint and refers to what is called the interplay of luck or fate in one's life. It does not necessarily indicate good luck, but a tendency toward either a positive or negative reaction to life's unexpected challenges, both good and bad.

The Fate Line can be used with other lines, especially the Apollo or Fortune Line, which can be a branch off it. At its clearest and longest, it extends from the base of the hand to the Finger of Saturn, and indicates not, as traditionally thought, that fate will always favor the possessor, but that the offered pathway will be successful, because of an innate ability to change difficulty into challenge and to adapt rather than be defeated by outside events.

A very pale or wavering Fate Line can indicate uncertainty and a tendency to be easily discouraged, but often improves dramatically once this characteristic is acknowledged.

A broken Fate Line can indicate that many external influences exist that must be accommodated or overcome. These may be caused by oversensitivity to the good opinion of others.

A centrally evolving line can suggest that many obstacles early on in life or a particular venture may be ones that, on reflection, serve to change the life course for later advantage.

If linked with the Heart Line, emotional pressures may be the source of limitations or challenges; while a linked Head Line implies that ambitions may be thwarted, but logic will present solutions that, in the long term, will prove advantageous.

A linked Fate and Fortune Line suggests financial challenges and setbacks that, with ingenuity and perseverance, can provide the roots of future prosperity.

Connections with the Life Line presage energy in meeting challenges and a breadth of perspective that can enable the avoidance of life's slings and arrows.

Links with the mounts accentuate the effects of that mount on the life path: for example, Venus, with its obvious attraction to, and maybe problems caused by, dealings with the opposite sex. Our fate is so often influenced by our own tendency to end up in certain situations.

 The Fortune Line or Line of the Sun This line, also called the Apollo Line, begins around the Mount of the Moon and is similar to the Line of Fate. Sometimes people have one and not the other, or the two join. The Apollo Line is the line of worldly success (not necessarily in monetary terms, although the gold of the sun may provide a tangible reward).

If the line is long and well-defined and reaches the Mount of Apollo, it indicates recognition in one's chosen field, usually through the sheer determination, hard work, and optimism of the possessor.

A pale, meandering, or nonexistent line can suggest a tendency to wait for fortune to smile and to entrust one's future success to others. A short line, especially one beginning higher in the hand, can mean that success will come later in life, perhaps as a result of a second career.

A broken Fortune Line shows great talent spread over many fields, but—less positively—an eagerness to try to pursue too many pathways to success and fortune without working out their long-term implications or checking their viability. Cracked Fortune Lines can heal once clear planning is added to life's fortunes.

A Sun or Apollo Line beginning at the center of the hand may indicate that success will come later, after years of effort, and could involve sacrifice or some temporary hardships. This success, once attained, is usually permanent and substantial.

A line beginning even lower tempers the desire for success with an aim that is worthwhile and may be linked to spiritual satisfaction or the good of others rather than personal achievement.

Links to the Heart Line indicate success either in love or in dealings with other people (for example, as a social worker or teacher).

Links to the Head or Life Line add determination and focused efforts that can reap great financial benefits.

Double Apollo Lines either indicate dual and often parallel success or two talents merging in a single goal.

 The Health Line or Line of Mercury This line is perpendicular to the Head and Heart Lines and crosses the center of the hand into the Mount of Mercury or Upper Mars. It is sometimes known as the River Line and refers to physical health (although it is also connected to mental and spiritual well-being). Rather than foretelling ill-health, as once thought, this line is the indicator, in the inactive hand, of a tendency for health to be affected by environmental or stress factors. In the active hand, if the energy is negative, it is a sure sign of current stressors that have built up over time.

If the line feels positive, it shows energy manifest in good health and emotional balance. This is therefore a line very sensitive to change and can be a good benchmark of positive and negative attitudes in the possessor and of deep-seated instinctive reactions to the unexpected, good and bad.

At its clearest and most defined, the line indicates that sharp memory, especially in learning, is a powerful asset and that flexibility, serenity, and receptiveness to the ideas of others ensure that stress is at a minimum and optimism prevails. Above all, especially in conjunction with well-developed Mounts of Mercury and the Moon and the Life Line, it can be a strong indicator of healing abilities. If present in the inactive hand, this line can suggest that it may be a good time to develop healing powers more formally.

A long, thin, pale line can indicate a great communicator, especially verbally, but also a perfectionist whose anxiety levels can be affected by shortcomings in others and self.

In contrast, a short line can indicate the damming up of emotions and, therefore, a tendency to have migraines or problems such as eating disorders, smoking, excessive drinking, or other ways of stifling negativity.

Breaks in the Health Line can indicate minor health problems from exhaustion or insomnia caused by longer-term unresolved anxieties that are not tackled and may be seen by the person concerned as a sign of weakness. They may be manifest in allergies, frequent colds, or cuts that do not heal.

A line in the upper part of the hand suggests that a person is happier with facts and figures than people and may find social interactions difficult. If the Health Line is in the lower hand, it signifies a deep thinker who reflects before speaking and tends to be emotionally stable.

The most significant mount linked to this line in terms of nervous energy is Mars. Like the Life Line, it can give great physical energy and enthusiasm. But a constant flow of nervous energy can also make relaxation difficult.

 The Intuition Line This line, also known as the Line of the Psychic Self, extends in a curve from the center of the Mount of the Moon, passing through the Head and Heart Lines, almost to the Marriage Lines. It represents, at its clearest, a well-developed intuitive sense of highly evolved psychic abilities. If it fades, is broken, or is absent from the active hand, or even from the inactive hand, it may be an aspect that has not been trusted or developed. As people begin psychic development work, this line can develop over a period of months. It can also emerge at other times of psychic awakening: for example, adolescence, childbirth, and times of crisis such as divorce or bereavement.

The following are considered tertiary lines.

 Marriage and Child Lines These "family lines" can appear in the left hand long before they emerge in the active hand and can indicate a stirring of intention or a change of emphasis that will take time to work its way through to the real world. The Marriage Lines lie horizontally directly on the outer edge of the hand immediately above the Heart Line, below the finger and Mount of Mercury. Their clarity, depth, and number do not predict the number of permanent relationships, but a desire or need to enter a deep relationship and relate to people on a meaningful level.

Immediately above are vertical lines called the Child Lines that, again, do not refer to the number of children, but a desire to bear children or to nurture others who may be vulnerable. Nuns who work in the community often have clear Marriage and Child Lines, as may a man "married to his job."

Family conflicts may be reflected by a disintegration or disappearance of these lines. But this is not an indication of permanent damage, and the inactive hand will reflect potential healing and happiness. Changes on the active hand can indicate long-term unacknowledged problems in the family.

Marks on the Hand

These can be the most transient elements in palmistry and yet can indicate very vividly what is happening on an individual line or mount. They are especially good to assess by using a pendulum, as they can either indicate a blockage or a new opportunity or emerging talent. The new opportunity can be felt as a bubble of energy, like a miniwhirlpool, whereas a blockage seems heavy or inert. These marks can occur on either hand as potential unfolds, but they are especially prevalent and changeable in the dominant or most active hand. In Oriental palmistry, they are of great significance. They are also very predictive of short-term events.

See whether the marks are repeated or mirrored by other marks along a contour of the hand: for example, if a square (limitations and protection) and dots (prosperity) are ranged along the Head Line, it might indicate that a consolidation of resources and efforts into realistic short-term projects, rather than short-term schemes, will ensure success.

Branches or Forks

These are the great connectors, linking different aspects of the hand, and can indicate changes of direction (usually positive). A great number of branches on a hand indicates great versatility and also harmony between the different facets of personality. Downward-pointing branches can indicate worries. These may be unacknowledged if they appear on the potential hand.

The most famous fork is known as the Writer's Fork—an indication not only of writing ability and optimism, but of great intellectual capacity. It occurs at the end of the Head Line, branching horizontally across the Mount of Mars. Traditionally, forks can represent a loss of energy, but this is clearly not the case with the Writer's Fork. Instead, this can imply a late flowering and the newfound energy diverging into new areas—such as writing or other creative work. A branch to the Moon from the Heart or Life Lines can be a sign of prophetic ability.

Chains or Islands

Chains are small circles linked by a line, while an island can be an area on a mount or line, larger and more separate. These represent linked stages or steps in a venture or life path, not in the sense of an enslaving change, but in the sense of unity and acquisition, for example, accumulating along the Apollo Line. They may indicate support or strength in unity. They are not at all the harbingers of gloom or an early fixed fate.

Islands can represent sanctuaries or a feeling of isolation or a period of waiting. Whether this is stagnation or creative waiting depends on the general feel of the palm. Islands can also be an indication of traveling to get away from pressures or when personal identity is becoming blurred or threatened by the demands of others.

stars

Lines can sometimes cross each other to form a star shape. These can occur anywhere on the hand or a line and tend to herald unexpected events beyond the control of the subject. Such events might not necessarily be bad, but could be unexpected opportunities or challenges. Although unexpected, they may be related to past actions or even old contacts. Like wishing on a star, stars may indicate dreams that can be made to come true, maybe through a change in direction and a realization of hidden ambitions. Stars are also secrets that should be revealed only sparingly and wisely.

DOTS

In all forms of divination, dots are frequently an indication of money, property, or prosperity (usually through the success of one's own ventures), and in clusters, they can be especially promising. Less positively, they can be distracting factors that must be dealt with, after which they disappear. On the inactive hand, they can indicate either possible financial avenues to be explored or irritations that can be avoided if acknowledged before they hit the everyday world.

squares

Squares can form from the intersection of lines. They are a sign of the reality factor, tempering ambitions, and ideals with an awareness of the limitations of the practical world. This is not necessarily bad. Rather, it is a protective sign, indicating that crises will be limited. The possessor probably has protection from the malice of others through the love of loyal friends and family and also a built-in ability to withstand unfair criticism or gossip. Squares may be present in the inactive hand immediately before a difficult situation emerges.

crosses

These are another sign of favorable change. For example, on the Heart Line, they can indicate a desire to form a permanent commitment and may be mirrored in a partner's hand.

Crosses can naturally indicate a crossroads, at which choices could be considered rather than allowing fate or other people to take a hand.

They accentuate any area's characteristics, positive or negative, according to the intuitive feel of the reader. For example, a cross on Mercury can indicate either deviousness or versatility—both characteristics might be necessary at different times.

GRILLS or GRIDS

Grills or grids are traditionally a sign of obstacles, relating to the particular mount or nearest line. These can be internal obstacles, for example, a fear of commitment on the Mount of Venus or the Heart Line. They should be considered carefully, as self-imposed obstacles are sometimes there because a course is not right, especially if accompanied by a protective square.

Grills on the left hand can indicate a natural inherent caution that again needs careful consideration, as caution may be a good approach to certain events moving into one's life. Use your pendulum or fingertips to understand whether the energies are a blockage or a protective wall. With practice, you will be able to use the marks and areas of the hand as a template for your own intuitive wisdom, much as you will use the basic meaning of a rune or tarot card to explore the inner world of the questioner and to indicate potentially fruitful paths.

STRIPES

A series of stripes, however faint, traversing a line or on a mount indicates a repository of hidden resources. You should feel a surge of power over them. They indicate hidden strengths, talents, and sometimes a secret world of dreams, ambitions, or emotions pulsating beneath a seemingly smooth Heart Line.

BRACELETS

The Chinese especially value what they call the magical Triple Bracelet, three clear parallel horizontal marks around the wrist, seeing these as indicative of not only intellectual, but moral greatness. One or more unbroken bracelets, especially if marked with a cross, augur a charismatic personality and great charms in love.

Broken, pale, or irregular bracelets suggest that disappointments can be overcome and turned to advantage, especially in love that may blossom later in life.

Chained bracelets are a sign of synchronicity, a series of coincidences that direct the life path in the right direction, if followed. The possessor is a child of fortune and a natural psychic.

Vertical lines around the wrist, pushing upward to the palm, are the sign of the traveler.

Intuitive Palm Reading

Sketch the two hands on paper, drawing in lines, mounts, and marks in black. Then use a red pen and a dotted line to plot the courses of energy. A palm print, made by rolling paint or lipstick over the hand and marking paper, does not allow you to record the living palm and its energies and so offers only a partial picture. You can use a blue pen for interconnections between mounts and lines.

* Begin first with the left hand, using this to assess both potential opportunities and setbacks and also what is coming over the horizon. Is this hand relatively smooth and unmarked, indicating stability or maybe a lack of challenge, or deeply lined? What unacknowledged factors can offer keys to present action and possible solutions, mirrored in the right hand?

* Either finger the contours, lines, and mounts, or run a pendulum over the entire hand slowly, feeling for any blockages or surges of energy, especially over a mark. Are these positive, negative, or just inactive?

* Look next at the lines and their relative strength, length, and continuity. Is your current potential in the area of Head or

Heart, and does the Life Line offer a store of energy or indicate exhaustion and anxiety?

* What about the minor lines of Fate, Fortune, Intuition, and Health? What avenues offer potential opportunities or potential hazards?

* Which mounts are prominent or undeveloped? Why? Is this a natural characteristic or one shaped by circumstance?

* Are there many marks or distinctive marks for travel or family? Are these interconnected?

* You do not have to read every aspect of the hand to get an overall picture, and you will soon acquire an automatic feel for what is relevant.

* Look next at the right hand to see what is happening in the present. This reflects current questions, areas of importance and conflict, and, most importantly, the strengths and weaknesses that allow a positive response to both opportunities and challenges. Once more, run your fingers or pendulum slowly over the whole hand to gain a general impression. This may be startlingly different from the left hand, which can indicate that current events are having a marked effect.

* As with the left hand, note the individual features and any con-flicting elements that may make decision-making more difficult. Do the Heart or Head aspects (the reason or intuition areas) predominate, and is the life force concentrated or dissipated?

* Compare the two hands. This is the most important stage. What has developed in the right hand that was presaged in the left, especially markings such as dots or squares, breaks, and forks?

* What is absent in the right hand that was present in the left? Could this aid the questioner? Have forks not been pursued?

* Has a potentially strong or developed Mount of the Moon (with its intuitive strengths) or a powerful Head Line been neglected in the real world so that these potential strengths have not been utilized?

* If in doubt, close your eyes and use the contours as a map of the psyche to give you the overall impression. Nowhere in divination

is it truer than in palmistry that the whole is greater than the sum of the parts.

★ What suggestions for future action can be made from the combination of potential and actuality?

★ Keep a copy of the palm drawings and, in three months time, take new images. You will be surprised at the changes. Over a year, you can discover the stable factors in your own hands and the hands of those for whom you read regularly.

Sample Reading

Clare, a single parent, was suddenly and unexpectedly laid off from her job as a book illustrator with a large company. She found herself working night and day to keep the family together and stave off her creditors. What, if any, hope for the future lay before her?

I looked first at her left, potential hand, as she was right-handed, and ran my pendulum over it.

The Left Hand The hand was full of blockages, especially over the Life Line, indicating that Clare had become increasingly exhausted by fighting life's problems over a long period of time, so that her potential was not flowing naturally into her everyday life.

Clare had always had a hard life, but she had continuously coped. The current problems, she explained, had been getting consistently worse over the previous two years, with constant backbiting at work and difficulties since an international company run from Canada had taken over the firm. Her pale Life Line merged with the Head Line, which was chained along its length. It suggested that her built-in logical, achieving nature was strengthened by her own slow but sure successes as a book illustrator over the previous years, although her efforts were not appreciated by the new bosses. The Head Line and especially the chain pulsated with energy in spite of her feelings of exhaustion, indicating that her latent as well as manifest talents offered the potential to energize the Life Line that was now being challenged by a survival situation.

The Heart Line disappeared abruptly at the Mount of Jupiter. Clare found this surprising, because she had always considered herself a heart person. Her well-developed Mount of Jupiter was a repository of determination and a refusal to compromise, indicating that Clare had the strength of character to fight, as she had fought all her life, for her family, and that this overrode her innate concern for others' feelings.

Equally, the Mount of Saturn was well-developed, promising that the setbacks could be met as challenges. Another well-developed mount was Mercury, promising that versatility and ingenuity would see her through, even if the short-term prospects seemed disastrous.

Her Fate Line met a large chain on the Head Line and had branches to the Mounts of Saturn and Apollo, promising that her strongly creative potential would offer her a way out of her problems.

All these were strengths she had within her. Because the Fortune Line joined the Fate Line early on, the two were intrinsically linked as part of her makeup, and so she had the innate power to turn limitation to fortune.

The Health Line running right to the Finger of Mercury promised deep reservoirs of physical and emotional strength that would help her through the coming weeks, despite her current exhaustion and fears.

Of the marks, apart from the chains, the most significant were stripes over most of the major areas, suggesting reservoirs of untapped power and hidden resilience.

It was a promising hand, showing that she was much stronger than she felt at that moment.

The Right Hand This gives clues to the current situation and reactions to it. The pendulum again picked up blockages. The most significant feature was the deeply grooved Fortune Line joined to the Fate Line. These were far deeper than those on the other hand and scattered with grills or grids and islands. Clare's current loss and fears for the future had clearly made their mark. The islands indicated her isolation because of her layoff, but also, ironically, sanctuary from the pressures. The continued link between Fate and Fortune reminded Clare that her present and future Fate and Fortune lay in her own hands and that only she, through sheer hard work and determination, could claw her way back as she had done on other occasions.

Her Mount of Mars was particularly prominent and showed that anger was pulsating, but also courage. The pendulum was positively throbbing at this point.

The Life Line was actually stronger than on the left hand, surging with energy in response to the immediate challenge threatening her children's future, and was fused with the Head Line.

The Heart Line was not surprisingly shattered, because she felt betrayed, and again this reflected concern for her children's future happiness. However, it made an unexpected fork at the Mount of Mercury and still touched the Mount of Jupiter at the end, adding the power of versatility and ingenuity.

The Solution—Putting the Hands Together Clare's left hand revealed untapped potential and talents and an underlying determination, not only to survive but to thrive. The right hand betrayed her fears, but her Life Line in this hand was actually energized by the crisis. Adding the powers of Mercury and Mars to the wisdom and determination of Jupiter, her active hand could draw on the reservoir of latent power in the left hand to create a new way of life. The right hand had great energy and the blockages, even as we talked, began to pulsate. Clare told me she had applied to various book publishers for freelance work.

When we met six weeks later, Clare said she had found her work was greatly admired and that she had secured several contracts. Once she utilized the tax benefits of being self-employed and saved on full-time child care, she was actually in a stronger position—and she had met a very nice single editor who had asked her out for dinner several times. The grills were fading on the right hand, and the faintest cross was emerging on the left hand (a future romance?).

FURTHER READING

Crystal Divination

Cunningham, Scott. *Encyclopedia of Crystals, Gems and Metal Magic.* St. Paul, Minnesota: Llewellyn, 1991.

Eason, Cassandra. *The Crystal Directory.* New York: Sterling (Vega), 2003.

General

Eason, Cassandra. *The Complete Guide to Psychic Development.* Berkeley, California: The Crossing Press, 2003.

Radin, Dean. *The Conscious Universe: The Scientific Truth of Psychic Phenomema.* New York: HarperCollins, 1997.

I Ching

Baynes, C. F., R. Wilhelm (trans.) and Vary F. Baynes (trans.). *I Ching or Book of Changes.* Princeton, New Jersey: Princeton University Press, 1967.

Tzu, Lao, and Robert C. Henricks. *Lao Tzu's Tao Te Ching.* New York: Columbia University Press, 2000.

Numerology

Crawford, Saffi, and Geraldine Sullivan. *Numerology: The Power of Birthdays, Stars, and Numbers.* New York: Ballantine Books, 1998.

Goldschneider, Gary, and Joost Elffers. *The Secret Language of Destiny: A Personology Guide to Finding Your Destiny.* New York: Penguin USA, 1999.

Palmistry

Altman, Nathaniel. *Little Giant Book of Palmistry.* New York: Sterling, 1999.

Cheiro et al., *Palmistry: The Language of the Hand.* New York: Random House, 1999.

Pendulum Dowsing

Schirner, Marcus. *The Pendulum Workbook.* New York: Sterling, 1999.

Webster, Richard. *Dowsing for Beginners.* St. Paul, Minnesota: Llewellyn, 2002.

Playing Cards

Sophia. *Fortune Telling with Playing Cards.* St. Paul, Minnesota: Llewellyn, 1996.

Webster, Richard. *Playing Card Divination for Beginners: Fortune Telling with Ordinary Cards.* St. Paul, Minnesota: Llewellyn, 2002.

Runes

Peschel, Lisa. *A Practical Guide to the Runes: Their Uses in Divination and Magick.* St. Paul, Minnesota: Llewellyn, 1989.

Thorsson, Edred. *Runelore: A Handbook of Esoteric Runology.* York Beach, Maine: Red Wheel/Weiser, 1988.

Tarot

Bunning, Joan. *Learning the Tarot.* York Beach, Maine: Red Wheel/Weiser, 1998.

Eason, Cassandra. *Complete Guide to the Tarot.* Berkeley, California: The Crossing Press, 2001.

Tea Leaf Reading

Mizumoto Posey, Sandra. *Café Nation: Coffee Folklore, Magic, and Divination.* Santa Monica, California: Santa Monica Press, 2000.

Tree Alphabet, Ogham Staves

Blamires, Steve. *Celtic Tree Mysteries: Practical Druid Magic and Divination.* St. Paul, Minnesota: Llewellyn, 2002.

Eason, Cassandra. *The Modern-Day Druidess.* London: Judy Piatkus (Publishers) Ltd., 2003.

index